THE SEVEN QUEENDOMS

A SoulMap for Embodying Sacred Feminine Sovereignty

RIMA BONARIO, TH.D

FLOWER *of* LIFE PRESS

Praise

"Once in a great while a book comes along that speaks so deeply to my own soul's journey that I find myself breathing more deeply, crying and laughing intermittently, while nodding my head with familiarity. Dr Rima Bonario has given birth to a powerful mystery school for our times that has roots as well as wings and calls forth the true Queenly sovereignty in all chakras and realms. I will use this book as a reference for my own shamanic work with my women's circles."

—Linda Star Wolf, Ph.D., www.shamanicbreathwork.org

"Dr. Rima Bonario is a master synthesizer. Fusing personal experience, vast research, and academic education, she brings forward critical missing links in embodying feminine power. *The Seven Queendoms* is a revelation in understanding how to live as a sovereign woman, providing extensive tools and practices to make personal sovereignty a real, daily, body-felt experience. A must-have for every woman!"

—Rev. Stephanie Red Feather, Ph.D., Author or *The Evolutionary Empath: A Practical Guide for Heart-Centered Consciousness*

"Dr. Rima Bonario is a force of nature driven by her passionate dedication to seeking the Divine in all realms. Her most recent work, *The Seven Queendoms,* is world changing; in that, with each woman who changes her life given the wisdom and tools available here, the deep effects will be felt far beyond the immense personal shift. Rima has an exceptional ability to weave the academic with the esoteric, the practical with the spiritual. This work is what a generation of women has been waiting for, a light illuminating the power to lead ourselves and our world to greater wholeness."

—Robin Rose Murphy, Teacher, Author, Priestess, and Ceremonialist

"*The Seven Queendoms* is a portal to feminine empowerment, liberation, and flourishing in our personal lives and leadership as women. It is a comprehensive resource full of rich personal stories, grounded research, practical tools and invitations to inquiry. It contains timeless wisdom you will return to again and again for years to come."

—Joni Advent Maher, Creator of the popular *Trust Your Sacred Feminine Flow* podcast

"The wisdom in *The Seven Queendoms, A SoulMap for Embodying Sacred Feminine Sovereignty* comes right on time! With so much talk about sovereignty in the personal growth space, Dr. Rima Bonario demonstrates what it takes to live out loud, unapologetically. She breaks down emerging divine feminine archetypes tailored for the times we are living in. I could not put this book down!"

—Lettie Sullivan, Priestess of the Sacred Arts, Bestselling Author and Life Coach

"Rima Bonario is lifting the veil and bringing light to the otherwise mysterious and perhaps esoteric path of Sacred feminine Sovereignty. A potent blend of both mystical and practical wisdom, *The Seven Queendoms* deliver's on its promise to be a SoulMap for the seeking sister. This book shows you not only that it can be done, or that it must be done, but it also tells you where to look in your own life for clues and how to work with what you find to reclaim your power."

—Anahita Joon Tehrani, Embodied Leadership Mentor

"This book is for all women who want to understand how to access their feminine power. But it is far more than that. It is a roadmap for how you are going to live from now on. Dr. Rima helps you to look at where you have come from and, with new awareness about yourself, how you can step into the Queen inside you just waiting to be expressed. You will recognize yourself in all of the seven Queendoms and identify all the things you can do to nurture and develop each one. Rima shares her personal stories all the way through and her courage to share so vulnerably and authentically makes her book so powerful."

—Geraldine Bown, Women's Empowerment and Gender Balance Consultant, Author, and Interfaith Minister

"Every once in a while someone writes a book that is so insightful and so practical that it shows one a path to a new land. Dr. Rima Bonario has accomplished this with her book, *The Seven Queendoms*. She shares personal experience in a way that enhances her message of healing and empowerment. This is a beautiful integration of wisdom, experience, and deep skill. I will be recommending this book to my clients. Thank you Rima for the deep dive on the path to wholeness."

—Victoria Wilson-Jones, MS, Certified advanced clinical hypnotherapist, Ordained Interfaith Minister, and Transpersonal Coach

"Dr. Rima Bonario writes in such an accessible, powerful way about the most important subject we women can address today: the calling to our own sacred divine feminine work on this planet, which starts within ourselves. *The Seven Queendoms* belongs right up there next to Tricia McCannon's *Return of the Divine Sophia* or Sophia Bashford's *You Are a Goddess*. Rima's work has informed my own expanding awareness and education of this side of our divinity. *The Seven Queendoms* will surely be an important guide for your own spiritual and personal growth."

—Halle Eavelyn, Transformational Coach, Author, and Tour Leader

"In the business world, women are often expected to minimize our feminine characteristics as we navigate male-dominated corporate systems and cultures. Dr. Rima Bonario's gem of a book makes it clear: trying to work and think like a man has not only put us in deep dissonance with intimate relationships, but has stifled our intellectual and creative genius. And we're worn out. Rima reminds us that it's time to let go of exhaustion as a status symbol and productivity as a trophy for self-worth. She gives us sweet permission and practical instruction to end the inner spiritual battle, to open and receive, and to resurrect our authenticity. This book is raw and real, beautiful and transformative, but mostly, it is necessary."

—Cyndi Swall, Author of *Bliss In the Wild: The Intentional Woman's Guide to Creating Everyday Joy*

"The Divine Queen is back and Dr. Rima Bonario is one of her messengers with her new book *The Seven Queendoms: A SoulMap for Embodying Sacred Feminine Sovereignty*. What brings you vacation happiness? Find it in the daily practice connecting yourself with your divine nature. We are at the evolution crossroads and our inner queen is calling us forward."

—Francie Desmone, Board Certified Acupuncturist and Wellness Coach

"As Dr. Rima Bonario says in her new book *The Seven Queendoms*, 'The good news is, we can change our hair-trigger responses, the choices we make, and direction of our life. Even pervasive habits that seem stubborn and beyond reach can be softened. But it is no small feat.' I say, you can do it ladies, we can do it, it's our place, and our time and our true liberation. This depiction of her journey and the path she offers will awaken the power of surrender and potential in all of us."

—REV. DR. MARTHA CREEK, ORGANIZATIONAL CONSULTANT

"Dr. Rima Bonario brings to light the pressing issues for women today and shares her journey, which gives the reader permission to accept and own their story without judgement. Rima embodies the state of oneness in her writing and gives a freeing perspective of the work it takes to feel genuinely connected with our feminine self while balancing our sovereign power. She empowers the reader to understand that surrender is the cornerstone to feminine power. She reveals the lifelong struggle women face in aspiring to be Super Women and discovering the real Queen that is within all of us. Having had the privilege of teaching with Rima, I know she truly lives by and epitomizes what she offers in this book."

—SYLVIA GUINAN, AUTHOR OF *THE RICHNESS OF DIVORCE*

"The writing and design of *The Seven Queendoms* is so beautiful. Dr. Rima Bonario has tapped into every aspect of her Queenly discoveries and the energy pours right from her soul into the reader. Here is what deeply touched me. In recent months on social media, Black American women will often address each other as, 'Hey Queen.' So when I read about the missing archetype of Queen, my next morning meditation was elevated to another level of posture, stature, and presence. Thank you for the education, her-story, and knowledge that will certainly be acclaimed as a must-read and resource for all levels of educators and those looking for answers on self-discovery, awareness, and self-worth."

—BUKEKA BLAKEMORE, SPEAKER/SINGER/SONGWRITER AND ENTREPRENEUR, TALK SHOW HOST OF *WORTHY OF WONDERFUL*

Visit **TheSevenQueendoms.net/dissolvetheblocks**
to access a free masterclass:
Understand and Dissolve the Six Blocks to Receiving

The Seven Queendoms: A SoulMap for Embodying Sacred Feminine Sovereignty
Copyright ©2021 Dr. Rima Bonario

All rights reserved. No part of this publication may be reproduced, distributed, or transmitted in any form or by any means, including photocopying, recording, or other electronic or mechanical methods, without the prior written permission of the publisher, except in the case of brief quotations embodied in critical reviews and certain other noncommercial uses permitted by copyright law.

The content of this book is for general instruction only. Each person's physical, emotional, and spiritual condition is unique. The instruction in this book is not intended to replace or interrupt the reader's relationship with a physician or other mental health professional. Please consult your doctor for matters pertaining to your specific health.

Published by Flower of Life Press
Old Saybrook, CT

To contact the publisher, visit www.floweroflifepress.com
Cover and interior design by Astara Jane Ashley
Cover and interior Queen art by Jenny Hahn, www.JennyHahnArt.com

Library of Congress Control Number: Available Upon Request

ISBN-13: 978-1-7349730-8-2
Printed in the United States of America

Table of Contents

Introduction 2
Part 1: Seeking Sovereignty 5
    Chapter 1: Myth, Mystery, and Muck 9
    Chapter 2: The Curse of Un-Sovereignty 17
    Chapter 3: Surrendering SuperWoman 23
    Chapter 4: From Cape to Crown 35
    Chapter 5: Parents, Patriarchy & Personality 45
    Chapter 6: Remaking the Past 55
    Chapter 7: The Toll of Trauma on Intimacy 63

Part 2: The Path to Feminine Embodiment 73
    Chapter 8: Reclaiming the Divine Feminine 77
    Chapter 9: Your Body As a Pathway to Enlightenment 85
    Chapter 10: Understanding Your Energy Body 91

Part 3: The Seven Queendoms 101
    Chapter 11: Introducing the Soul Map 105
    Chapter 12: The Grounded Queen 111
    Chapter 13: The Passionate Queen 121
    Chapter 14: The Empowered Queen 133
    Chapter 15: The Loving Queen 149
    Chapter 16: The Expressive Queen 165
    Chapter 17: The Visionary Queen 177
    Chapter 18: The Divine Queen 191

Part 4: Embodying Sacred Feminine Sovereignty 205
    Chapter 19: Maintaining Your Sovereignty 209
    Chapter 20: Sovereignty in Action 217
    Chapter 21: Finding Sisterhood 225
    Chapter 22: Remember to Rest 231

Afterword 235
The Seven Queens Energy Practices & Affirmations 236
Master Summary Charts 244
Bibliography 247
About the Author 249

*"There is a void felt these days by women and men—
who suspect that their feminine nature, like Persephone,
has gone to hell.
Wherever there is such a void, such a gap wound agape,
healing must be sought in the blood of the wound itself.
It is another of the old alchemical truths that,
"No solution should be made except in its own blood."
So that the female void cannot be cured by conjunction with the male,
but rather by an internal conjunction,
by an integration of its own parts,
by a remembering of a putting back together
of the mother-daughter body."*

—Nor Hall, The Moon and the Virgin

*Offered in honor of
The Sacred and Holy Divine Feminine,
Goddess of 10,000 Names,
Who lives in us all.*

With deep love and undying gratitude to:

*My parents and family,
especially my husband Tobias and daughter Sophia*

*My teachers, mentors, and colleagues,
especially Tj Bartel and Angela Blanchard*

*My friends and supporters,
And most especially, my students,*

All of whom made this book possible.

Introduction

It is my pleasure and honor to welcome you to the realm of the Seven Queendoms. My intent is that this book will serve as a resource guidebook or manual that you can return to many times for inspiration, information, and potent practices that will support you in deepening your connection to your inner sovereign.

Inside these pages you will find a combination of brain science, developmental psychology, and shadow work which will shed light on how our early years may continue to hold us back from living life at our best. I also offer milestones and route markers from my own personal journey to illuminate the path forward. And, through the use of poetry, art, and interactive exercises you will have the opportunity to mine the holy wisdom found in your body, mind, heart, and soul to activate your sacred feminine sovereignty.

As we start this journey, I must note that language has its limitations. While I use the terms masculine and feminine, and discuss sexuality through the lens of heterosexual interactions, and woman's bodies and terms associated with them traditionally, these teachings can certainly encompass all forms of expression and choice. These two archetypal energies are at the core of the human experience and should not be confused with the concept of gender or sex (male and female) which are entirely different. All people have some amount of feminine and masculine energy as part of their make up. We can gain mastery over how we use that energy and find a balance that suits us best.

WHAT TO EXPECT ON THE ROYAL ROAD AHEAD

Part One: Seeking Sovereignty begins by defining the common dilemma modern women face as we seek to embrace our personal power while maintaining a connection to our inherent feminine qualities. It also delves into the psychology and physiology underlying our social conditioning and how that evolves from our early relationships to overlay our adult relationships.

Part Two: The Path to Feminine Embodiment first invites us into a reclamation of the feminine face of the Divine, a critical component of restoring respect and honor to the feminine archetypal energy and, by extension, women. From there it focuses on how early childhood trauma forms the baseline for our body's response to our life experience. It offers a look beyond the physical body into the energy body as a pathway for healing and expansion.

Part Three: The Seven Queendoms will introduce you to the SoulMap that encompasses each of the Seven Queens and her two shadow forms. This section of the book is the most interactive, with art and exercises that bring the Queens to life inside of you. It is your invitation into the practical and the mystical aspects of your inner sovereign.

Part Four: Embodying Sacred Feminine Sovereignty weaves together the threads from previous chapters and offers some practical tips and tools for integrating the Seven Queens and the broader Queen archetype into your life.

Embodying this power and nobility of the Queen archetype is a life-long journey. I find her to be a delicious life-companion as she urges me to live into my most authentic, powerful, passionate, and loving self-expression. I hope you will come to treasure her presence in your life as much as I do.

Part 1
Seeking Sovereignty

It is a dangerous thing to be a self-possessed woman.
A woman who is not owned but owns herself.
Not possessed by society, fashion, or conformity.
Dangerous because that woman cannot be controlled
By shame or doubt or fear or hate.

Dangerous because saying yes to herself means confronting
Always and forever choosing, choosing, choosing.

But I say to you it is more dangerous for a woman
not to possess herself.
To give others the right to take her sovereignty
To twist it, bend it, break it
Until she forgets it was ever hers in the first place
That she is the Queen of herself, her life, her soul.

I ask you, sisters:
Will you die dispossessed of your body?
Will you abdicate the throne of your heart?
Will you hide from the wisdom of your soul?

No lovely. You will not.
You will rise.
You will find and reclaim your
wild, wise, sexy, smart, sovereign self.

Take the hands of your sisters and rise.

We will not cut ourselves into a thousand pieces
to try to take up less room
Or fit in the space we have been told is ours.
This is our life; This is our castle.
And it longs for our Queen to come home,
to awaken, to sit down, to be here NOW,
To lead and to love.

Heed the call sisters: Come home to your heart.
Come live in your skin.
Come dance with your soul.
Be truly, deeply, madly home.
For you have waited long enough.

*"Make yourself a myth and live within it,
so that you belong to no one but yourself."*

—Roshani Chokshi

CHAPTER 1
MYTH, MYSTERY, AND MUCK

We are living in mythic times.

It's as though the ground beneath us, which used to be solid, reliable, and comforting, has fallen away and been replaced by shifting sands. How do we find our bearings when everything around us is unfolding, exploding, and downloading at dizzying speeds? Hardly a day goes by without some new challenge to face, some new insight to assimilate, or some new adaptation to master. It can feel as though we don't know up from down, in from out.

This is what it means to be incarnated during a time of epic change. The evolution of consciousness has gained so much speed and momentum that we can no longer sit on the sidelines of life.

In these epic times, we are asked to make epic choices. First and foremost, we are being asked to choose to step up to this challenge. And while it may seem overwhelming, I can pretty much guarantee you that you were born for these times if you are living on planet earth right now.

You, my dear, have been cut from the starry night sky. Your beautiful and tender heart is designed to break itself open to create a portal through which your glittering soul can shine through. Your cells are literally made of stardust, and your body is just plain magic. Yeah, baby!

What? You mean that's not your daily experience?

Or maybe you see it, then lose it; you feel it, then you can't.

I can relate.

In the spring of 1998, I was fresh off of a painful divorce. I had spent nine months in a 12-Step recovery program for people who make very poor relationship decisions. I had also started attending a new, more supportive church. At one of my first Sunday services, Senior Minister Howard Caesar offered a lesson called "Be Impeccable with your Word." It was the first of a four-part series based on Don Miguel Ruiz's book *The Four Agreements*.

The lesson really moved me, so right after the service, I went to the church bookstore to buy the book. Lucky for me, the book was sold out. Lucky because I bought Ruiz's other book, *The Mastery of Love*. I took the book home and began reading. I didn't stop until I finished that evening. One of the most spiritually profound experiences of my life happened about four pages before the end of this precious little book: I had a Oneness Moment.

Something, somewhere inside of me, clicked in deeply with what Ruiz was saying. I looked up, and suddenly *I knew* my absolute oneness with every living thing on the planet and beyond. Tears of joy began to flow. I looked out of my window and saw the swaying trees and knew that I was them and they were me. When I touched the roses in the vase on the table, I could feel I was also touching myself. I placed a petal on my forehead, wanting to know this "me" more fully. For about twenty minutes, I was the Infinite, and the Infinite was me. I knew my life would never, ever be the same.

The next day when I went to Borders to buy *The Four Agreements*, I received another gift. As I said, "Have a nice day," to the young man at the register, he looked up and suddenly smiled the biggest, most enthusiastic smile I had ever seen. I was so surprised and affected by it that I can still see his face to this day. In the next moment, I realized he was smiling that way because I was smiling that way. And so it went for five full days—moments of deep connection with perfect strangers and feelings of love for everyone I saw. Whether I was at work, running errands, or visiting with friends, I found myself feeling completely connected to everyone and everything. When I would see someone different than me because they had a pink mohawk, or baggy pants, or drove a Hummer (back then, I thought people who drove Hummers were killing the planet), rather than feeling a separation or having a judgmental thought, I said, "Oh look! I get to have a pink mohawk, wear baggy pants, and drive a Hummer!" On the fifth day, I wondered how long this state would last. Sadly, within two hours, it had faded. I began to forget again.

Even so, the experience was so very inspiring it radically changed my life. I became committed to having that sense of oneness be my everyday experience. I learned that what happened to me was called a "state-change." I had an expanded state of universal consciousness. But to make it permanent, I would have to have a "stage-change," meaning achieving a change in my stage of spiritual development. As philosopher and father of the Integral Movement, Ken Wilbur says, "State changes are cheap; stage changes are expensive."

In the twenty-two years since that day, I have dedicated my life to my spiritual development so that I could experience and hold that sense of interconnectedness in my day-to-day life. Eventually, my quest grew into a calling to help others to do the same. On my journey, I have been abundantly blessed. This 20-minute miracle was only the first of many profound moments of meeting the Divine.

Seeking Sovereignty

I have come to understand the necessity of the gift moments like this offer us. They help us develop an increased capacity to clearly see what I call, *Truths of the Heart*. These truths reach far beyond the mundane sense of reality generally available and open a door into a profound mystery, a place where we come to know ourselves in a whole new way. Truths of the Heart are essential to living a life on our own terms. They give us permission to change course, sometimes dramatically, so that we can more fully embody a more deeply heartfelt, soulful version of ourselves.

My journey included cultivating a relationship with my body and my soul, two parts of myself that previously I did not relate to well. I needed to access the wisdom they contained so that I could receive guidance on matters of importance and make authentic choices that fit with this interconnected understanding of reality. While that may sound cool, the journey hasn't been all sugar and spice and everything nice. Like mucking out a horse stall, it took years to separate the horse shit from the wood shavings. And let me tell you, there was a lot of shit to shovel. Yet, this mission, this labor of love, has been worth every bit of effort it has required.

My studies eventually led me to pursue a doctorate in transformational psychology at a graduate seminary. Technically, I am a Reverend Doctor, having earned a Doctor of Theology degree. During my studies, I explored everything from developmental and transpersonal psychology to brain science and the treatment of trauma to perennial wisdom and the deep mysteries of the world's religions. I learned that there are reliable maps of the human psyche and repeatable processes through which we can access and develop the psyche—and that they have excellent odds in helping people increase their level of happiness and overall functionality.

What surprised me most in my journey was the powerful role the body played in the developmental process. For most of my life, my body has been a bother to me at best and an enemy at worst. But in these last few years, I have come to love her deeply. And as a reward, I can now hear her clearly. I have developed the practice of paying very close attention to what she is asking of me.

> *Becoming conversant in our bodies' language is essential if we are to survive and thrive in these mythic times.*

In March of 2020, I was leading my third spiritual pilgrimage to Egypt when the Covid-19 crisis began closing down country after country. Despite the growing craziness, we managed to keep ourselves tightly wrapped up in our spiritual bubble for the entirety of our magical journey. But somewhere on the trip home, my co-facilitator and I contracted the virus. I don't think I'd have made it so well through my 17-day quarantine or recovered from my illness so quickly if I hadn't eaten massive amounts of oranges and celery, consumed copious amounts of hot tea, detoxed entirely off of sugar, and avoided meat and carbs. By listening to and honoring what my body wanted, I could now give her what she asked for.

Of course, the pandemic was just the tip of the iceberg we were asked to deal with in 2020. Dangerous political and racial divisions deepened across the globe. These divisions found their way into our communities, and many of us found ourselves at odds with people we loved and respected. Misinformation is everywhere, and it has eroded our sense of certainty, our faith in our institutions, our leaders, each other, and maybe even our own views. It's a confusing time. But by looking at life through a mythical or archetypal lens, we can bring into focus the foundational energies operating beneath the visible world. Humans have done this for eons through the power of myths and stories. Long before the emergence of modern science, these stories helped us make sense out of our experiences. As we head into a new age, we will need these stories—and the characters and plotlines they illuminate—to navigate the uncharted territory we are facing.

From the archetypal perspective, we can see that we are in a time of diminishing returns from the masculine dominator or warrior energy and Father archetype as our primary form of leadership (often called Patriarchy), especially its more shadowy aspects. Most religions and nation-states are founded on and laud this archetype, centering male leadership and masculine forms of power as the only way to create safe, functioning societies. But the dominator warrior energy and his sword are being misused and coming up short with the kinds of complex, whole-systems issues we face as a species. We just can't kill our way out of the challenges we face. An emerging spirituality and a new, more collaborative approach to public policy are required for us to survive the existential challenges we face with the climate crisis, the pandemic, and global economic distress. The approach needed is founded on the more feminine energy available in the nurturing power and possibility of the Sovereign Queen archetype. That's where I'm working and playing. She gets *all* my energy... *all* my devotion.

The transition to this energy is inevitable. What is still unknown is how much will need to be blasted out and die to make way for nurturing and receptivity, for slower rhythms and communal care. While I often lament at the continued chaos and pain coming from the unhealed masculine presence within each of us and in our collective, its failure is required so that we can accept emerging feminine power patterns and leadership skills. It must become completely clear that leadership based on the model of dominate or be dominated, kill or be killed, simply won't work now. There is a place for healthy warrior energy, but it must be in service to the feminine, to the Sovereign Queen. Only then can we heal the masculine-feminine split first within ourselves and then in our communities and institutions. This is an epic quest. It is for men and women alike, and it is essential if we are to survive and thrive.

As Within, So Without

It is tempting to focus all our energy collecting evidence for and feeding the outrage we feel at the mind-boggling ecological and human injustices that are accepted as the standard in our world. No one could blame you for doing so. Goodness knows I have. Yet eventually, those of us wanting to effect lasting change in the world must come to understand that part of the effort is an inside job. Perhaps even most of it. But there is a real danger in saying so because some people will use this powerful esoteric teaching as an excuse for dropping out and copping out. Performative Oneness, or the more well-known spiritual by-passing, is a real danger to those in need of help. I did my share of by-passing until I found and embraced shadow work.

The term "shadow" was coined by famed psychologist Carl Jung, who also identified and popularized the understanding of archetypes. We will dive more deeply into shadow work in later chapters. For now, it's useful to know that in the context of this book, shadow work is a type of deep spiritual inquiry that asks us to become aware of the unconscious beliefs that run like computer programming below the surface of our conscious minds. Our shadow is the part of us that we have disowned, denied, and hidden from ourselves. Very often, it takes the form of unhealthy limiting beliefs about oneself and the world. It's the stuff that got swept or placed under the rug, often without our consent, most likely in our early years. Although it is unseen, it has a significant impact on how we perceive and interact with the world. By lifting the rug and looking into those shadowy places, we become capable of seeing the root causes of our destructive behaviors so that they can be addressed. It's messy work. Yet, it is an absolute necessity in order to find and live from oneness—because *true* oneness makes space for the good, the bad, *and* the ugly. Far from advocating for toxic positivity, true oneness includes the capacity to acknowledge and sit with pain (ours and others) so that we can re-make our inner and outer world in a more kind and just way.

If you have hung in here with me this far, I will assume that you are not interested in avoiding these glaring injustices. Instead, you are here because you know in your bones that it is your absolute responsibility to address these injustices. Perhaps you sense that often the most potent path to being of service in this way is to embody your own sacred feminine sovereignty. It can feel so delicious to feel the profound peace of oneness. However, it can also be deeply disorienting, intense, rageful, and full of agony as we burn away what no longer serves.

Many of us have found our way to personal transformation work because we have been appalled at the state of the world we see around us. Or maybe our relationship failed, our families are in crisis, or our jobs aren't going well. In any case, the time eventually arises when we see that we can't *really* make any progress *out there* without first addressing what is *in here*.

Why is this so?

In her seminal book *Hands of Light: A Guide to Healing through the Human Energy Field*, Dr. Barbara Ann Brennan, former NASA physicist and world-renowned teacher of energy healing, writes that each of us arrives in this life with a personal task and a world task. She notes that the life we experience is designed to help us along the way. Sometimes we experience the exact opposite of our personal task's aim in order to bring forward the skills we will need to accomplish it. Other times we are surrounded by what we need to make our connection to it stronger. Either way, she says, the personal task must be resolved before we can go on to complete our world task. It is the personal task that prepares us to give our gift to the world. This is why we are charged to become healed and whole and step fully into self-mastery and self-sovereignty. Along the way, we may find our lives becoming more meaningful and magical as well.

The many profound experiences of oneness I have been blessed to experience all keep pointing me back to the same underlying fabric of reality: My job is to *be* the new way, *be* the new pace, *be* the new frequency *now*; to embody it and help anchor it; to be the Queen I need, the Queen we all need. This kind of embodiment is not about mood-making. It is about developing a sovereign relationship with *What Is* and moving from there. We cannot be truly sovereign if we continually cut ourselves such a narrow path of life to avoid bumping up against our own, and humanity's, horseshit. The sovereign is not afraid of horseshit, not afraid to see it or name it. She also doesn't try to pass some sort of royal decree that the horse should never shit again. She recognizes that horses are powerful, beautiful, and strong. And horses shit.

One of the beautiful things about having regular brushes with the Divine is the comfort of knowing that the cast of characters populating my world are playing out roles I can't fully understand. So while I am often called upon to locate and use my holy HELL NO, I am at my most potent and powerful when I can do so from a place of non-judgment. Ignoring the horseshit of life just makes it worse. It will just keep on stinking if I refuse to tend to it. But there's no point in burning down my stall in anger or outrage. I simply need to become masterful at mucking it out or find someone who is.

Analogies aside, the pain-body within us and around us is real. My heart breaks every day for the suffering in our world. I pray that we will make this shift with just the requisite amount of suffering necessary—and not one drop more. I'm both aching *and* calm, accepting of it *and* devastated by it. In the end, though, I'm deeply hopeful. We are in a death and rebirth process. There will be a baby at the end of it. But it can't happen without pain, contractions, and the ring of fire being activated.

Once again, we can look to story and myth to help us understand the energies at play. The ancient Greeks told the story of the phoenix, a magical bird that dies and is reborn. It lives a cyclical life that includes a fiery ending followed by the spectacular act of regeneration. The theme of death and rebirth is a common one in human history. Death and resurrection is an integral part of Egyptian Mysticism, features in Greek mythology and other Near East non-Abrahamic religions, is found in Buddhism, and is at the core of Christianity. There's a reason that humans look to this story for illumination in times of challenge: it offers comfort inside of a predictable path forward.

But the phoenix can't rise from the ashes if it is holding on to even one feather. It must let go and allow it all to burn to ash. Yet, what people most often miss in this magical tale is that it's not the fire that is the moment of truth (that's the big, bright, attention-getting part.) Instead, it's the pause after the fire, the stillness, the moment of not knowing (the three days in the tomb) when the burning is over, and nothing new has yet emerged, that is the Transmutation. This is the true initiatory moment. This is the time when we decide who we are. And then we can rise into what we have chosen to be. If there is no fire, no stillness, no hopelessness of ever going back, we cannot choose to be something new.

I believe stories and metaphors of transformative becoming, like the phoenix, are crucial for navigating these mythic times. They have left clues for us as we seek to find our way forward, and I look to them for comfort and meaning.

So, where are you in the burning cycle? In what ways has your world burned down? What feathers are you still holding on to? Let's dive into those fiery moments and the potential of the ashes next.

"I am not free while any woman is unfree, even when her shackles are very different from my own."

—Audre Lorde

Chapter 2
The Curse of Un-Sovereignty

Sovereignty is defined as supreme power and authority, free from external control, a state of self-governance. How many of us have felt deeply, truly sovereign in our lives? As children, we live under our parents' rules and structures based on the structures they were taught to live by. This can mean religions, philosophies, shadow beliefs, ignorance and biases, and all the great stuff, like hopes and dreams, love and kindness, care and concern, encouragement, and support. In school, we also find ourselves under someone else's dominance, someone else's plan for our day, our life, our soul. Same thing if we attended services or classes at church, in temple, synagogue, or mosque. In our teen years, we often seek to differentiate from these outside influences.

We may dissolve ties to our childhood authority figures and seek solace in our friends. But our social circle is also an external influence. It often acts as a golden cage as our peers' expectations can cause us to curb essential aspects of who we are. The fear of feeling outcast or separate from the group can be overwhelming and follow us the rest of our days into our jobs or careers. Once again, we give ourselves over again to the ideals and expectations of our environment. And finally, this giving over of self follows us into our intimate relationships. If we enter our intimate relationships under the sway of outside forces, out of need, out of expectation, unaware of who we are, or unwilling to expose ourselves to create true intimacy, we may find ourselves locked inside golden handcuffs of our own making.

For most of us, who we think we are isn't our truest self. It's a mask of some sort that hides the brilliance and beauty of who we are from the world and maybe even from ourselves. Our society is not set up to allow for soul-level inquiry and exploration as part of the process of growing up, especially if you don't have the resources necessary to engage effective teachers or take the time and space to meet your soul. There is some sense that things must change. I am heartened to see that those with the means are choosing to take a gap year between high school and college so that they can explore the world and themselves before committing to a path that might stay fixed for decades.

The struggle for sovereignty is even more challenging for women. While it is fashionable for western women to feel powerful now that we have greater access to the power places that were once reserved only for men, that access just opened us to a new kind of dilemma, a new form of subjugation. We needed access to the economic opportunities the work world provides so that we could chart our path forward and avoid or leave unhealthy relationships. Yet the work itself often became another master to which we tied ourselves. Life has improved, but in the end, this access has not made us any happier overall.

According to what researchers at Yale University dubbed, *The Paradox—Declining Female Happiness*, women's sense of well-being and happiness has fallen significantly even though women have experienced substantial economic gains over the last thirty-five years *and* despite the fact that when asked, women say their lives are indeed better now, with greater choice and more opportunity. This drop is both in relation to happiness reported by men and in general when measured against previous levels of happiness among women.

Interestingly, researchers were puzzled that increasing wealth did not correlate with increased happiness once it moved past a certain point. In addition, it seems that even in countries with less discrimination or improvements in the gender pay gap, women's overall happiness has not increased. It appears the women's movement may have not yet translated happiness gains for women. The authors of the study provide several possible reasons for this:

- The mega-trend of increased social disunity seems to disproportionately affect women over men.
- While women got more economic power, it came with more economic responsibility.
- Despite the increase in responsibility outside the home, many still hold the vast majority of the household and parenting responsibilities.
- Marital happiness is lower among women who work than those who don't.
- Even in households where men "helped out" or even took more ownership of home and parenting, women's happiness levels did not improve, while men's happiness did!
- Women may be feeling less happy because they are now comparing themselves and their lives to male colleagues, whereas before the 1970s, they mainly compared their life with other women.
- The increase in social media has also increased the instances of negative life-comparison.

I have seen this sense of dis-ease in myself as well as in my students.

Joan came to me for support with her unhappiness at work. She was a high-level executive in a non-profit organization. She loved the organization's mission and the people on her team, but new leadership had arrived, and she was being asked to track all sorts of new metrics. All this translated into lots of hours at work, lots of pressure in her system, and lots of frustration and exhaustion. She was also newly married to a wonderful man and concerned that the extended focus on her work would interfere with their connection. Not new to marriage, she was determined to extend the "honeymoon" phase of the marriage as long as possible.

Christine was a brash and animated spitfire who showed up in one of my energy classes. She'd arrived at middle age with well-constructed armor and the battle scars to prove her life had been challenging, to say the least. In college, she was at the forefront of women's leadership, particularly in the arena of public policy. After college, she headed to Washington DC as a policy specialist advising public officials in high office. She moved in impressive power circles and began a relationship with an older man that turned toxic. After the devastating breakup, Christine fell into a deep depression. Then she had a spiritual awakening. She packed up everything and moved back to her home state of Florida. By the time I met Christine, she had spent years nursing her mother through her transition. She was exhausted and struggling financially. She was working in a low-paying job, but one with a spiritual focus that she enjoyed. She had been celibate for twenty years. Her body was numb. She was carrying a fair amount of extra weight, what I call "shielding" weight that is consciously or unconsciously designed to provide safety and distance from men and the possibility of partnership. Yet, she knew that she was meant for more in this life.

Jasmine was a young woman in a new marriage with a young child. While her marriage started out well, things had gone south pretty quickly. Jasmine was dedicated to her child and had done a lot of spiritual study. She knew that she had so much to heal from her abusive past. To her credit, Jasmine took responsibility for how her past experiences, including sexual abuse, were causing her relationship challenges. She was working hard to hold the relationship together, doing all she knew how to heal herself and therefore improve her marriage, but it wasn't enough. Before long, Jasmine asked her partner to come with her to get help for his traumas so that they could create a new, healthier relationship for both of them and their child. She was devastated and full of anger when he refused. She felt trapped and struggled with how to manage all the competing tensions.

Each in her own way, these women sought a more authentic, whole, and decidedly more feminine way of living and working in the world. They sought greater sovereignty over their life circumstances, greater connection with themselves, and the resulting rewards. However, if you asked them what they needed, self-sovereignty would not be the answer. At first, it appeared they needed a better boss, an available man, or a more engaged partner. This is often how it goes. At first, the answers to our problems seem to be outside of ourselves. Or we make someone else, or the lack thereof, the cause of our discontent.

It's not unusual to sometimes struggle with feeling inadequate and unsatisfied despite all our efforts to create a successful, healthy, and happy life. No one talks about the toll it takes on us to keep all the balls in the air. We sacrifice sleep. We postpone our dreams. We ignore our needs. We lose connection with our bodies. We settle for less than what brings us joy. We work ourselves harder and longer than is healthy. And it never seems to be enough.

Many of us have become unwitting members of the *Not-Enough Club*:

- not enough energy to complete the never-ending task-list
- not enough time to tend to what's *really* important
- not enough support to allow the moments of rest you deserve
- not enough money to cover the growing cost of living
- not enough love to meet the deep longing in your heart
- not enough freedom to create the life of your dreams...

I used to be a card-carrying member of the Not-Enough Club. As a wife, mother, and entrepreneur with three businesses to run, I was constantly on the go. After years of pushing myself to succeed, I had the kind of life that looked like a dream on the outside: A loving husband, a beautiful daughter, a lovely home, and meaningful work. Yet, there seemed to be something inexplicable between me and my joy. Despite investing thousands of dollars in business training, self-help books, personal development workshops, and goddess retreats, none made a lasting difference. Every gain I made eventually faded, and I found myself right back where I started: feeling like there was simply not enough time, money, love, etc. Eventually, I began to believe the problem was ME and that I must not be enough.

It wasn't until I learned that the lifestyle we have inherited as modern women is energetically a "net-negative" that it all began to make sense to me. In truth, we have landed in the Not-Enough Club through no fault of our own. We were told that we can do it all and have it all–and we can! But we've been trained to get it in a way that drains rather than fills our energy reserves. The quest for success has us operating in a way that runs counter to what works for us as women: for our body, our heart, and our soul. We are paying a huge cost to be part of this club which we never intended to join. Here are some indications you are in the club:

You feel constantly driven, operating at high speeds on an empty tank.

- You feel frazzled or frustrated, overworking, and overdoing.
- You feel drained, cranky, or irritable—and not in the mood for lovin'.
- You feel tired and run-down, perhaps even facing significant health challenges.
  You feel overwhelmed, undervalued, and unappreciated.
- You feel shut down, numbed out, or disengaged.
- You feel hopeless or trapped.

These symptoms are the curse of un-sovereignty. And the worst part is we have gotten so good at hiding it from ourselves and others that we fear we may never get what we need to live a sovereign, self-directed, sustainable, and joy-filled life. Deep down, we may be terrified that it's just too late for us. My work with women has offered me the opportunity to learn from so many unique situations. But if I boil them all down into the underlying issues, they usually fall into one or more of these three problem areas:

Problem #1: We have been trained to work like men

We live in a world energetically more suited to men, so most women have been trained to operate energetically like men. Perhaps you have created some success in your life by mimicking masculine power patterns. You are not alone in this. But as women, our energy system is unsuited to this. You simply *cannot* be a more powerful man than the men. You can, however, be a more powerful woman!

Problem #2: You don't have the help you need to slow down

If you are a high achieving, capable woman, you may be unknowingly closed energetically to receiving help, which is why you may sometimes refuse, shrug off, or criticize the help you get. The truth is that most women don't get the support they desperately want because they simply do not know how to be completely open to and fully receive the help that is available.

Problem #3: You don't know how to stop doing

This is not your fault. As a woman, you have a heart made for doing. Yet, it's problematic if you don't also tend to yourself or accurately measure how much you really have to give. This leads to over-giving, and before you know it, resentment, criticism, contempt, and defensiveness, all of which threaten to poison your thoughts and wreak havoc on your love.

I know these three problems well. I lived them for much of my life. But like the phoenix who can't be reborn until it has first burned to ash, I couldn't break the curse of un-sovereignty and renounce my membership in the Not-Enough Club until I was first willing to part with the version of me that kept me entrenched in these unhealthy patterns. Something had to die so that I could be reborn.

"Of all the nasty outcomes predicted for women's liberation ... none was more alarming than the suggestion that women would eventually become just like men."

—Barbara Ehrenreich

CHAPTER 3
SURRENDERING SUPERWOMAN

She stood looking out the kitchen window, transfixed, proud, and maybe even a tiny bit jealous, as she watched her 8-year-old wisp of a daughter. The girl was struggling to teach herself to ride a bike. The bike she had was adult-sized, making it incredibly difficult. Over and over, she tilted the bike toward the ground, put her foot on the pedal, and tried to mount the bike. Over and over, she fell. Until, at last, she didn't.

I have no recollection of this story, but my mom tells me it was the moment when she knew beyond a doubt that I would be okay in the world. I would find a way or forge a path if there was none yet. I may not remember it, but I know it. It feels like me. Getting over on that bike. Fighting my way onto it and making it bend to my wishes.

That trait, that persistence and sense of "I can, and I will," served me well over the years as I stacked up significance and accomplishment. Until it didn't anymore; until it became a master that stole my freedom and my joy.

I have a confession to make. For most of my life, I have had *no idea* how to be a woman.

Growing up in my home, it was clear where the power was. My father was the axis around which the entire family spun. He was the dominant force, busy, emotionally unavailable, and often harshly critical. My mother seemed completely stumped by this. Her father was the sweet, kind one in her family, and her mother was the tough one who ran the household. I guess that's how she thought it would be for her. She had no skills for holding her own in the face of my father's domineering energy. From where I stood, it looked as though she had ceded her power on all fronts—except with us kids. (Shit, as they say, rolls downhill.) As a mother, she alternated between being lovingly engaged and angrily abusive. It was a mixed bag for sure. Looking back, it's easy to see and appreciate all the wonderful things my parents did for my siblings and me, but at the time, emotional and physical safety was never a given.

Somewhere along the way, I grew determined to never become powerless the way I judged my mother to be. It rankled me to see it. I became a classic tomboy helping my dad with his projects, watching football games with him on Sundays, facing down bullies for my older brother at school, and being spunky and tough in every possible way. My mom used to complain that I had my dad wrapped around my little finger. It made me feel powerful. I learned to see everything in life as a fight or a challenge, and I intended to rise to every one of them.

I was always more comfortable hanging out with the boys than the girls. I had crushes on boys, but they never liked me back. While it was a source of frustration and pain for me at the time, having studied the human energy-body, it's not at all surprising to me now. Boys just didn't think of me "in that way" because to them, my energy just didn't read "girl."

I had no idea that I had already begun taxing my body by habitually running too much masculine energy. While it helped me feel strong and safe, it came at a cost. I remember going to a birthday swim party in fifth grade with a bunch of girlfriends. The birthday girl suggested we style ourselves with our towels and some props and do an impromptu beauty contest. We had a swimsuit, evening gown, and talent rounds. I tried my best and thought I had done okay. As she announced the contest results, I got a lump in my throat when it became clear she wasn't just going to choose the winner and runner up. First, second, third, fourth place... As she went down the line, I felt the sting of her judgment and the burn of humiliation when I came in last.

I ached to be like the other girls, but I felt clueless. They had something I didn't, and I had no idea what it was. Later that summer, I found the secret to soothing that ache in a TV commercial for the perfume *Enjoule*. It ran constantly that year. I can still see the woman and hear the jingle in my head.

> *I can bring home the bacon,*
> *fry it up in a pan,*
> *and never, ever let him forget he's a man,*
> *'cause I'm a woman!*

It's laughable as I watch it now, but at the time, it cut me to my core. I wanted to be both powerful and beautiful. Both respected and desired. I wanted to be the woman in the ad—but I had no idea how to get there.

I wasn't about to give up the safety I felt with my tomboy power, but with the help of puberty and hormones, my body became womanly. My energy grew exponentially. This got me into huge trouble by the time I got to college. I was outgoing and powerful with my *I can do anything* mentality and also running a lot of feminine and sexual energy. But I had no idea how to handle it. I attracted bad boy types who felt the challenge to best the tomboy in me and get the reward of my womanly goods. They would woo me intensely and I'd fall into bed with them, always mystified as to why they never wanted to be my boyfriend for long (if at all). It was a painful and confusing time.

My tomboy energy was a boon at work, though. I could hang with the guys and do, do, do like the best of them! I became a SuperStar at every job I had. It wasn't uncommon that workplaces would need to hire two people to replace me after I left. But as I grew older and sought to have a family of my own, my tomboy energy got in the way.

My first husband was a marine who served in Desert Storm. He was man enough for both of us, so my tomboy went underground for a while. He was good-looking and popular, and I felt like I had won the lottery. The first year and a half with him was like heaven. I worked days and he worked nights, but our weekends together were enough. I still was a boss at work, but eventually, that energy started seeping into my home life, and our marriage began to suffer. I was still unconsciously treating everything like a competition, and since we had so little time together, I wanted all of his attention when we were off work. He preferred watching football and mowing the grass. We fought a lot. And our sex life was a wreck. He rarely initiated sex, even though he said he always enjoyed it once it got going. During sex, he'd often wonder out loud why we didn't do it more often. I wondered the same thing. It hurt. I internalized the issue and agonized over what was so wrong with me. Was I too fat, too thin, not a good lover, not sexy enough? Weeks would go by without intimacy if I didn't initiate. My self-esteem plummeted. I didn't understand that the energy between us was completely off. It didn't matter that I found him deeply attractive and wanted more sex. Because I pursued him, it actually made it worse.

We were depolarized, with too much masculine energy in our space. At the time, I had no words to describe this dynamic, just a gnawing, painful awareness that something was wrong. I blamed myself and then I blamed him. I became critical and he criticized me back. He began drinking—a lot. Our fights became more intense. To my horror, I grew meeker and more afraid. I collapsed in on myself when I was around him, ceding my power just like my mother had. When I asked him to come with me to get help for our relationship, he told me he wasn't interested in personal growth. It was everything I had hoped to avoid, yet this was my life. I felt like I was dying in slow motion, and I didn't know what to do about it. I was twenty-eight and felt like a failure as a person *and* as a woman. Eventually, I left the marriage. But it took the attention of another man to pull me out of it.

About six months before I exited my marriage, I developed a crush on a young man I worked with. At a work happy hour, he caught me making an angry gesture toward him after he cracked a particularly funny joke. It was born out of frustration. I was angry with myself for the growing infatuation I felt and angry at him as well for being so damned good-looking. He pushed me to tell him what was going on. I hedged, but eventually, he got me to cough up the truth. I told him that I had a crush on him and that I wished that I didn't. He was seven years younger than me, funny, handsome, with a girlfriend I knew he loved, although she lived in another state at the time. I thought he would say he was flattered, but no thanks. Or perhaps he'd just laugh at me, and that would be the end of it. I was wrong. To my utter shock, he told me he was into me as well. After that, he went out of his way to flirt with me. No one had ever pursued me with so much skill and effort before. It was intoxicating. There was a lot of sexual energy between us. I was so starved for attention; I allowed the intrigue to grow. We spent time together outside of work several times. Even though nothing beyond one very passionate kiss happened until after I left my marriage, I was mortified by my behavior. And it only got worse.

One of the things I discovered about myself in that marriage and my effort to exit it was how much I looked to men to tell me I was worthy of love. For me, it was like an addiction. It took the form of co-dependency, but it didn't stop there. I was so hung up on this young guy that even after discovering he was a real player and regularly cheated on his girlfriend, I continued seeing him. Over the next eight months, I was in this un-relationship with him. We really liked and respected each other, but he was utterly incapable of having a committed relationship, and I had no desire to be one of the women in his harem. So we agreed just to be friends. Weeks would go by and it would be fine, and then one or the other of us would reach out, and we'd end up in bed together again. After a few days, we'd come to our senses and resolve to go back to being friends. *Lather, rinse, repeat.* The attraction was so strong, neither of us seemed able to resist it for long.

A friend suggested I read Pia Melody's powerful book, *Facing Love Addiction,* and I saw myself all over the pages. Who knew there was such a thing as Love Addiction?! Fortunately, Bill W's powerful 12-step program for alcoholics, Alcoholic Anonymous, had been adapted to help addicts of all kinds. I discovered that there was help for codependents and love addicts, too. Sitting in those groups, I began to understand myself better. Between my meetings and the help of a good therapist, I was able to see that I had related to all of the men in my life in the same way. I had wanted them to help me feel better about myself. If they just loved me enough or in the right way, it would prove I was good enough. I would finally know I was desirable and worthy of love. I had no sense of my own sovereignty. I had located what my therapist called the "locus of control" outside of myself, usually in the man of the moment. Once I saw this, there was no unseeing it.

I felt like I had woken up from a bad dream. I broke off the un-relationship with my young friend for good and got to work on myself, making significant progress and deep changes in how I saw myself and related to others. I learned about boundaries and how I lacked them and began to do the hard work of setting healthy boundaries for myself. I looked unflinchingly at the coping patterns I had taken on to survive my early years and how they contributed to my inability to hold my power around men. It helped a lot. But it didn't get at the energy imbalance that was at the root of my relationship challenges and my lack of self-sovereignty.

Even so, within a few years, I was happy again, feeling more empowered and successful in my work. I had taken a nice long break from men and had found salsa dancing which gave me a safe and structured way to feel like a woman. Latin men responded well to my body type, and I felt beautiful and desirable, possibly for the first time in my life.

Learning to partner dance was a significant first step toward straightening out my energy body. My role was clear: I needed to follow the man's lead. I got immediate feedback when I tried to lead, and I was able to surrender to the dance and to my partner on the dance floor. It was such a powerful experience. I absolutely loved the feeling of being surrendered in this safe and structured way. I dated here and there, mostly younger men, mostly fleeting romances. But nothing too disastrous. I was still learning how to hold my own with men. But for the most part, I was focused on my career and my personal growth. And I had a large circle of dance friends who got together several nights a week. I worked hard, and I danced. And that was enough.

After my divorce, I left the Catholic church. There was really no place there for a young, divorced woman. No matter the parish I attended, the predominant view was that a woman's value was as a wife and a mother. I was neither, so that left me out. I started attending Unity, a New Thought church with a focus on positive spirituality. It was a welcoming and loving spiritual home. I joined a prayer group. We met in a large hall with several other groups. It was there I was blessed to meet my husband Tobias, a wonderful man. In less than a year, we were married, and we started our family right away. It felt wonderful being pregnant. Growing my daughter Sophia inside me was such a delight. There was no denying my womanhood with her inside me. I LOVED IT. And I loved her. She brought some much-needed feminine balance to my life.

After she was born, life took on new meaning. She opened my heart and made me want to be a better person. I was determined to be the kind of mom I had always wanted—strong, capable, loving, and present. I was committed to being a SuperMom! As you'll read later, I threw myself into my self-growth so that I could give Sophia the kind of childhood I knew she deserved. It was a rich time of expansion, and it paid all sorts of dividends.

Now I was a SuperStar at work and a SuperMom at home. Perfect life, right?

The problem is that, like a career, the act of mothering requires us to *do, do, do*. It is hugely draining and requires tons of energy. And the only source of power I knew was my tomboy energy. As my daughter grew and the mothering took more out of me, the same power struggles I faced in my first marriage began to surface in my second, some of which I'll share in more detail later.

But this time, I was determined not to fail. I had done heaps of work on myself. And I had learned how to surface the hidden beliefs that ran in the background, my unconscious operating system, that would scuttle this relationship too if I allowed it. When competition reared its head once again, I used my newfound tools to make it visible, writing in my journal:

"Today has been a good day, and so was yesterday...More major aha's have come through for me. Like how one of my habits is turning everything into a competition ~ every conversation, every job, every decision on what to wear, what to order in a restaurant, what to cook for my family, etc... they have all subconsciously been about speaking RIGHT, choosing RIGHT, acting RIGHT, performing RIGHT so that I would win, so I would come out on top because if I don't, you will. And of course, you will most certainly shove my failings in my face, clearly demonstrating my unworthiness to exist and making it painfully clear how unlovable I really am. Whew! So glad to bring that festering wound to the surface so it can dry up and blow away! It is a good sign to see this stuff coming out of the woodwork where it has been hiding and eating away at the foundations of my self-concept."

Shadow work is now one of the go-to items in my Medicine Bag, more on that in chapter five. It was a painful process learning to stay present to these ugly, hidden beliefs. But I wasn't going to be beaten by these shadowy lies.

I intuitively began to organize my life in a more balanced way. I left the corporate world. I pursued a doctorate in Transformational Psychology as an appropriate place to focus my "doing energy." I collaborated with two colleagues to develop a powerful 21-day shadow work practice that supports people in surfacing and resolving un-healed childhood wounds. I began speaking and teaching workshops at spiritual communities across North America. It was work I deeply enjoyed, and it was making a real difference. For a decade, I was living and breathing shadow work. Not only helping others but also helping myself. Much of my inner child found her way home to a place of safety within me. It was truly a beautiful time in my life, filled with expansion and healing.

But, old habits die hard, and I eventually grew my work into two businesses and then a third! My challenge-loving tomboy energy was back on top and once again creating huge amounts of tension in the house and causing problems in my sex life.

I attended women's workshops to try to fix what felt off. I developed a *SuperMe* who was now supposed to find time to do yoga, paint, and find other ways to nurture myself, along with being a *SuperStar* entrepreneur and a *SuperMom* to my now pre-teen daughter. As if that wasn't enough, I was determined to get our sex life back on track, so I headed off to workshops and therapy so I could be a *SuperWife*, too. And it worked! Tobias and I began to have sex more often, and more importantly, it was more fulfilling sex. We were connected and loving, and in tune for the first time since our early days together.

Finally, at the age of forty-six, I had it all. I was the woman in the commercial! I was bringing home the bacon with meaningful work I loved. I was caring for my daughter and being the attentive and loving mom I had always wanted; I was loving on my man, and *BONUS!* I was loving myself too.

I had made solid progress in overcoming shadow conditioning that had made it hard for me to live fully in my body. I passionately wanted to share the lessons I was learning about my own embodiment and self-sovereignty with my students, so I expanded my focus and work with women to include teaching and coaching on feminine embodiment practices. The problem was that my tomboy energy was still as hyperactive as ever. I had just overbalanced it by ratcheting up my feminine energy so that I felt and looked more feminine. Yet, in reality, much of what I did, including at times being feminine, was coming from a place of meeting and beating a challenge.

Congratulations to me! I had now graduated to full-on SuperWoman status. I was flying high! Little did I know it was all about to come crashing down.

It took something big to convince me to give up the fight I started as a little girl getting over on that bicycle. My teacher came in the form of chronic pain. Not mine, but my husband's. He developed a rare nerve condition which led to consistent and chronic face pain. His pain level kept increasing until one day he came home from work in tears and admitted he didn't know if he could continue on living if this was going to be his new normal. It was so crazy painful to watch my beloved suffer. I was afraid of losing him, our quality of life, and the quality of our relationship. I was afraid for myself and for my daughter. And I had the mistaken idea that I had to minimize this, or at least manage it, for all our sakes. I was SuperWoman, after all, and I was determined to fight this thing and make it all go away.

But this illness was determined to show me the truth. It unceremoniously made me see that I did not, in fact, have the power to make it all better, even if I believed that I did. It forced me to look at some very hard things, to own that I dragged my husband through numerous edgy, all-natural, holistic, and in some cases just plain weird treatments—because it's what I would have done. But my efforts only led to tension, spoken and unspoken criticism, and resentment between us.

Finally, after one treatment went really wrong, I made myself stop. I saw clearly how my SuperWoman had taken over and squeezed my beloved out of his own life. My actions caused real harm, not just by adding to Tobias' physical pain but by hurting his psyche or sense of self as a man. My energy had grown so big and so masculine that to keep the peace, he either had to ramp up his energy high enough to beat mine back (which he couldn't do in his state of pain) or abandon himself in the face of it. Super Ouch! Once I saw that, it didn't take long for me to connect the dots and see that my enormous energy hadn't left much room for my daughter either. Super-Duper Ouch!

I sat with the results of my behaviors and the underlying energy pattern. I looked deep within myself. And I finally allowed myself to feel how utterly exhausted I was from fighting for every single thing my whole life. I had been living on the verge of collapse for longer than I cared to admit, holding it all together by sheer force of will. It was time to stop fighting. I was terrified. I had no idea how to live without being Super.

My soul-sister Allison Conte, founder of Sophia Leadership, was doing deep work in Feminine Leadership, and she began sharing some teachings with me that would change my life. Eventually, she pointed me to a deep dive workshop called *The Dance of the Masculine and Feminine* taught by two masters of energy, Lynda Caesara and Tj Bartel. Sitting in circle with Linda and Tj, I finally found the structures that sat at the foundation of my core issues. Years of confusion and mystery fell away, and my life experience finally began to make sense to me. But it wasn't a cakewalk. Despite the fact that I had more than a decade of experience as a shadow work facilitator and had been exploring feminine practices with my students, *I got my ass handed to me in this course.*

Taking the course was no small thing. The program consisted of ten full days at a retreat center on the east coast. It meant a significant investment of time and money. But I had already learned that deep immersion work with a competent teacher was the fastest way to supercharge my growth, so I packed my bags and headed east. Even before I left home, I began to feel a kind of nervous excitement building in me. This intensified as I arrived. It grew even stronger as the first day of the program unfolded. I felt completely ungrounded and out of my body, and at the same time, I had this terrible knot plaguing my solar plexus.

As a women's empowerment coach, I was baffled by how hard it seemed to be for me to be at peace in my body and show up powerfully within the group. I had no problem understanding the material intellectually. Outwardly, I am sure nothing looked amiss, but there was a battle going on inside my body. It brought up feelings of fear and anxiety and the shadow beliefs of inadequacy and unworthiness. I often found myself intimidated by Lynda and sometimes the other students. Everyone was very friendly and super professional, so there was no rational reason for my response.

This raised the stakes for me as I furiously leaned into each lesson she taught and gave my all in the exercises we undertook. By the end of the day, I found myself feeling a little more embodied and had intermittent success dissolving the knot. But when class resumed the next day, it seemed I had to start all over again. This pattern repeated itself day after day. It turns out that Lynda had put in place an energetic field with a very high vibration which she increased day by day. She had set the intent that, while in the course, the students would be challenged to stay embodied and in presence for the purpose of having to work deeply with the tools she was teaching.

It was brutal, and it was beautiful.

I decided to book a private energy session with Tj to help me. The session was powerful and made a significant difference in my experience. But I was still struggling to feel at peace. The turning point for me came in the middle of a sleepless night on Day 7—when I used my shadow work practice to help me get at what was under the experience I was having. As I found and released an old story about power, sexuality, and shame and moved into the healing, a profound awareness came forward from my heart. It showed me how all week I had been trying to use my masculine power to *make myself* get into my feminine power. That gave me a good laugh.

I decided to simply surrender to what was appearing in my body, to welcome every sensation, every failed effort, every moment of struggle, and then shift my focus toward what I wanted to experience (feminine power) and away from managing what I didn't want to experience (my masculine energy). The change in my body was instantaneous and completely palpable.

Surrender is a cornerstone of feminine power. It took three more days of focused practice to hold it, but by the end of the course, my skill sets had grown beyond anything I could have imagined at the start of the course. I was able to understand feminine energy and actually feel and hold it in my body. I felt soft and comfortable in my own skin for the first time in my life.

When I returned home, I was confronted with the consequences of living almost exclusively from my masculine. It broke my heart to see my daughter bracing for my energy as I came through the door. She had come to expect the fiery feel of my SuperWoman. But my system was now exquisitely balanced, so my energy was much quieter. I watched her from a distance as she sized me up, trying to figure out what was different and likely wondering if it was a trick. Within the hour, her energy had settled and attuned to mine. I could see the anxiety melt from her face and body. She seemed open, happy, and comfortable, so much so that the next evening she came to me seeking advice about a boy at school. Unbeknownst to me, she had been struggling with this for months. The boy had a crush on her, and she wasn't sure how to deal with the confusion she felt. We had the most beautiful talk about what it means to be a woman. I was able to teach her some of what I had learned about the dynamics of masculine and feminine energy so that she could untangle her confusion. It was a moment I will always cherish.

My husband also felt the difference in my energy. He, too, was waiting for my tomboy energy to show up in a state of challenge. He would later say that on some level, he always felt that I was resisting him, which I was. In this new state, there was simply me being me and him being him. I felt safe and secure in my feminine power and ability to manage my energy skillfully. Our first big challenge came a few days after I got home. He announced that he had invited a couple and their two small children over for dinner. The man was a friend from his men's group. I had met this couple once or twice, and they were friendly people. But I was still feeling protective of my new energy and not keen to prepare the house for guests and cook a big meal for our two families.

Rather than being angry that he invited them without checking in with me, I calmly said I thought that sounded nice but that I wouldn't be attending. I explained I would leave the house in the afternoon and come back after they left, probably around 10 pm. He went ballistic. This was not something he was used to. He figured he'd have to hash it out with me but that I would acquiesce, choosing to rise to the challenge he issued. Not this time. I listened to him rail, but rather than get sucked into a confrontation; I used the skills I learned from Lynda and Tj. I stayed in my feminine energy and repeated that it was fine for him to have them over but that I would not be participating. When he started yelling again, I planted my feet and, just as they had taught me, imagining my words coming from the floor up and looking him right in the eyes, I spoke evenly but firmly saying, "Honey, don't be a dick."

His mouth dropped open and he went silent. I had delivered a nugget of truth in the way only The Feminine can do. It was not a challenge. It was a fact. He turned on his heels and left for work without saying another word. The whole thing was over in about 3 minutes. I marveled at the power of communicating from my embodied feminine sovereignty. Two days later, we dropped in and unpacked what had happened so we could learn from it. He acknowledged that I had held up a mirror to him regarding his behavior with a kind of power and grace that left him unable to refute it. He didn't like my choice, but ultimately he could respect it.

I continued my practices to stay in my feminine sovereignty and as disagreements arose, I was able to put into practice all I had learned and quickly deescalate the situation allowing us to find respectful resolution in minutes. I remain forever grateful to have found the teachings I needed to shift from a SuperWoman to a sovereign woman, to open to and explore a healthier archetype, one better suited to my time in life: The Queen.

It's time to hang up our superwoman capes and don our Queen crowns.

"The world will be saved by the Western woman."
—HH The Dalai Lama

"In every woman there is a Queen. Speak to the Queen and the Queen will answer."
—Norwegian Proverb, Barbara Ehrenreich

CHAPTER 4
From Cape to Crown

If you have been around the block a time or two in your development as a woman, you may have heard of the three stages of a woman's life: Maiden, Mother, and Crone. These stages have their roots in the three-fold image of the Goddess popularized in the early to mid-1900s. The Triple Goddess is based on the interpretations of various texts and archeological discoveries from cultures that worshiped the feminine divine. Some eighty years later, the return of the Goddess is driving enormous cultural shifts, or it's just as possible that the enormous cultural shifts we are experiencing are driving the return of the Goddess.

Either way, the act of looking backward for truth is relatively new in human history. The rediscovery of beautifully preserved sites such as Pompeii and Herculaneum caused quite a stir, awakening a hunger for the history of humankind. Hidden under copious amounts of ash from Mount Vesuvius's eruption, the life of ancient Romans, from their luxurious homes to their public buildings, was revealed in great detail. Having recently emerged from the dark ages, the Renaissance looked to the Greco-Roman era for inspiration and information on how to move forward, and Neoclassicism was born. Renaissance art, literature, architecture, and music all pulled heavily from Greek and Roman cultures of antiquity.

The hunt for lost civilizations began in earnest. By the late 17th century, archaeology shifted into its modern form of utilizing corroborating ancient texts to discern the correct use and context for everything from everyday items to architectural monuments. Knowledge of this treasure trove of discoveries became a benchmark for all wealthy gentlemen and men of noble birth who, for about 200 years, were expected to set out on "The Grand Tour" of key sites for their own education. Not far behind that came the mind-bending discoveries of ancient Egypt, launching a whole new level of interest in lost spirituality, stealing much of the thunder (and mystery) from the Greco-Roman sites.

By the late 1800s, these discoveries were being shared more widely through the paintings and writings of artists and formal study of archeology in Universities across Europe. The Cambridge Ritualists were one of many academic groups intrigued by these discoveries. They sought to understand these cultures more deeply by looking through the lens of religious rites and rituals to get a foothold on the cultures in question. This group, in particular the scholar Jane Ellen Harrison, deeply influenced poet, novelist, and mythographer

Robert Graves, whose work we owe much of our understanding of the three-fold Goddess that we have today.

What we know about the Mother, Maiden, Crone trinity is relatively new. In fact, the Triple Goddess largely entered into modern consciousness in the 1940s, though Grave's novels and the assertion that there was one universal, cross-cultural three-fold Goddess worshipped in antiquity is still contested. For our conversation, it is worth knowing that the three aspects are also in part related to the phases of the moon (an ancient symbol of the Goddess).

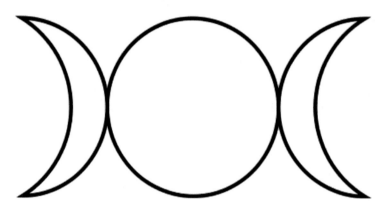

I found the Mother, Maiden, Crone teaching as I was seeking a new model of feminine power that would rescue me from the myth of the SuperWoman. But I found this three-fold model deeply lacking. And it didn't sync with a new awareness I was having around sacred geometry and the shift from the energy of the potential of the triangle (Divine Feminine Portal of Life) into the manifestation of the square (Human Expression), representing a time of the union between the Divine and the Human. This is reflected in the ancient architecture in which temples were built as square buildings (human) topped by a triangular roof (divine) to facilitate the connection between them. I was finding all kinds of clues that were pointing to humanity entering the time when Heaven and Earth are to become one.

For example, in my personal development work, I had been exposed to the way of looking at human consciousness through the lens of Body, Mind, and Spirit. This model worked for me for many years until I had an intimate encounter with my Soul. Where was She in this equation? I was also beginning to question my understanding of the Divine Trinity as I had been taught in Catholic School: Father, Son, and Holy Spirit as the three-fold God. Where did Mary fit in? She was kind of a pseudo-Goddess for Catholics, worshiped in her own right by many of the faithful. And finally, I had my own life experience, which told me there was something deeply lacking in the Maiden, Mother, Crone model.

As I entered into my 50th year of life, my role as a mother was changing. As a young teen, Sophia no longer needed me in the same way, and I was clearly not ready for Crone! Nope. Not. At. All. But as hard as I tried to find my footing, it eluded me. The SuperWoman energy was failing me. The exhaustion was no longer ignorable. My work life was fraught with stress and frustration. The moments of passion and pleasure in my marriage were far too few. And my body was... well, not the same.

It wasn't until I focused on self-sovereignty using the missing archetype of The Queen that it all began to make sense to me. As I dug into my research, I found many other women who had themselves intuited that something important was missing from their lives. I found authors and scholars who picked up nearly invisible threads and began to weave back together the HER-story that painted the picture of our inner Queen energy. When Robin, one of my circle-sisters, gifted me with the book *The Queen of Myself: Stepping into Sovereignty in Midlife* by Donna Henes, I felt like I had found the missing piece! There it was, on the pages of her book for me to see, a new model that worked: Maiden, Mother, Queen, Crone. Donna called her the Four-Fold Goddess. Her words flowed over me like a healing balm, and I knew the truth of it instantly!

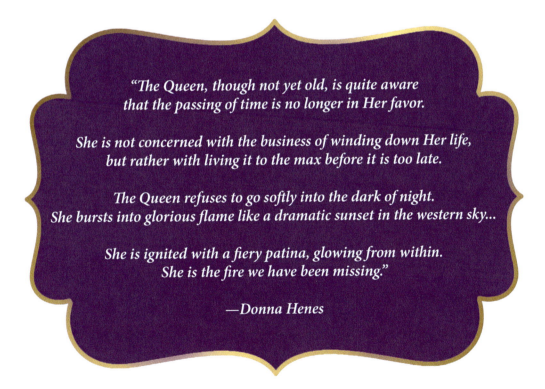

> "The Queen, though not yet old, is quite aware that the passing of time is no longer in Her favor.
>
> She is not concerned with the business of winding down Her life, but rather with living it to the max before it is too late.
>
> The Queen refuses to go softly into the dark of night. She bursts into glorious flame like a dramatic sunset in the western sky...
>
> She is ignited with a fiery patina, glowing from within. She is the fire we have been missing."
>
> —Donna Henes

The moon actually has *four* phases, not three: waxing, waning, full, and new (or dark). This fourth phase, which is hidden, has been missing from the sacred teachings about the phases of a woman's life. I created this graphic to illustrate what I was finding in my research:

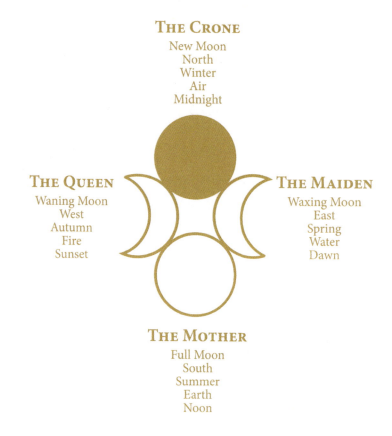

I have come to believe that every woman is a Queen, or has one inside waiting to be expressed, no matter where she is in life. Whether you find yourself balking at this assertion or feeling the "shiver of truth" moving across your skin, there is no denying that every single one of us is The Queen of our Life—or should be.

Being the Queen doesn't mean we get to boss everyone around or have riches dropped at our feet. It means that we recognize ourselves as the Sovereign Ruler of our inner and outer landscape—what we see within and without and how we experience life. We step up and out by taking complete responsibility for ourselves and our lives.

The Queen represents power and authority in all women. Symbolically, her court can be anything from a corporation, to her home, to her body. If we have unhealed ideas about our self-worth, power and agency, or sexuality, we may find it challenging to find and own our Queen energy. The archetypal energy of the Queen becomes activated through our own maturity and growth—through the act of self-healing, which allows us and guides us to claim our full sovereignty.

Between Mother and Crone is the missing phase of Queen. And while it is a beautiful thing to have a croning ceremony, I firmly believe that you just cannot fully embody the wisdom of the Crone without first embracing and embodying the power and self-sovereignty of the Queen.

The subtle patriarchal message of the missing Queen is, "Raise the kids (Mother) or settle into your rocker (Crone) and leave the world to us men." Well, we can all see how that is turning out. Don't get me wrong; I love men. But the voices and hearts of women are desperately needed in leadership arenas everywhere we look, as is a more feminine approach to leadership. It's time for us to prepare ourselves to take a more active role, but we must learn to lead ourselves first. It is essential that we women wake up to and embrace our sovereignty so that we can make the difference we are called to make. It's time for us to take center stage in our own lives and in the world.

Center stage can be a scary place. It requires that we lean into ourselves and listen to the whispers of our hearts, to the guidance of our souls, and choose ourselves.

I was terrified to make this shift, but there was no denying it. I knew it was where I was supposed to be. I knew it was time to choose me. I invested significant time and money to deepen my studies with Lynda and Tj. I began the deep healing work of coming home to my body, mind, heart, and soul and learned so much more about harnessing the power of my energy body through the study of Tantric practices. I discovered the Life Force Energy (Shakti) that is my birthright. I learned how to let it flow in and through me, and miraculous things began to happen.

As I claimed my right to focus on my sovereignty, I had to navigate through tremendous internal resistance. The critical voices inside my head tried to sabotage my efforts out of fear of being seen as selfish or weird. They used guilt and shame. They insisted I should stay small and play it safe. But my Soul had other plans for me.

Since stepping fully into my sovereignty, I have experienced a kind of life I didn't know was even possible. I feel alive and in love with myself and my life like never before. My relationship with my husband is both full of fiery passion and tender love. My daughter and I are closer than ever as I now know how to give her the space she needs to become her own woman. Even my work with women has become more potent, and my business has become more fruitful. Everything is different now because I remember who I am:

I AM A QUEEN.

What makes a Queen a Queen?

In reality, every woman, at every age, needs access to the Queen archetype. The gift of The Queen archetype is experienced in varied ways, but it is always dependent on the ability to receive. The Queen knows two things, and they are inextricably linked. She knows her authority and right to her power and she knows how to receive, which is where she actually gets her power.

This is a problem for most women because we are not skilled in receiving. Why? Because we've been told we need to give, give, give! In truth, during the Mother phase of life, giving is essential in carrying out that role. In my work with younger women who are still in the Mother energy, I teach them to start cultivating the capacity to receive immediately rather than waiting until arriving at Queen. But once we arrive at midlife, the balance needs to shift dramatically if we are to manage the changes in our bodies.

Perhaps you are finding yourself filled with fire (and a few hot flashes too!) for the passions you put on the back burner as a Mother and are ready to bring them forth now that your kids are getting older. Or maybe you are still feeling exhausted, drained, and disconnected from your dreams, unable to find your joy. Perhaps you are yearning for a new focus and the time to reclaim your space and yourself. While recovering from my life as a SuperWoman is an ongoing process, I am using all I have been taught to help me stop being a SuperWoman and take responsibility for the quality of my life as a Queen and to inhabit the throne of my Queendom.

Trading my Cape for a Crown: Capturing My Own Attention

The first big step was wooing my attention away from others and bringing it back to myself. It was a revelation to truly experience myself as worth tending to *first*. Only when I was fully connected to myself could I see that who I am is enough. I didn't stop working or being a mom, but on an energetic level, I learned how to tune in more deeply to myself and my own needs, wants, and desires in order to stop trying to take care of or save everyone else. In other words, I had to commit to saving myself. Think of it as putting your own oxygen mask on first. In order to do that, I had to reprogram many of the childhood messages I got about what it means to be a "good girl," a worthy person, and instead, find my authentic and sovereign self.

Sitting on my Throne: Inhabiting My Body

With my attention firmly on me, I began using deceptively simple energy practices that strengthened my self-connection and supported me in keeping myself energetically in my own body. I studied the seven energy centers known as the Chakra System so that I could balance and access the wisdom they hold. I learned how to keep myself clear and energized so that I could be a safe and loving place for myself and a safe and loving person for others. Having clear and effective energetic boundaries allowed me to be around others without losing myself or invading their space. I was able to be more open and connected without being mushy, more effective without being abrasive, more present without being anxious, and more focused without being critical.

Beating my Sword into a Scepter: Balancing My Polarity

The final step was learning to balance my masculine and feminine energy poles. I learned that a little bit of Tomboy is not only good but necessary for a healthy life. Yet as a woman, my real power is in my feminine energy. With a little practice using two very simple techniques, I was able to access and unleash an exquisite pool of deep feminine power that I never knew existed. Through these magical and mighty practices, I have been able to find my way back to my natural feminine state. And it feels amazing in my body, heart, mind, and soul.

Perhaps you, too, have lived your whole life unaware that you have within your body a limitless source of energy and power and relied instead on "force of will" to keep you going.

There is another way.

I am so grateful to have learned how to tap into a natural form of feminine energy designed specifically for a woman's body. This form of energy is every woman's birthright. And it's a game-changer.

Here are just a few of the ways this work has changed my life:

I feel soft and comfortable in my skin

- I feel more balanced energy and healthy vitality in my body
- I have soul-sourced creativity and potent productivity with my work
- I experience life as a supportive partner rather than a foe to conquer
- I am kinder and gentler with myself
- I experience more pleasure and delight in life
- I have more harmonious relationships with my loved ones, friends, and colleagues

- I feel the exquisite juiciness of being a woman
- I have lots of fulfilling sex with my beloved
- I have a sweeter and safer connection with my daughter
- I am more at peace in myself
- I am more skilled at handling upsets and disagreements with men
- I am more open and connected with women
- I take better care of myself, and it doesn't feel like a chore
- I am a more effective teacher for my students
- I am in love with my body
- I can feel others are more relaxed and at ease in my presence
- I welcome life as it comes
- I am finally, finally satisfied

As I began to share the tools and techniques I was using with other women, I wove them into a coherent teaching I now call the Seven Queendoms: A Soul Map for Embodying Sacred Feminine Sovereignty. I use seven forms of the Queen archetype to help myself and my students access and embody the fullness of our sovereignty so that we can navigate the challenges we face in an increasingly complex and chaotic world.

What exactly is an Archetype?

An archetype as defined in Jungian psychology is a universally available idea, a pattern of thought, or imagery that is collectively inherited by all individuals and available to us in our psyches (conscious and subconscious mind). Both Jung and the fields of comparative anthropology and comparative religious studies extended the understanding of archetypes from something accessed by individuals through the mind to the art, literature, and mythology found across human cultures. Like a set cast of characters who repeatedly appear in apparently unrelated stories, myths, and legends, they illustrate common themes, instinctual responses, and characteristics that seem to be embedded in the human experience and underlie much of human behavior. For generations, these archetypes have helped humanity make sense of ourselves and our world. It's like a shorthand that bypasses the conscious mind and works directly at the subconscious level. I like to think of archetypes as the language of the soul.

So why do I need seven Queens instead of just one? Well, first off, there are as many ways to be sovereign as there are people on the planet. That is at the very core of self-sovereignty is the understanding that, while there are some universals involved, there is also a Divine uniqueness to each and every human. And the right to self-determination must be granted to all if we are to respect and encourage self-sovereignty. The Seven Queendoms SoulMap offers a way to organize and examine a vast amount of content so that we can pull from each the right amount of each to support our most unique and healthy expression.

Sometimes we need to access our deepest wisdom with clarity or hold a detached and divine perspective. Other times we may need to access our inner dragon's breath and use our holy HELL NO! Some days we will traverse the spectrum of love from motherly, grounded, and nurturing love to the wild and playful temptress. Or what's needed is deep truth-telling or loving healing. The Queen is responsible for all of it. And so, she must have the necessary breadth of sacred skills to rise to the task of ruling over her Queendom. Through these seven forms of the Queen archetype, we will seek to bring balance to ourselves and our world.

As we look out at our world broken and ravaged by unchecked domination, it's obvious how desperately we need sovereign women who can embody regal grace under pressure. We must embody the new way in order to bring it into being. It starts with us. We cannot abdicate our power at this potent moment in history. Not only for our own sake but for the health of our planet. It will take the uniting of our masculine and feminine energies under a single banner to get the job done. We must leave behind the shadowy fears and limiting beliefs that we inherited. We must break the curse of un-sovereignty. The work starts now.

*"Watch your thoughts; they become words.
Watch your words; they become actions.
Watch your actions; they become habits.
Watch your habits; they become character.
Watch your character; it becomes your destiny."*

—*Lao Tzu*

Chapter 5
Parents, Patriarchy & Personality

If we are to break the curse of un-sovereignty, we need to understand how it first came to be. Why do we become disconnected from our sovereignty? How is it that we become the people we know ourselves to be? Is it a unique combination of qualities and characteristics that make up who we are? If so, where do we come by these qualities and characteristics that "define" us to ourselves and others? Are we born with them (nature), or do they come to us over time as we experience life (nurture)? This is a common and unnecessary fight, an either/or proposition that need not trap us. When recent advances in brain research are considered alongside research in the psychotherapeutic domains, it's easy to see that nature and nurture work in tandem, like two sides of the same coin, to shape us into who we become over time.

This combination of the character traits we were born with and the environment we were raised in form the foundation of who we become. But what happens if we decide we don't like some aspect of who we have become and want to change it? In order to fully become self-determined, self-sovereign, to govern ourselves consciously, we have to have the capacity to grow past the limitations of our past. We need tools and processes to consciously examine who we have become and then systematically challenge what we find so that we may alter it. We have to understand the impact of our family dynamics on the person we have become and find ways to reconcile unresolved wounds that may still linger and fester.

Each of us is born with a unique set of physical traits that form a clear base from which our development will necessarily unfold. Yet, that unfolding doesn't happen in a void. Rather, that base set of traits is molded and shaped by our interaction with our environment, the sum of which becomes the lens through which we perceive and respond to life. Increasingly, research shows that even the earliest interactions infants have with their world, especially with their caregivers (primary attachment figures), significantly impact the development of the child, physically, emotionally, and intellectually on every level. For this reason, the level of physical, emotional, psychic, and spiritual safety we experienced in our relationship with our parents, especially in our earliest years, has the most significant impact on how we develop as adults.

Family Systems Theory (Murray Bowen) and Attachment Theory (Mary Ainsworth and John Bowlby) both make clear that it is impossible to fully understand the emerging or fully grown individual without understanding the context in which they grew up—to understand the individual, you must look into the inner workings of the family. Emerging neuroscience confirms that the brain has specific functions within the neocortex designed to support our healthy connections (attachments) with others. Dr. Daniel J. Siegel, clinical professor of psychiatry at the UCLA School of Medicine and executive director of the Mindsight Institute, has written extensively on this. In his seminal book, *Mindsight,* he notes that this part of the brain is not fully developed in young children, so the child's brain develops in part by tuning into the brain of its caregiver where "the adult provides much of the modulation of infant states, especially after a state disruption or transition between states." In effect, "a child uses the state of mind of the parent to help organize her own mental processes." Children born into homes with adults who are unavailable or unsettled are at a significant disadvantage. Adults who can self-regulate are better able to support their children in developing their own self-regulating mechanisms.

As an infant, the need for safety is all-consuming. Initially, it was thought that if we have adequate food, clothing, and shelter as children, we would be safe enough to grow into healthy adults. Studies of children raised in orphanages have proven that this is not enough. Beyond physical safety, we must have a loving connection with our caregivers to feel emotionally safe. The absence of this (emotional neglect) threatens and thwarts the child's emotional and cognitive development and can even interrupt our physical development. Alternately the presence of emotional abuse (screaming, yelling, berating, and belittling a child) and naturally physical punishment (hitting, slapping, spanking, grabbing, etc.) all register in the child's body and mind as dangerous and even life-threatening.

Each individual goes through their own unique process of ego development as they age. According to Zweig and Abrams in *Meeting the shadow: The hidden power of the dark side of human nature,* key stages are developed in the first half of life within the "psychological atmosphere created by parents, siblings, caretakers, and other important sources of love and approval." This process allows our growing consciousness to develop by embracing what is rewarded as positive behavior and whittling out what is judged to be negative behavior, thereby reducing the experience of anxiety and earning positive regard. As a growing plant will bend itself toward the sunshine, we bend our growing ego (and sense of self) toward that which brings nourishment (secure attachment) from our caregivers/institutions and away from that which disappoints, unconsciously forming a conditioned self.

Fundamentally, the body-mind is hardwired to identify and cope with threats to its existence. Survival is the goal; therefore, it makes sense that we would need to assess the environment to determine how hospitable a world we have been born into. Our earliest relationships teach us about this world and our place in it. Throughout childhood, those moments when our needs aren't met serve as tests for us to discover how the world will respond to our cries for help, attention, or affection. To the child, if the world seems good and safe, then the child is good and safe; if the world seems bad and unsafe, then the child is bad and unsafe.

The experiences we have and messages we receive become the default settings for our emerging "alarm system," which helps us navigate our world. These default settings become the neural firing patterns in our neural net profile. Over time this forms a complex neuropsychology and self-view often referred to as the "persona" or the "conditioned self." As we age, we experience feedback from the people and world around us as the behaviors and responses of the conditioned self are expressed. Our parents, extended family members, teachers, and clergy are some of the most impactful people in our lives; their feedback can take on disproportionate significance. Some are likely to be skilled at providing corrective comments and gentle guidance, while others may fall woefully short. Over time their words and actions help to shape the way we see ourselves. That feedback either confirms the current sense of self, making it stronger, or disconfirms the sense of self, offering us an opportunity to adjust how we see ourselves.

But safety in the family setting is just the first layer of consideration. The family itself may or may not hold a position of safety within the larger social context. The family's socioeconomic standing impacts the container in which the child is raised. Issues of race, religion, education, sexuality, and able-bodiedness will naturally add to or take from the family's sense of safety. Patriarchal influences have long run under the surface of society's fabric, often driving what is embraced as acceptable societal norms. Over centuries, these influences have simply become the water in which we swim, often drowning out the voices and bodies of those who would question or rebel against the norms. Knowing this, parents have the difficult task of teaching their children how to survive in the often-inhospitable world in which they live.

For parents who themselves feel safe, the task of creating a safe space in their family is quite a bit easier. It is possible to grow up in a family environment that is physically and emotionally safe but be bombarded with trauma outside of the family setting. Furthermore, most parents recognize that they have an obligation to produce a child who will be an asset to society as a whole. Like all functioning societies, we must have a clear sense of which behaviors will serve the group and which should be avoided. Part of the role of parents is to help children temper behaviors that threaten group harmony.

There is a constant dance in the human family between the need to have room to express the self and the need for those forms of self-expression to increase the health of the group (society) rather than threaten the social contract. And it is a rare parent who can see the longer arch of oppression that is worth questioning. It takes the most conscious and mindful parent to find the sweet spot between allowing children enough room for authentic self-expression while still supporting them in developing the habits, skills, and behaviors that will help them succeed and better our community as a whole. If you or your child was born with a soul designed to shake up the system, the ride might be a little rough.

Some parents may be inclined to over-indulge childish habits in an effort not to bruise the child's ego. This can have the tragic outcome of cutting short their child's forward progress into adulthood. These children are rarely asked to consider the needs of others, not just their own. They lack practice making choices between the two, leaving them in an infantilized emotional state.

Other parents may over-preference social norms and subvert their child's sense of sovereignty. It goes too far when the parent seeks to "break" the child's spirit and remake them in their own image. This often happens when parents don't understand the importance of criticizing the child's behavior rather than the child herself. How skilled our parents/caregivers were at supporting us in walking this line between living a life in alignment with our authentic self-expression and curbing impulsive and disruptive behavior sits at the root of our life conditioning. As we age, our experiences with extended family and authority figures at school and our places of worship also come into play.

You can think of your personality as the sum total of your life conditioning. But there is more to it than just the parts of ourselves that are easy to see. Because safety and survival are so dependent on our caregivers' pleasure, children learn quickly what impulses of their emerging self won't be tolerated. If parents are only seeking to change undesirable behavior rather than seeing the child herself as bad, the child adjusts and changes her behavior. This is a natural and necessary part of helping our children grow up. But when we demean a child or imply that they, rather than their behavior, are wrong, children cope with the threat of losing the parent's love and approval by repressing or hiding aspects of themselves that would imperil the relationship. This can have dire consequences on our development process.

Enter the Shadow

In 1912, Carl Jung used the term "shadow side of the psyche" to describe the hidden side of the human psyche, according to former student and colleague Liliane Frey-Rohn. In his 1917 paper "On the Psychology of the Unconscious," Jung explained that the shadow is made up of energy patterns or sub-personalities that emerge due to fragmented, incomplete, or arrested development in critical and pivotal stages of early childhood and adolescence. He found that it was like a receptacle for "not recognized desires" of our youth and "repressed portions of the personality" that were sent into hiding. Jung used the terms "social mask" to describe the habits we form and "shadow" to describe the disowned positive and negative traits we hide in order to get the love and safety we desire.

Jungian analyst John A. Sanford underscores this point by pointing out that the process of identifying who we allow, imagine, or want ourselves to be (athletic, sweet, sexually expressive, smart, creative, rebellious, shy, angry, etc.) creates an opposite quality which we exclude from who we think we are (weak, selfish, prudish, dumb, boring, agreeable, outgoing, calm, etc.). With good reason, parents and society encourage us to identify with positive traits such as honesty, kindness, and respect. However, if this is done without regard for our natural impulses to hide the truth, be unkind, or ignore, those darker aspects can get split off from our sense of self. Rather than owning our darker impulses and consciously choosing a healthier behavior, these impulses get repressed and form the basis of the shadow. They get swept under the rug. When our darker aspects recede into shadow and are no longer accessible or visible to our conscious personality, they become alien and threatening when observed in others. When we see in others what we have disowned in ourselves, we are ripe for all manner of undesirable outcomes such as jealousy, fear, judgment, blame, or anger. Research into this dynamic has produced evidence that people "feel threatened by undesirable features of others that they fear in themselves." This is at the root of the urge to judge others.

We project our hidden and rejected impulses, motives, beliefs, and behaviors onto others, and because we have deemed them unacceptable in ourselves, we deem them unacceptable in them, too. Most people are entirely unaware that they are often not truly seeing the person in front of them but are actually interacting with a projection of their inner world. This is a phenomenon that is almost impossible to avoid, so we have to learn how to navigate past our projections by not buying into the stories we make up about other people and instead, ask questions. This is especially important when we find ourselves purporting to know what others think and feel. Sometimes, our projections align with what is actually happening, but other times we are way off base. Maturing means being conscious of this dynamic and being willing to check it out to see if we have it right.

If we want to have any chance at improving our experience of life, we have to become familiar with these aspects of ourselves. We must accept that the personality is a combination of the physical ability, mental acuity, and emotional temperament we were born with and how those building blocks have been tempered and conditioned by our life experience. And we need to develop the ability to recognize when our thoughts and behaviors are being driven by that conditioning or by the hidden shadow material of our youth.

The good news is, we can change our hair-trigger responses, the choices we make, and the direction of our life. Even pervasive habits that seem stubborn and beyond reach can be softened. But it is no small feat.

Because the brain is wired to more easily assimilate information that fits with its current understanding, our conditioned self typically increases in strength and rigidity until it becomes our primary self-identification. It doesn't matter if our inner self-portrait is accurate. It can be wildly incorrect and still become the predominant way we believe ourselves to be. Since all perception is filtered through and interpreted by this self-view, we are at risk for serious distortions in our assessment of the world around us and our place in it. This can have tragic consequences for children raised in sub-optimal environments.

Did you endure and perhaps (mal)adapt to experiences of emotional, physical, mental, or spiritual abuse/trauma/neglect? Or was yours an inconsistent/unreliable experience of safety and connection? If so, you will have likely ended up with a distorted view of yourself, your sense of security, and even your value and worth. This distorted view can set the body-mind up for a lifetime of elevated levels of anxiety and hyper-vigilance or plunge the body into numbness and depression as a way of defending against overwhelm. Couple this with the modern dilemma of fast-paced, high-stress living, and it becomes easy to see why we have become, in the words of researcher Brené Brown, "the most in-debt, obese, addicted, and medicated adult cohort in U.S. history."

The recent onslaught of collective challenges has pushed stress levels to impossible levels. For many, just trying to get by in life is no longer satisfying; and, out of crisis or courage, a decision is made to find a better way to live. Whether we have a single defining moment that demands attention, are facing the slow drip of a dissatisfying life, or are in the natural phase of questioning that arrives with mid-life, the Queen finds the courage to examine those aspects of life that are no longer working.

Looking Under the Rug

The path to sovereignty includes understanding how the dynamics of shadow make it impossible to see directly. In other words, we have forgotten what we swept under the rug all those years ago. In some cases, it went under there when we were so young that our long-term memory wasn't even online yet. It is quite challenging to actively and intentionally look for shadow material. More often, we stumble over it.

When Sophia was about three years old, we were living in a two-bedroom apartment in the Midwest. We loved that little apartment with a nature trail right outside the door. The trail had a bridge we called the Troll Bridge, where we'd recreate scenes from *Dora the Explorer*. Next to the bridge was a wide-open field we called the Hundred-Acre Wood, where we acted out scenes from *Winnie the Pooh*. It was a magical time filled with beautiful family memories and a lot of spiritual growth.

While we lived there, I was working with my colleagues Rev. Drs. Jane and Gary Simmons to create a shadow work practice based on Gary's thirty years of teaching conflict resolution practices. We wanted to find a reliable way for people to heal childhood adaptive behaviors and shadow beliefs.

In my research, I found William Miller's work, which describes five paths for effectively revealing the architecture of our inner shadow patterns.

1. Soliciting feedback from others as to how they perceive us

2. Uncovering the content of our projections

3. Examining our "slips" of tongue and behavior and investigating what is really occurring when we are perceived other than we intended to be perceived

4. Considering our humor and our identifications

5. Studying our dreams, daydreams, and fantasies

The shadow work practice I was developing with Gary and Jane primarily focused on understanding what our projections, words, behaviors, and misperceptions show us about our shadow (items 2 and 3 from the list above) so that we can consciously engage in resolving old wounding and integrating disowned aspects. Consequently, we were focused on figuring out how to turn the shadow aspects that we stumble over into new stepping stones towards a more functional way of being.

I was pacing around one day in our little apartment, thinking through a tricky part of the program we were creating. As I circled around and around in our small living room, I kept catching my toes on this one spot on the carpet. After the third and most painful run-in with this spot, I knelt down to examine what I was tripping on. I felt a hard bump and realized that there was something under the carpet that didn't belong there.

In truth, I had stumbled over this same spot many times since we moved in, but I hadn't been bothered enough to look into it. Now that I had taken the time to examine it and knew more about it, I was faced with a decision. The only way to get rid of it was to pull up the carpet. (If you were raised to be a good girl like me, you might imagine that my inner voices had a lot to say about that!)

"This is a rented apartment, not your home. You can't just pull up the carpet! It's wall-to-wall carpeting. How will you get it back in place? What if it looks awful? What if we lose our deposit?"

On and on went the litany of reasons to let it go. But I was so done with tripping on that spot that I pushed aside the voice of my inner critic and ripped up the carpet. At once, I saw what was causing me pain. It was a plastic pen cap! Someone carelessly didn't make sure the space was clear or maybe saw the cap and didn't care as they installed the carpet. It wasn't my fault, but it was my problem.

I was so relieved to get that pen cap out from under the carpet. I did manage to lay the carpet back down and make it look alright. But most importantly, I never tripped over it again! This is precisely how shadow work unfolds to reveal and resolve hidden problems so we can make our lives run more smoothly. Just like I had to stop and examine what was causing me pain every time I tripped, and look for the root cause and do the work to uncover and remove it, we are called to do the same with our life experience.

Becoming sovereign means that when we trip over our painful moments, judgments, and criticisms of ourselves and others, we know these judgments are often rooted in what's been swept under the rug. If we take the time to become curious, to examine the root causes of our judgments, they will tell us more about ourselves than those at whom they are aimed.

It is important to note that the shadow, hidden below the surface in the subconscious mind, often contains brilliant aspects along with the darker aspects that may have been equally discouraged by our environment. In the introduction to their collection of essays on the shadow, *Meeting the Shadow: The Hidden Power of the Dark Side of Human Nature*, Jungian therapists and authors, are clear that a full understanding of our shadow includes knowing it contains "our infantile parts, emotional attachments, neurotic symptoms, *as well as our undeveloped talents and gifts,*" (emphasis added).

In his paper "Some Basic Propositions of a Growth and Self-actualization Psychology," Abraham Maslow noted that, "No psychological health is possible unless this essential core of the person is fundamentally accepted, loved, and respected by others and by himself." It seems we are not only capable of projecting our darkness onto others but our brilliance as well. This subject is explored extensively in William A. Miller's excellent book, *Your Golden Shadow, Discovering and Fulfilling your Undeveloped Self*. Knowledge of the self, including all that we have excluded, seems to be a pre-requisite for healthy integration, so we must first come to terms with our past and how it shaped us in order to consciously create a new future.

No one escapes childhood unscathed. We all have stuff hidden in our psyches that trip us up from time to time. Maturing into our sovereignty allows us to develop the ability to see the parts of us that trip us up as a gift that opens the door to healing. Become curious about your conditioned self and your shadow material, acknowledging how it impacts what you see. Develop a practice of looking under the rug to remove past hurts, echoes of old threats, and shadow material. In doing so, you can minimize the potential for tripping, see more of what is really there, make better choices, and create better outcomes. Our sovereignty and capacity for true self-governance must include this kind of deep self-knowledge and the often more challenging task of self-acceptance. When we arrive at the point where there is no longer a desire to be rid of our shadow, a new level of integration has occurred. As Carl Jung stated eloquently in his article, "Modern Man in Search of a Soul,"

"We cannot change anything unless we accept it. Condemnation does not liberate; it oppresses. I am the oppressor of the person I condemn, not his friend and fellow sufferer. I do not mean in the least to say that we must never pass judgment when we desire to help and improve. But if the doctor wishes to help a human being, he must be able to accept him as he is. And he can do this in reality only when he has already seen and accepted himself as he is."

For those who were not raised with viable models of self-acceptance by loving and accepting caregivers, the work of embracing and integrating the shadow aspects of the self may be quite painful or difficult, even bringing on temporary depression—as John A. Sanford says, "When one first sees the shadow clearly, one is more or less aghast." As the awareness dawns that we have seen the enemy and the enemy is us, we add a new layer of threat that must be managed—the inner critic. Self-compassion is an absolute must if we are to be successful in coming to terms with the shadow.

We are so different he and I
I think someone such as him would never befriend me
I am maddening to him
I cannot see the truth—there is right and there is wrong
I appear lost and confused
I seem to tolerate anything and everything
What has happened, he thinks
Has he failed me in some way?

We are so different he and I
I think someone such as me would never befriend him
He is maddening to me
He cannot see there are many truths—that context and paradox exist
He appears rigid and self-righteous
He seems to tolerate only that with which he agrees
What has happened, I think
Have I failed him in some way?

Yet we would die before parting.
We love each other beyond reason,
We need no reason—we love as only a parent and child can

It is this love that makes the connection sweet and the conflict sting
Despite the upsets, misunderstandings, and arguing
This unlikely relationship continues

And so it will
Until the moment when my heart will break beyond imagining
When I will no longer have my brilliant, generous, brave, loving,
and flawed father to argue with
And I will know, even more than I already do,
that nothing but the love ever mattered.

Chapter 6

Remaking the Past

As adults, we have the opportunity to cultivate the capacity to separate "who we are" from what we think and how we feel. Doing so gives us the room to consciously examine our conditioning, notice our habits, and reclaim our lost aspects. This can feel like a daunting task. It takes courage to risk losing whatever stability we have crafted for ourselves based on our conditioning. Yet, it is this conditioning that also stands between us and a consciously integrated and resilient self. When we do what's needed to heal from past hurts, we find we can respond to life in more flexible and creative ways.

We can live from the scar, not the wound.

By the world's standards, I grew up with a tremendous amount of privilege. My parents were college-educated. My mother stayed home with us, and my dad was a professor at the local University. While we didn't have a lot of money, my parents were determined that we would get a good education. They sacrificed so that all three of us kids attended private Catholic schools. And we all went on to graduate from college and even earned advanced degrees. We all have managed rather well financially, surpassing our modest childhood living conditions. I am eternally grateful for this good start in life. But on the soul-level, a lot was missing for me.

My work began by looking at the worst parts of my childhood, starting with the emotional tenor in the house. My parents did not offer me an example of a thriving, loving, high-functioning partnership. With their constant clashes over even the simplest things, it felt to me more like living in a war zone with periods of tenuous peace. I had a constant sense that our family life balanced each day on the edge of a knife, and at any moment, that balance could be lost, and we'd fall and get cut. Happiness wasn't encouraged or well-tolerated. From my perspective, it seemed as though my happiness was considered dangerous. So rather than build up hopes that might not be realized, my father, in particular, loved us by discouraging what he felt were fanciful thoughts. Growing up, his harsh criticism was an ever-present force in my life. Rarely did I feel that I (or anyone in the family) lived up to his expectations or made him proud. In truth, I always knew he loved me, and if the chips were down, I could go to him with an issue I had or a mistake I had made. But I also knew there would be hell to pay in the doing of it.

When it came to connecting with him daily and the small stuff of life and everyday childhood mistakes, the price tag of correction was too high to produce a sense of intimacy or safety. There just wasn't any room to get it wrong. When I was fifteen, one night at dinner, I mentioned that a girlfriend had just pierced her ears a second time. My father looked right at me, and with the full force of his sizable personality, he warned, "Don't bother coming home if you do that." It was chilling.

My mother also seemed to live in constant fear of angering him, as we kids did. I had a recurring dream that summed it up:

My father was a giant who was about 40 feet long. He slept upstairs 24/7. The entire second floor was his sleeping room, and the roof was built directly over him. We kids were supposed to stay quiet. One day, we were playing with musical instruments. My mom got angry with us and reminded us to stop it or else we would wake him up, and he would sit up, hiccup, and blow the town to smithereens. But for some reason, we refused to stop. We headed up to the landing at the top of the stairs and banged away on our little drum and tambourine. Within moments he woke up, sat up (smashing through the roof), hiccupped, and just as predicted, blew the town to smithereens.

When the dream would come, I would always wake up gasping for air, in a cold sweat, frightened out of my mind, and wracked with guilt.

As for my connection with my mom, she could be soft and loving at times. But she could also be far more violent than my father in her response when upset. While my dad was consistent in his harshness, we never knew what we would get with mom. She simply had no control over when her rage would surface. One time a friend and I were playing in the basement. My friend accidentally knocked over my mom's craft shelf. It came crashing down, and all her stuff went flying out across the room. We were so scared, not only of being hit by the falling shelf but by the sound of my mother's footsteps on the stairs. Once she saw what happened and that we were not hurt, she picked up a bright orange Hot Wheels track and whipped me with it. One particularly nasty strike left a wide purple welt on the inside of my thigh that lasted for four weeks. I was just six years old when that happened.

Another time my brother and I were playing in the basement. He was six, and I was four. He asked if I wanted to play barbershop. I said, "Yes, but not for real." Then I handed him the scissors, and he proceeded to cut off a chunk of my hair. I ran upstairs crying to my mother, who flew into a rage upon seeing my hair. But rather than marching downstairs and disciplining my brother, she roughly scooped me up, stomped her way to the upstairs bathroom, slammed me down on the counter, and cut off all my hair to within a half-inch of my head.

I was shorn.
By my own mother.
Like a criminal, or a witch.

I couldn't understand it. I was the one who had been wronged. How could I trust this woman who was the only real source of nurturance in my life? I remembered looking at her stomach while it was happening and realizing that I could kick her in the stomach and make her stop. As I contemplated defending myself, I knew that would just make things worse, so I buried the impulse. The technical term for this is a truncated defense response. It happens when we can't or don't defend ourselves when under attack. Unable to defend myself, something at the core of me shattered. I shut down, gave up, and chose to leave my body instead. It was the best I could do at the time.

As we have already discussed, the bonds or attachments children form to their caregivers are essential to their sense of safety. Healthy bonds are called secure attachments. The bonds can also be dysfunctional to greater or lesser degrees. The three known forms of dysfunctional attachment currently diagnosed and treated are anxious attachment, avoidant attachment, and disorganized attachment (both anxious and avoidant combined.)

Children who both fear their parents and see them as their sole source of comfort often develop the disorganized attachment style. This means that the child is afraid of the parent but also needs that same parent to help with quelling that fear. It's a profound dilemma for a young heart and mind. Attachment researcher Mary Main coined the phrase "fear without solution" when referring to this experience. The child has a primal need to seek love and reassurance from the parent, but at the same time, s/he can feel anything from uncertainty to terror when thinking about how the parent will react once s/he draws close. I developed a disorganized attachment bond with my parents. To this day, I cope with the fallout from this form of attachment, although to a much lesser degree than I used to.

Attachments styles manifest on a spectrum. It's possible to be highly functional in many areas of your life and still face challenges in having successful intimate relationships, particularly with children and spouses. But if we are willing to put in the work, we don't have to stay stuck in these patterns.

When I became a parent, I vowed never to hit my daughter. I was surprised at how hard that was. On occasion, I could fly into a rage, yelling over small things just like my parents did. But when she would start crying, I would be crushed. I would grab hold of myself and pull myself together. I spent more time than I care to admit kneeling beside her, wiping away her tears, asking for her forgiveness, and repairing the ruptures caused by my temper.

I hit Sophia twice, using a single pop to the bottom when all my other parenting tools failed me. Both instances were traumatic for her, even though they seemed measured and mild compared to my experience. As a two- and three-year-old, they were the worst, most fearful moments of her life. I have no illusions about this. I have wounded my daughter just like I was wounded. Seeing myself hurt her was what led me to shadow work in the first place. I wanted to stop this cycle. I had to look under the rug, inside my mind and its neural connections, and inside my body and the nervous system habits and truncated defense responses that lived there in order to find a way out.

The kind of love I longed for as a child was more than a roof over my head, healthy food on the table, and a good education. I am acutely aware that I had it better than so many other children. I am immensely grateful for that and for the many other very positive experiences my parents provided. But what they didn't give me, and what every child needs to thrive, was a consistent sense of safety and connection. They didn't understand the critical importance of fostering a healthy emotional bond and a secure attachment. They were unaware of just how damaging the physical abuse was—and so was I until I started unearthing my own trauma. I could have left it buried there in the past or hidden under the rug, but I was unwilling to tolerate the tripping any longer, especially when it was causing my precious daughter so much pain.

I saw great results from using the shadow work practice we created and decided to enter a doctoral program in transformational psychology to study its efficacy. I learned so much more about positive parenting and alternatives to what I had experienced growing up through my research and coursework. Through my commitment to my own personal practice, I was beginning to change.

When Sophia was four years old, we took a family vacation to Las Vegas with my brother, sister, and their partners. On the trip, Sophia kept doing things a four-year-old does. Once, she tried wandering off to explore something while we shopped. Another time she started climbing into a fountain. A third time she pushed her stroller around erratically. Each time I called her by name and asked her to make a different choice. If needed, I reminded her that I would start counting, and if she didn't make a new behavior choice by the time I got to three, I would make a choice for her. Inevitably she would make a new, more acceptable choice and the day would continue unfolding in harmony. On a couple of occasions, I had to say, "One..." and she would change her behavior. This allowed her to have a significant measure of control over her actions and still kept the family vacation on track peacefully.

At one point on the trip, my brother told me he was amazed that asking Sophia to make a new choice was so effective. Naturally, he compared it to how we were parented (anger, yelling, threatening, spanking, etc.) when we acted out. I explained that my parenting hadn't gotten that way overnight. I had been working on it consciously and with great intention for at least two years. As a result, we had structures in place that supported Sophia in being able to self-express and be mindful of what worked in her environment. It was a commitment to seeing her as a sovereign being. My task was providing loving boundaries that weren't overly controlling. By the end of the trip, my brother had caught on. I loved hearing him reminding her to make good choices. It was a healing experience for all of us.

Before I started this work, I would have said I had a pretty happy childhood. I could recount dozens of stories of fun times and good memories. My mom threw the most amazing birthday parties for us kids. She spent hours sewing stunning costumes for Halloween and school events. One time she made me the most excellent jester costume, and I won a prize. She was always doing arts and crafts with us and teaching us new things. She took me to get a makeover and bought makeup for me when I was an awkward pre-teen. When I was seven, she stood up to a doctor who said I would have to stop eating tomatoes in order to quit wetting the bed. I remember her saying to the doctor, "This child loves tomatoes, and I would never ask her to stop eating them." I felt so seen, so important. It meant the world to me that she showed up in such strength and put my preferences before this man who was the "expert."

One of my favorite childhood memories was collecting leaves with my dad for a third-grade project. I can recall feeling so happy and joyful one afternoon when he drove me all over the neighborhood looking for different leaves. We would drive along until he spotted a tree that "looked good," and he would pull over right there and jump out and grab some leaves. It felt like being on a secret mission with him, one that was a little daring and even a tiny bit dangerous. And we were doing it together! We did other fun things together. I loved doing the New York Times crossword puzzle with him on Sundays. Or we would work on his stamp collection together. We enjoyed watching football cheering for his hometown team, the Houston Oilers, in the "run and shoot" Warren Moon days. We did projects around the house together. He helped me with my homework, and I can still recall several reports that I earned high marks on with his help. I felt proud and supported.

We had some wonderful times as a family, including a magical summer we spent with my mother's family in Italy that is the stuff of family legend. I always felt that my parents believed I had a good head on my shoulders, and they gave me a lot of freedom as a teen. Of course, it had been drummed in that mistakes of any significant proportion would be met without mercy. And I suppose in some ways that fear was useful. But it came at a huge cost to my body and my heart. Diving in and looking at that cost had an unexpected consequence.

I had pushed down much of the emotional and physical chaos I experienced. As I began to see all the stuff I had repressed or swept under the rug, for a time, all my childhood memories turned to shit. There were several years that I simply couldn't remember any of the good stuff. I was flooded with memories of moments of fear and anger—stuff I had forgotten about but still lived on inside of me. I can't tell you the number of times I found shocking beliefs and old hurts that left me curled up in a ball, sobbing my eyes out as I allowed myself to come back into the little body of my inner child and feel everything she had tried to avoid by leaving.

"I am a very bad girl."

"The people who love me hurt me, and I deserve it."

"I am ugly and unlovable."

"I don't matter." "I am not safe."

Why would anyone want to dredge up such things? Isn't it better to leave well-enough alone? Not for me, it wasn't—not when my own rage and hurt was still coming out sideways and hurting those I loved.

There's no escaping it: Hurt people hurt people.

I was determined to minimize the wounds I passed on to my daughter. And beyond that, there was no way for me to fully enjoy all life had to offer if I continued to live an unembodied way. Now that I have healed significantly, when I think of those hurtful moments, they no longer trigger hidden pain in my body. It has been felt and released. So now, I can recall the memories like a neutral observer. I have regained my access to the happy memories and can once again enjoy the memories of joy, laughter, connection, learning, and adventure. I trust these memories now because I know they aren't covering up anything. This kind of truth-telling is critical if we want to be able to establish real and loving connections. To get the loving relationship with my parents that I always wanted, I had to tell myself the truth that I didn't have it when I was young.

In my healing journey, I listened to an audiotape a friend gave me by M. Scott Peck called *On Blame and Anger*. On the tape, he said any real forgiveness or reconciliation process with our parents would require that we first put them on trial and convict them where they were guilty. Without trying and convicting, there can be no clemency as there is nothing to forgive. Truth and reconciliation must go together if we wish to return to wholeness.

As an adult, my relationship with my dad continued to be fraught with pain and power struggles. I loved my dad dearly but being around him left me feeling drained and beaten down. I respected him as a human being and saw all the amazing and thoughtful things he often did for me and others, but I didn't respect how he expressed his views with such anger and bitterness. I admired his intelligence, but not the way he used it as a weapon. I honored that he never shirked his duty as a father or husband but judged him harshly for not carrying them out with loving-kindness or humility.

Regardless, I wanted the relationship, and I was willing to work for it. I had moved away at that time, so we didn't see much of each other. We did talk on the phone a few times a month as I'd call home wanting to be a good daughter. At that time, I discovered that even though I had moved away, there was a dad living in my head, and he held my attention in painful ways. As I was growing and evolving as a spiritual being, I found myself having imaginary conversations with him. I'd continuously practice new and better ways of communicating what was in my heart in hopes I could share my journey vulnerably, and I'd be heard, understood, accepted, respected, and loved.

It took a lot of effort to kick the habit of arguing with him in my head. I finally successfully interrupted my monolog of self-explanation and defense when I realized I could replace it with the very thing I wanted. Silently in my mind or out loud while driving in the car, in bed before falling asleep, and again upon rising, I would envision my dad's face and say over and over and over until I really felt it: "I love you, I honor you, I accept you, I respect you…just the way you are." If I noticed I was carrying on a conversation with my head-dad, I'd say these words. I began practicing extending loving-kindness to him at every possible opportunity. It became my devotional practice, and I kept it up for more than a year. Slowly, the need for him to show up for me in a certain way lessened. I didn't need loving-kindness *from* him in our encounters because I was giving it *to* him.

> *It didn't seem to matter which way the loved flowed,*
> *either in or out; I felt it.*

And then the most remarkable thing happened. My daddy softened. He started calling me sweetheart and saying, "I love you" at the end of every phone call. He often shared that he was proud of me and complimented my parenting. When we would see each other, he always had a warm hug waiting for me and some cash in an envelope! He had always been a generous man, but the increasing generosity of his heart was the real prize. It was a healing balm, and it felt like a miracle.

My mom and I have had dozens of clearing conversations. She has fully owned her failings and asked for forgiveness. It's been wonderful to have her acknowledge how much it pleases her to see me mothering my daughter differently. She and my father still have their relationship issues, which the entire family sees when we are home for holidays. As painful as that is, I am grateful that she has found her own way of growing and evolving through prayer, reading self-help books, and seeking to find some inner peace despite her circumstances. And while I have let go of the belief that I need to rescue her, I have been willing to speak up and set boundaries with my father when he acts out in my presence.

I am so fortunate. For more than a decade now, I have been able to truthfully say that I *adore* my parents. My REAL parents. Not some idea of them I have in my mind—good or bad. I can see them for who they are: flawed yet precious human beings who did what they thought was best. I can deeply appreciate them for that, even as I acknowledge it wasn't enough. I can admit that their mistakes had consequences, but I can also see that the work I have done to heal has been the greatest gift of my life. In many ways, it was their mistakes that became their greatest gift to me and ultimately my own family.

"Freeing yourself was one thing, claiming ownership of that freed self was another."

—*Toni Morrison*

CHAPTER 7
THE TOLL OF TRAUMA ON INTIMACY

My childhood conditioning didn't just impact my parenting behavior, it impacted my partnering behavior too. Learning how to form secure attachments with my romantic partners was a long and winding road. In the beginning, my focus was on being a better mom—and then, a better daughter. I wasn't too focused on being a better wife. In fact, I had grown comfortable with my somewhat distant and occasionally volatile relationship with my husband. It mirrored my childhood family dynamic but was healthy enough that I could feel smug.

In truth, I simply had never been able to feel fully safe in any of my intimate relationships. It didn't matter if they were good, I was always waiting for the other shoe to drop. I was fortunate to realize about five years into my marriage that I wasn't fully committed to the relationship.

Even though I had said my marriage vows and we had bought a home and begun raising a child, from the moment my husband made his first major blunder (back in year two), I always told myself not to worry, that I could leave at any time if things got too bad. It was a form of protection I sought when I once again had determined that my home environment was not safe. But the thing about having one foot out the door is that it didn't just keep things from getting too bad, it kept things from getting too good!

Since it was my second marriage, I didn't want to mess this one up. While I was researching the impact of childhood conditioning for my doctoral dissertation, I read something about securely attached children that knocked me for a loop.

- Securely attached children believe:
- The adults in my life love and care for me.
- The adults in my life love and care for each other so that I don't have to care for them.

This last sentence brought home in a powerful new way that it wasn't enough to have a loving secure relationship with Sophia. I needed to cultivate one with my husband as well so that she didn't feel the burden of our emotional upheavals or fear the people we became in those moments of conflict.

Just like I had with my parenting, I needed to dig in and shovel through the layers of shame, blame, guilt, and goo that were at the heart of my partnering. I likened it to opening a magician's black bag filled with colored scarves. The scarves were my beliefs, and as I pulled on one, an endless string of these colored scarves all tied together came forth. I recall spending many hours journaling about these beliefs. I'd imagine myself untying each scarf and asking myself, "Where did this belief come from? Is it serving me? Do I want to keep, alter it, or get rid of it altogether?"

I found a few more toxic, irrational beliefs lurking in my shadow:

- I am not worthy of love.
- I have to be perfect, or I'll die.
- It's dangerous to have too much fun or feel too good.
- Not knowing is dangerous.
- Kindness is for saints and sissies.
- Punishing yourself and others and withholding love from yourself and others is virtuous and Godly.

Yuck! It's pretty easy to see I wasn't going to create a very healthy relationship with these beliefs hiding under the rug. It took massive doses of self-compassion to invite in these awarenesses and hold them with love. I saw that how I treated myself was how I treated others. At first it looked like I loved others better than I loved myself. I certainly prioritized them over myself. But the expectations I had of them in return weren't exactly loving. I subconsciously kept score in my head and let it be known when I felt unattended. As I kept on with my shadow work, I discovered that it was virtually impossible to create a world of love outside of myself if I was anything less than loving within myself. I was going to have to listen closely to the whispers of my heart and treat my own needs with love. I would have to be worthy of and capable of creating a secure attachment *with myself*.

I learned that the knot I would feel in the pit of my stomach or in the middle of my chest was a sign that I was bumping up against something that needed my attention. I would feel frustrated, angry, sad, guilty or resentful and knew that this was so because I believed something was true, and that the world was going against that "truth." What hidden agreement did I have to be "broken"—causing me to feel this way? I could see that within my marriage there were many agreements that no one had agreed to.

Intimate relationships are often the most fertile ground for shadow work because they are one of the places where we have the greatest difficulty drawing personal boundaries. At first, our relationship was fairly balanced with few power struggles, but it didn't take long before the complexity of family life increased, and we fell into the age-old pattern of domination and control, mimicking that which we both had in childhood. This isn't unusual.

Since we spend so much time in close proximity with our partner, we see them in countless body postures and facial expressions, some of which are bound to mimic a physical stance or facial expression that triggers past trauma from childhood.

Our mates usually embody, carry, and express some of our hidden shadow qualities. These are like lost pieces of ourselves. We see them in our mate and find them deeply attractive. According to the work of Harville Hendrix and his Imago Therapy approach, this is because we have an unconscious desire to restore ourselves to wholeness by claiming our disavowed qualities we see in our mate. We are seeking healing.

Initially though, qualities that should be shared, are held by just one or the other. If we don't learn how to process our own shadow material it could forever be like one of us has to do all the breathing in and the other has to do all the breathing out— all the while resenting each other for it. In our case, I expressed the anger and Tobias expressed the shame. Each one of us had anger and shame to process, but I wasn't comfortable with shame and he wasn't comfortable with anger. In my first marriage it was reversed. I had felt subservient (kind of like my mom had been). In my second marriage I was determined not to repeat that mistake. But that just pushed me to the other end of the spectrum. In my relationship with Tobias, I was the dominant energy in the house (kind of like my dad had been), at least in the beginning. I usually played the "heavy," making most decisions and pushing for things to go my way. Since Tobias grew up with a domineering, controlling mother, he was comfortable with the dynamic. It worked for a while. But underneath I longed for a more present partner and he ached for the space to be more fully himself. Neither one of us wanted to repeat the patterns of our childhood.

As grace would have it, Tobias found his way to the Man-Kind Project's New Warrior Training. It's a men's initiatory weekend in which he got in touch with his wants and desires. It helped him step into owning his voice and his power in the relationship. When he found his anger, it triggered my unfelt shame. It rocked our relationship boat considerably. I was frozen in place by his angry outbursts and his requests to have his needs met. They mirrored both my fear of being dominated again (which felt like facing death) and my inability to powerfully ask for what I needed (bringing up feelings of invisibility from my childhood). It pushed up all of the anxious/avoidant aspects of my attachment style.

Like many couples, we had hit the place in our relationship when the things that attracted us to each other now felt insanely annoying. We were fortunate to understand that we were being asked to own and integrate disowned aspects of ourselves, therefore the annoyance is actually a form of self-rejection. Unfortunately, most couples don't see it this way. Rather than facing the internal conflict of integrating the disowned qualities within themselves, partners tend to avoid the work by making the conflict external, as in the problem is with the relationship. What is really an intrapsychic problem becomes an interpersonal problem. The only way forward is to uncover our previously disavowed traits and love ourselves back into wholeness. As we become capable of loving these quirks and qualities within ourselves we are then able to love them in our mates.

Sometimes what we see in our mate is real. Sometimes it is not. This is true for both positive and negative attributes. But we must be on guard for those most dangerous moments of projection where we (or our mate) ascribe our own motives, thinking, and behavior to another when it's not really there. If our denial is strong enough, we can actually convince our partners that the problem we see in them is really a part of who they are. It's so insidious that partners can actually be trained by their spouse to identify with his or her partner's expression of the repudiated thoughts, feelings, and emotions. It is an "off-loading" of our shadow material. For example, if you are the one who has trouble owning your anger, you may be very adept at triggering an explosion of anger and hostility in your partner. You may then criticize the explosion in the same way that you criticize and repudiate the anger within yourself. And then, in a strange turn of events, you feel justified enough to be angry.

Ideally, our mates are an agent of healing. If we know that our upsets are a sign that our biology and biography have been triggered, we can become curious about the upset and dive in to see what's under it. When both partners are aware of their own behavioral patterns, as well as their patterns as a couple, each triggering episode offers a chance for deep healing. If we are to be successful we have to be able to have both self-respect and respect for others. This is especially difficult when our needs appear to compete or conflict with one another. Who wins? Who Loses?

The Queen seeks the path forward where everyone wins.

She helps us develop the skill to balance respecting and honoring ourselves and our needs with respecting and honoring the needs of our partner. Our house is much different these days. My husband and I know our stuff inside and out. We still have the occasional flare up, but we are gentler with ourselves and each other. We know when we are stuck in a shadow story. We prize our connection above all, so that means we don't allow things to stay salty. We may allow for a short cooling off period, but then we seek to work it out.

One of our favorite tools is the "re-do." This family practice is implemented if someone has said or done something reptilian style (fight, flight, freeze) so that they get the chance to say it or do it better. It's amazing the therapeutic effect this has on both the one triggered and the recipient of the triggered behavior. Sometimes when everyone seems grumpy and out of sorts, one of us will say, "Do we need a family scream?" It is incredibly cathartic to do a family scream. Jumping is also one of our favorite techniques. And we do our best not to carry on lengthy discussions or make any decisions when someone is still "running hot."

Our lives and our relationships benefit greatly from understanding how our past programming and our shadow qualities are constantly at play in our connection to ourselves and others. In order to show up in our relationships as a Sovereign Queen, we must develop deep awareness of the unconscious patterns that run on auto-pilot, as well as deep mastery of the tools and techniques that can effectively interrupt those patterns. Finding them can be a challenge. Sometimes they reveal themselves in surprising ways.

A few years back I was having coffee with a sister-friend when I was struck with a soul-shaking realization. As we chatted about the evolution of our spirituality and the changes we noticed in our relationships and in our career choices as a result of our growth, I saw with great clarity that if I wanted to continue evolving and move past the old conditioning I took on as a child, I would have to acknowledge something hard to grasp: *Deep at the heart of human existence is the reality that we are all fundamentally alone.*

The aloneness I am referring to is not the physical state of being alone or without company. I am talking about the psycho-spiritual condition that all humans face as a result of being birthed on planet Earth. As the saying goes, we come into this life alone and we will depart from this life alone. This seems to conflict with my earlier "Oneness Moment," when I felt viscerally that we are all one. And we are. When we contemplate our spiritual nature and our spiritual consciousness, we know we are all indeed inextricably linked. We even now know that physically we are connected in ways we are just beginning to understand. These connections at the unseen atomic level demonstrate that all matter is simply layers and layers of overlapping energy fields—interconnectedness. Knowing that this is true gave me the strength to explore when it is not true. Like all spiritual truth there is a paradox here.

We are One, except when we are not.

For the last six or so years, my husband Tobias has been suffering from what appears now to be chronic pain in his teeth, mouth, and jaw. Without going into too much detail, after a grueling slog through many health and healing professionals, false diagnoses and all manner of treatments, he has finally been diagnosed with Burning Mouth Syndrome (BMS). As you might expect this has taken its toll on our family. We all have this diagnosis now, but in our own way. And what a teacher it has proven for me.

It has taught me over and over how much help I can be, and how much help I can't be. It has unceremoniously made me see that I do not in fact have the power to make this all better, even if I believe that I do. I have had to learn that the healing journey I would take is not the healing journey my husband should take. It has forced me to look at some very hard things, to own that I have dragged Tobias through numerous edgy, all natural, holistic, and in some cases just plain weird treatments—because it's what I would do. I did many of these holistic treatments too, and often I got more out of it than he did. I finally realized that guidance I thought I was getting for him was really for me. It's been painful to see that; and even more painful to acknowledge that I probably would not have sought out these treatments for myself. I wouldn't have given myself permission.

But the most painful thing of all has been to see how my faith in these things, in my "guidance," was so convincing that I unconsciously used my force of personality to dismiss or drown out my husband's voice. I often judged him harshly as not understanding how consciousness works, and not believing enough to get well, not wanting it badly enough. I am not proud of this. Yet I have compassion for myself knowing that I was desperate to help him find relief.

Accepting my aloneness has dramatically shifted my experience of living with a chronically ill person. First, it helped me see that my seemingly uncontrollable need to continue to "problem solve" this for Tobias (despite his repeated requests that I stop) came from an attempt on my part to avoid feeling pain and sadness. Watching my beloved suffer is brutal. I feel such incredible sadness. I feel utterly powerless. And I unconsciously side-stepped feeling all of this by going into problem solving every time these feelings popped up. That behavior led to tension, spoken and unspoken criticism, and resentment between us. Second, it helped me see that I was afraid of losing him, our quality of life, and the quality of our relationship. I was afraid for me and for my daughter. Before I understood Aloneness, I had the mistaken idea that I had to minimize this, or at least manage it, for all our sakes.

But after accepting my aloneness, something unexpected happened. I stepped fully into the feelings I had been avoiding, and I faced the fact that I am already alone. I could see that all this time I had mistakenly believed that my husband could understand me and I could understand him. That we could understand and love each other so much that we would finally feel safe. That our childhood wounds would heal and there would be no more pain. It was a nice fantasy, but not much more than that.

Accepting aloneness helped me see that we would never ever fully understand each other. We've been married eighteen years now and I can tell you that the more I learn about my husband, the less I understand him. I can barely understand myself! Yes, we have offered each other moments of understanding and lots of love, and yes we have used that to further our healing. But we were each responsible for doing the healing work for ourselves.

Accepting aloneness has liberated me in so many ways. It has helped me to stop messing around in my husband's territory and instead, tend to my own ignored feelings. This skill arrived just in time to keep me from wrecking my relationship with my daughter Sophia. What teenager wants a mom mucking about in their interior space? It has also helped me see all the ways I was still, after years of conscious relationship-building, hoping my beloved would fulfill certain needs for me and then feeling hurt, sad, scared, and angry when he did not. And much to his delight, it has helped me see how impossible it is for me to guide him on his healing journey.

But most importantly and profoundly, accepting my aloneness helped me to see what my real job was: to simply sit with him, in the pain, in the sadness, in the crushing fear that it might never get better, to be alone together. It was a turning point for me and for us. I accessed huge pools of self-compassion, compassion for him, and for us as a couple. I found a reservoir of loving kindness I never knew I had. I have been able to form new habits of attention, and practice new, healthier behaviors.

I invite you to consider your own aloneness, the hell and heaven of it. Because it is of course both hellish and heavenly: hellish because we have to do something with the longing to not be alone and heavenly because it liberates us to focus on our own work, our own healing, as our primary task. Whichever way we see it, we are alone in our hell and we are alone in our heaven. Simply put, no one is coming to save you.

While others can join us to celebrate our heavenly moments and empathize deeply and compassionately with our hellish ones, the path that is our life is ours and only ours. We may share a part of our path from time to time with others, our parents, our spouses, our children, our colleagues, but if you have lived any length of time at all, you know that these co-journeys are not permanent. At any given moment, without warning or preparation, those we hold most dear may come to the end of their journey, or at least the end of the part of the journey we were sharing with them. And we grieve those losses. Sometimes the grief seems endless and utterly overwhelms us. I suspect we get dragged under at times by grief because the losses force us to see this unwanted truth that we are ultimately alone.

But we aren't alone in our aloneness. Every single other human on the planet is also deep down alone. We are alone together. Being alone together makes it so much easier to stand by each other in our pain and sorrow, as well as our joys and triumphs. When we recognize our experience is ours alone, and theirs belongs to them, no jealousy or comparison is possible. We can celebrate another's success without negatively comparing ourselves. We find relief from the need to fix someone's pain or hurry them over their grief. We feel more comfortable around hurting, grieving people if we are willing to acknowledge our own grief and sadness, and if we recognize that we, and they, are alone in working it through. Our responsibility is our *response*, and we can be with them tenderly, vulnerably, alone together.

Seeing this allowed me to stop abandoning myself (all aspects of me) in pursuit of things, people, and situations outside of me that can never ever take away or fix my aloneness. Just like I had to commit to being fully present in my relationship, I needed to commit to being fully there for me, myself, and I. This provided a deeper healing than I ever imagined. I no longer felt alone. I had ME! All facets of me: The wounded me, the ego of me, the soul of me, the heart of me, the mind of me. Plus, I have the Queen in me—all seven versions of her.

I feel grateful to have cultivated the capacity to feel deeply satisfied with my own company and increased my skill at meeting my own needs. It's a crucial step if we are to embody our sovereignty. It has also allowed me to see that, in my aloneness, I truly need others. But I need them in an entirely different way—not to prove my worth or to assuage some insecurity, but to share this journey of life and the burden and blessing of aloneness. It's brilliant really, this thing called Life. We must learn to face the joys and tragedies of it all on our own, and we do that best in the company of others who are also learning to do the same.

When all our healing work is said and done, we find the sweet spot of being both self-reliant and interdependent. We have faith in our own ability, and we are open to having help. We know we are the source of our own safety, and we can receive and give care without losing our connection to ourselves.

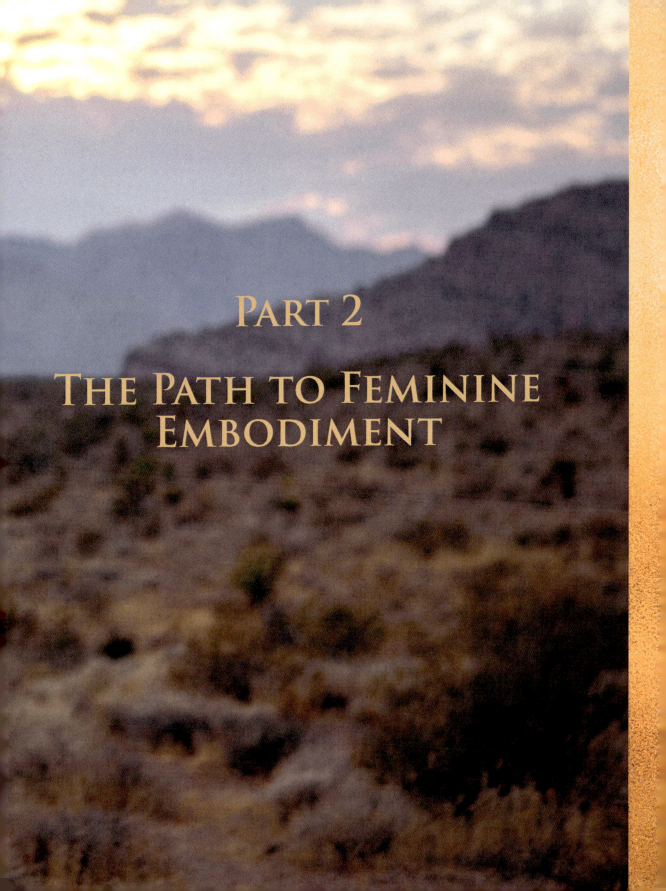

Part 2

The Path to Feminine Embodiment

*Something is rising from the muck and the fog and the dark of life.
Something that scares the holy hell out of most everyone it touches
at first.
Something so powerful that it threatens to upend every single thing
about the way we live and move in the world.*

*But there is no stopping it…
no stopping HER.*

*The Wild Feminine is coming home,
home to our hearts and our bodies,
home to our souls.
Finally.*

*The only question is whether you will willingly offer all you have to
the Her that is You
or whether you will burn in the fire of your own resistance.*

*We know we must make the conscious commitment
to let the Wild Feminine into our lives.*

*We know well the assets and limits of our egos and have placed
both in service to the She-go.*

*We are rolling out the red carpet for the Queen of Fire that has
begun to smolder in our hearts.*

*We know we are not perfect, and we don't mind.
We know our magnificence but are not fooled.
We know our shadows but are not controlled.*

*We know nothing we do matters, and everything we do matters.
And we're down with that. In fact, we are turned on by that.*

We get still enough to hear the guidance of our inner compass,
liberated enough to act on it,
And sovereign enough to invite others to join us.

We are tuned in to our inner Pulse.
We see the inner weaving that is being asked of us.
We understand that any outer weaving we do is the second
act of our life-play.
And when we find ourselves hooked by the fray of life,
we move inward, joyfully or grudgingly.

We have been asked to let go of everything we thought mattered.
She has demanded that we give it all to Her, without reservation.
And we have.
Or we have watched in horror as it was ripped from our hands,
claw marks and all.

Some of us feel nearly dead from slow dripping poison and pain
of a life bereft of authenticity.
Others have been broken hard on the rocks of our life
so that our very bones seem to have disappeared.
All so She could have Her way with us.

And like the Phoenix, we have begun, slowly,
to rise from the ashes of her WildFire.
We have been transformed, our bodies and blood transmuted.

The blood of the Wild Feminine now courses through our veins,
beats our hearts.
She has brought new life, new meaning,
and new focus to our world.

And we honor her by Weaving Her Dream into Reality.

*"We all come from the Goddess, and to her we shall return,
Like a drop of rain, flowing to the ocean."*

—Zsuzsanna Budapest

CHAPTER 8
RECLAIMING THE DIVINE FEMININE

I began having "visits" from the Goddess in 2017 when I made my first spiritual pilgrimage to Egypt. Inexplicably, I burst into tears as soon as I exited the airport into the warm Cairo night. I wiped away my tears, attempting to hide them from our tour leader, who I had met just moments before. He looked at me kindly and said, "It happens often to daughters of the Goddess when they come home." I had no earthly idea what he was talking about, but it soothed me none-the-less. Two days later, when the tour was in full swing, we made our way to the Afandina, where a gorgeous private sailing vessel called a *dahabeya* awaited us. We were about to start a seven day sailing journey down the Nile, stopping along the way to visit temples and other sacred places where the Goddess flourished. From the moment I set foot on the boat, the conversation between us began.

I stood on the top deck looking out on the dark blue waters of the Nile. I could hardly believe that I was actually in Egypt sailing peacefully down this luscious river, the Mother of Life. It was a dream come true and felt like a miracle to be soaking in the Egyptian sun. Several months earlier, I had felt a call from deep in my soul to travel to Egypt on a spiritual quest for my fiftieth birthday. I shared this with a group of girlfriends who were part of a monthly circle I ran that we jokingly called a book club. The response was electric. We all felt the power of it zip around the circle. Everyone was excited and keen to go. I reached out to my friend Halle Eavely who led transformational tours of this kind, and we booked a date for the trip. Three of my friends signed up immediately. Three more were seriously considering it. I was feeling pretty great about filling the spots I had agreed to fill. Unfortunately, by the time the trip rolled around, things had changed. I was bringing just one other woman and me. I felt like a failure. The trip went forward because Halle filled the slots I couldn't.

But on the deck of that boat, every negative judgment I had toward myself was erased. I heard the Goddess whisper, "Welcome home." My heart swelled with so much love I thought it might explode. Then my insides melted into pure pleasure. I lost track of time and have no idea how long I stayed in this altered state of communion and connection. When it passed, I knew something radical had shifted in me. This is just one of a dozen spectacular experiences I have had in Egypt. As we explored the ancient and powerful places where the Divine Feminine was acknowledged, something began to wake up in my cellular memory. We walked the halls and ground of Hathor's temple at Dendera. We conducted rituals in ancient power-centers, including Isis' temple in Philae and in the Great Pyramid. No words can ever describe the deep and lasting transformation that happened for me on that trip.

The Mother Nile herself was one of my greatest teachers. As we sailed her sacred waters for six days and nights, I learned more about what it means to be in feminine flow than I could have ever expected. Before the trip was over, I heard the goddess's voice once more, "Bring my daughters home to me." I knew She was asking me to return to Egypt the following year with a group of sisters. I made a vow to do exactly that even though I had no clue how I would accomplish such a task. After all, the Goddess had asked, and who was I to say no to the Goddess?

After returning home, I booked the next trip myself and invited a colleague to teach with me. I was now committed to filling the entire trip. It was the highest-priced offering I had ever created. I was scared. This was no small feat as I needed to fill the trip while simultaneously moving my family across the country. We had to prepare and sell our home, pack and ship our belongings, and find and move into a new home. We were between homes for seven weeks, and I worked from Airbnb's and friends' basements all during the launch period. I doubted. I worried. I stressed. Until I remembered that this was not my trip. It was Hers.

I kept putting myself back on the deck of that boat, feeling the Nile river beneath me, remembering what I felt there, remembering what my cells learned in Egypt. Every time I sent another chunk of money to my Egyptian tour company, I prayed for guidance, for my part in the process. I listened for instructions on how to put the word out so that those who were being called home would hear it. I surrendered my plans, my ego's desires, my list of who I thought should enroll, and I focused on being of service to the Goddess and the sisters who felt called to come home to Her.

Eventually, I came to see my role as partnering with the Goddess Herself. It was exhilarating to feel Her presence in my life palpably as we worked together on the project. I didn't do it perfectly, yet She never withdrew from me. There were hiccups and delays. Some cancelations and fears needed to be calmed. But in the end, I headed back to Egypt with ten women. A ten-fold increase from my first attempt!

In November of 2018, on my first night in Abu Simbel in southern Egypt, I was sitting in meditation under a field of golden stars on a deep blue background painted on a domed ceiling in my room. I dropped in deeply and whispered to the Goddess, "I have returned home. And the daughters you have called to you will arrive tomorrow." I felt Her presence surrounding me. Suddenly my inner eye opened, and I saw Isis standing about fifty feet away from me at the altar in a colorful Egyptian temple. There were lighted torches on the columns that lined the aisle on both sides. Isis motioned for me to come toward Her. I had a moment of doubt and opened my eyes. Am I making this up? I wondered. Nothing like this had ever happened to me before. I had grown used to "hearing" Her and feeling her presence, but I had never had a vision of Her.

I closed my eyes again, and She was still there, beckoning me. I floated down toward Her, and She gestured upward, urging me to go up. I floated toward the top of the temple above Her. It was shaped like a pyramid. Across the apex was a stone tablet. It had a male name inscribed on it, and somehow I knew that the name was placed there first by Moses and then replaced by Abraham. I didn't fully understand, but I realized She was inviting me into a ritual of some kind. It had to do with passing on the lineage and access to sacred wisdom. I knew that I was being given the opportunity to erase that name and put a new male name in its place. But I had no son to pass it to. I thought about putting my daughter Sophia's name there instead. But that felt wrong. And then I thought, "It should be for all the children of the world."

I let out a wild roar from deep inside me, "It's for all the children! It's for all the children! It's for ALL the children!" In a flash, my body reeled around until my back was to the apex of the pyramid. My legs stretched and opened along the sides of the pyramid, widening out as all of creation began to tumble from my yoni. I felt the birth of the gasses and stars that make up the Universe; I felt galaxies and planets tumbling from within me. I birthed our beloved earth, Gaia. I felt all her plants and animals spilling wildly out of me.

The diversity of life was breathtaking. I was utterly mesmerized by the beauty of it all. Then the people came, in a parade of human history, the dark and the light, the good and the bad; it was all there. And then I gave birth to myself. It was trippy! My consciousness moved down into my own body, and the birthing continued as I gave birth to my daughter Sophia. I was so overcome with love for her, and in that instant, I knew how much the Goddess loved me and all of creation. At that moment, I understood that I was being shown the truth of who I am—a goddess who gives life. I saw the fractal nature of the Goddess of All and the goddess Rima. I realized this is who I am. This is who we all are.

Then everything disappeared but Isis and me and she said, "Now you know. Go and tell them."

"I will," I whispered through a flood of tears. This book is part of fulfilling that promise.

While Isis has come to me on many other occasions, none have felt as immersive and real as that particular visit. In the years since, She has encouraged me to study different faces of the Divine Feminine. I already had an affinity for Mother Mary from my Catholic roots and from a powerful experience I had at Chartres cathedral. She also brought the Magdalene to me to work with. All of these faces of the Divine Feminine have been woven together to support my work with my students. They are an essential part of my programs and my ongoing personal work.

My third trip to Egypt took place in March of 2020. We were sailing on the Nile in what would turn out to be the final week of free travel across the globe before the Covid-19 pandemic would suspend all flights and shut down airports, stranding travelers for months. We put safety precautions in place to help everyone stay safe and Covid-free as we finished our pilgrimage. The level of interference was palpable. Egypt was experiencing road closures, sandstorms, and even a flood of epic proportions. It took a lot of magic and help from the Goddess to make it to our final destination of Abydos before we were to return to Cairo and start the journey home. But She had planned something special, and She would not be deterred.

This stop was the highlight of the voyage for me. My beautiful soul-sister and tour leader, Doaa Bodawy, had arranged a private visit to the Osirian, an ancient structure located behind the younger main temple of Abydos. The energy in that structure rivals that of the Great Pyramid, and it appears to be structurally similar and of about the same age. The Osirian is considered to be the temple where Isis brought the rescued parts of her beloved Osiris to stitch him back together after his jealous brother Set murdered and dismembered him. I could certainly feel her presence in the space. It was mind-altering from the get-go.

The only hieroglyphs found in this temple are carved on the ceiling. Looking up, we saw a vast, incredibly well-preserved rendering of the Goddess Nut and her consort Geb holding her up as she gave birth to the world. I was immediately transported back to the vision I had with Isis eighteen months before. Here was my experience carved in ancient stone. I was dumbfounded. I slipped in and out of the time stream, finally snapping to—and almost too late. Months earlier, Isis had given me very explicit instructions for the ceremony I was to lead once we made it to the Osirian. But because I had never been there before, I wasn't prepared for the impact it had on me physically and energetically. I can't imagine how horrible I would have felt if I had not returned to myself in time and remembered what I was supposed to do there to do. As the ceremony completed, I could feel the enormous columns of rainbow light beaming outward and creating a connection between the ground where we stood and grid points in the sky. I don't pretend to know what all of this means or how it fits into the grand scheme of things. But I do know it was incredibly important, if only for me and the rest of the pilgrims in that group.

Since returning home, I have continued to commune with the Goddess daily. She is coming to me now as Isis, Hathor, Mother Mary, and Mary Magdalene. Sometimes I feel Her presence close by. Other times She seems farther away. Most often, She seems to be asking me to stand more fully in my own Divine Feminine energy rather than relying on experiencing it through Her.

When I went looking for my old writing on the subject of the Divine Feminine in preparation for writing this chapter, I found my scholarly research and writing to be dry and devoid of the warmth that I feel in my relationship with Her. It wasn't lost on me that it is one thing to read and write about Goddess culture and ancient rites and rituals. It's entirely something else to have direct and participatory experiences.

There have been several occasions where I have questioned my grip on "reality." What feels true for me is that there are, and likely always have been, two (or an infinite number) of realities happening here. There is what we can see and collectively agree on, and then there is the etheric, nebulous, mystical reality that is rarely made visible. In this alternate reality, I find myself having access to a wealth of resources that don't exist in my normal daily experience. This is what it means to recover and discover a personal relationship with the Divine Feminine.

It seems there was a time when many of us lived in this more mysterious, cosmically-connected world. If anthropologists' conclusions are correct, there was a time when humans felt completely woven into the fabric of all life on Earth and even beyond. Many indigenous cultures have never lost their connection with this reality in which we were one with nature—part of it, not superior to it. We worked within its rhythms rather than trying to ignore or tame them. We rose when the sun rose and slept after it set. We understood the rhythms of the seasons and the cycles of life. Our experiences were not merely the facts of life; they were sacred to us. We lived embedded within them. We were children of the Earth and therefore intimately connected with Divine Presence… and it felt feminine.

It is easy to see how we could conclude that the earth was feminine just by associating it with the sex that bears life. A woman becomes pregnant, nurtures life within her belly, and bears a child at the end of nine months, about the same timeframe it takes for a crop to be planted, grow to maturity, and be harvested. In earlier times, perhaps we saw the act of sowing the fields and planting seeds into the earth's soil as a mirror to the act of love-making and seeding a woman's womb.

But somewhere along the way, we lost the feminine face of God (at least in Western cultures.) The introduction of the sky-gods that replaced the earth-dwelling goddess may mark the beginning of our collective amnesia regarding the understanding of life as a sacred and cyclical act and the notion that the sacred is numinous. The Egyptian, Sumerian, Greek, and Roman deities included images of the Sacred Feminine. Hinduism still depicts God in various forms, including feminine forms.

The Judeo-Christian tradition offers its understanding of a singular form of God, and it is masculine only. The God of Moses is disembodied. It appears in a bush. There are to be no idols. No representation of it in the physical realm. Even God's name is unutterable, except for once a year by the High Priest in the holy of holies. And even then, if he is unworthy, he will die.

The sacred practices of the temples were to be left behind. Yet mystics in all spiritual traditions never lost sight of the importance of balancing the physical with the spiritual, the heart, and the mind. The Sacred Feminine was always at the Sacred Masculine's side in the true teachings of the mystics. It is only in the politicization and institutionalization of these teachings that the Feminine has been lost.

Christian cannon seemed to go even farther in denying the Sacred Feminine. In what seems oddly opposed to the life and teachings of Jesus, the Church interpreted his resurrection and triumph over death as evidence that the body and the physical are a loathsome prison to the spirit. Death is to be feared and overcome. The course of early Christian communities was altered dramatically when Rome gave up fighting against the growing popularity of the movement and subsumed it into their culture. There is ample evidence that both women and men shared liturgical and teaching positions within the early Christian community. Something that didn't sit well with either the Roman or Jewish male-dominated authority structures. Before the third century, Jewish scholars paid almost no attention to the story of Adam and Eve. In that same century, leaders in the now Romanized Christian church gathered to determine what the official Christian Codex would be. The version we all know of the Adam and Eve story was added to the official canon at that time. As part of what we now call The Bible, it became the new lens through which the feminine was, and is often still, viewed. It delivered a final blow to the Sacred Feminine by depicting Eve as the cause of man's fall from grace.

For millennia women of the Christianized world have lived their lives in religious and societal frameworks that disavow the female sex as evil—our bodies as a temptation offered by a temptress that must be tamed. Yet something new seems to be stirring, something bubbling to the surface in fragmented memories. Whether on sacred pilgrimage to faraway places like Egypt or while meditating on our couch, whether through the scents of ancient and holy oils used in anointing rites or the songs sung in sister circles while we dance around the fire: We Are Remembering. And we are coming home to reclaim the holy and powerful nature of The Divine Feminine as made visible by the magic of our very bodies.

It is to the body we now turn as a portal into healing and the gateway to restore the sacred to what has been called profane. As we embrace and heal the wounds stored in our bodies, we become safe and sacred containers for the feminine power within us to re-emerge.

"Let your body call you back into yourself, into your most deeply embodied self.

Land, dive, soar. Find the crumbs that lead back home."
—*Cheryl Pallant*

CHAPTER 9
Your Body As a Pathway to Enlightenment

In addition to having the psyche's shadow stories based on the biographical data we picked up in childhood about ourselves and the world, there is emerging science that indicates we have stories lodged in our bodies as well. The work of trauma specialists Dr. Peter Levine, Robert Scaer M.D., and many others reveals that the shadow concept is found not just in the psyche as described by Freud and Jung but also in the body.

The body's stories can go unnoticed for years until they get our attention through illness, disease, or dysfunction. It is most apparent in PTSD patients whose bodies involuntarily respond to stimuli that mimic past moments of trauma. You may not have experienced catastrophic trauma, but we all experience trauma of some sort—as evidenced by our imperfect caregiving environment. Whether that trauma is adequately processed on a physical level determines if it becomes shadow material for the body.

This was all news to me when I was first introduced to this work through one of my doctoral courses. At the time, I didn't have a two-way relationship with my body. I didn't understand how to hear it despite the fact it continuously talks to me. I was deaf and blind to what was happening with me physiologically. After developing body-based practices designed to help me interact with my body, I can now take the cues from my body sensations to track what I might be feeling—even before there are words for it. When we gain some skill at this, we can interrupt our stress responses before, during, or immediately after we shut down or overreact.

According to Babette Rothschild, trauma researcher and author of *The Body Remembers,* we can experience trauma as "a psychophysical experience even when the traumatic event causes no physical harm." Because there is often no physical harm, the body's response to trauma and the physical component of trauma has been largely overlooked in traditional talk therapies used to help trauma sufferers. Rothschild's work explores the importance of understanding the role of memory in patients' ongoing experience of trauma and helps to illuminate how information can be found in muscle memory.

Embodiment work is critical for our capacity to live healthy, happy lives because the somatic nervous system can store information instantly. Rothschild says this can be easily seen in the simple experience of forgetting why one entered a room and gaining access to the memory once we have returned to the posture and location when one first had the impulse to head into the room. The body posture may not fully account for the accessed memory, but many people can access memories, sometimes quite surprisingly when they find themselves in certain postures. This form of state-dependent memory can send someone into chaos if they are surprised by the activated emotions. So can certain movements, smells, or sounds. For years I had to close my eyes during love-making because I couldn't tolerate my husband's head near mine, particularly on the right side of my head. It was only after exploring our sexual successes and failures through the body-loving art of Tantra that I discovered this weird aversion. I have no conscious understanding of why it bothered me, but I was able to shift it anyway by repatterning my experience in a safe and therapeutic sexual setting.

Conditioning is another way we develop "body memory." For example, in a time of danger, the only concern of your body-mind is to "make safe." This is a primal, instinctual response that happens automatically from the reptilian part of our brain without our directing it (I call this part of my brain my lizard lady). When a particular defense response is successfully implemented, the body remembers this and is more likely to call on it again in the future. Similarly, if a defense response is unsuccessful, the odds of it being used also go down. There are times when we are under attack where fleeing or fighting back is impossible (when being spanked by a parent or attacked by someone). In these cases, our lizard self may enter a freeze response as a way of going numb and blocking out pain. This can be problematic as it can lead to habitual freezing at times when it's healthy to stand up for ourselves or leave an unhealthy situation.

Using body-based techniques to reset the nervous system can bring about resolution. Taking self-defense classes may help assist assault victims in turning the fight response back on after it has been overridden by the system that deemed it an unsafe strategy. The need to be awakened from the freeze response is very real. Robert Scaer notes that in some cases, severe freeze response can kill instantly, as in cardiac arrest brought on by an extreme response in the dorsal vagal complex. Studies by Peter Levine have shown that PTSD patients experienced a dramatic clearing of many of their symptoms when they were allowed to complete motor discharge of the freeze response through Levine's unique body-based therapeutic technique Somatic Experiencing.

Understanding how to settle ourselves when we have been triggered is essential because in states of high stress or perceived danger, the brain's instinctual reptilian part is in charge. The higher-level thinking capacities go off-line during these moments when instinct is in play. So, when I am upset, my lizard lady brain is all about trying to "make safe," and that can look like ripping someone's head off or running a mile away—both of which can have career-limiting consequences, not to mention damaging our children and our spouses. What I need most in those times is my rational, thinking brain (the neocortex) to come back online as soon as possible, as this is where all of my creative potential for problem-solving resides. In addition, I need to be able to access my capacity for empathy and understanding, none of which are of any consequence to my lizard lady.

The reality is that in today's world, we are far more likely to experience a stress response in times that aren't really life-threatening, like when our child is asking for a sugary snack in the checkout line in a particularly whiney voice, when our spouse is late getting home in time for a special event, or when our boss cuts us down in a meeting in front of our peers. The lizard brain kicks when moments like these touch some shadow belief or body memory that reminds us of childhood moments when we experienced what felt like threatening or shaming responses from our caregivers.

I learned four simple techniques from trauma specialist Geneie Everett that help interrupt the body's trauma response, calming my lizard lady and bringing my thinking capacities back online. She calls them Trauma First Aide. She has taught these techniques to first responders worldwide and to medics in the US military so that they could administer life-saving aid under life-threatening circumstances. These four simple techniques help to shift the body's focus to the peripheral nervous system and away from the central nervous system, which is where it is readying to fight or flee by pumping the heart faster, drawing in more air in the lungs, slowing digestion, readying the muscles to fight or flee, and pumping adrenaline and cortisol through the body. This shift in focus allows the body to naturally settle and then draw a natural deep breath as it rests and senses that the danger has passed. They can be used alone or together. Some will work better for you than others. It's important to try them and see which one(s) reliably help you "make safe" and then employ them when you are upset.

1. **Grounding**—focusing your attention on your feet, then hands, then back. This is done best in a chair with your feet flat on the ground, your hands in your lap. Tap your feet, then wiggle your finger, and finally lean back in a chair and release all your weight to the chair.

2. **Resourcing**—think of something that makes you happy inside, like your favorite vacation spot, your dream car, a speech that garnered a standing ovation, snuggling your grandchild or beloved pet.

3. **Tracking**—noticing the sensations in your body and how they are changing from moment to moment.

4. **Somatic Release**—shaking, jumping, pounding a pillow, going for a run, screaming.

These techniques allow the energy unleashed by the reptilian brain to be discharged in a safe and intentional manner. This is what animals do naturally when they need to recover from a dangerous episode.

Without a basic understanding of this physiological response, we may continue to believe that our shutdowns and outbursts are happening because of our spouse, our boss, our children, the traffic, the stock market, etc. The reality is that our shadow is in play. We need to have compassion for ourselves and treat ourselves gently. These are hardware issues that have come up for healing. They are not signs of weakness. Once we have negotiated the body's shadow stories and the psyche's shadow stories and we are back in our "right mind," we have a much greater chance of finding a true resolution to the trigger that set us off.

Working with the body is one of the most direct and effective ways to resolve old trauma and integrate new information. Many people do this naturally through exercising to stay calm, dancing or singing to lift our mood, and boxing or martial arts to off-load energy. Deeper trauma can often be addressed through body-based therapies such as EMDR, somatic release, psycho-drama, and even certain kinds of massage. In the next chapter, we will discuss how embodiment can be supercharged by working with the energy systems that support our physical systems.

"When we contemplate the miracle of embodied life,
we begin to partner with our bodies in a kinder way."

—Sharon Salzberg

CHAPTER 10
UNDERSTANDING YOUR ENERGY BODY

Western medicine has taken an approach to treating the body that relies on what can be directly perceived. Centuries of autopsies and cadaver dissection gave doctors a view inside the skin. They yielded illustrations of the body in beautifully detailed renderings that show the musculature, skeletal system, the nervous and circulatory systems, as well as the organ system. Much like a mechanic who diagnoses what is wrong with a car by examining and testing various parts in an engine, Western doctors use their eyes and increasingly advanced technology that allows for greater "seeing" to understand how the body's parts and systems are functioning, or not, in order to prescribe treatment.

Eastern medicine, however, followed a much different path. Long before the Greeks performed the first recorded dissections for medical purposes in the third century BCE, Eastern physicians used an entirely different, unseen system to diagnose and treat disease and illness: the body's energy systems. Like our physical body, our energy body has an anatomy made up of several distinct systems such as our Meridians, Chakras, and Polarity.

In our effort to embody our sacred feminine sovereignty, it is essential that we grasp how to interact with the components of our energy body and the resources it makes available to us.

According to eastern medicine and esoteric teachings, the body is said to exist in three forms simultaneously: The Gross or Physical Body, the Subtle or Light/Energy Body, and the Causal or Unmanifest/Seed. Western medicine recognizes only the first (physical) body. Eastern medicine works with disturbances in the physical body by addressing the body's underlying energy patterns and flows. It recognizes and seeks to understand the relationship between the physical plane (gross) and the subtle realm. The causal realm is largely undetectable and usually the domain of spirituality versus medicine.

THE CHAKRA SYSTEM

Within the subtle body is a large number of energy centers, referred to as chakras. The word chakra means spinning wheel. Each center is understood to be a sphere that spins and circulates energy throughout the body. Seven main chakras serve as the doorway that connects each of the three bodies—causal, subtle, and physical.

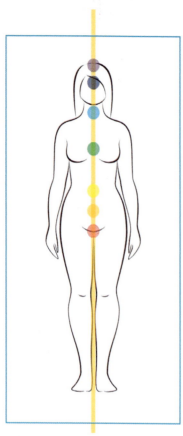

These chakras are said to influence the operation of various organs, hormones, and processes within the body. But more than that, these seven doorways or portals are a powerful way to make shifts within our physical, sexual, energetic, emotional, mental, and spiritual expressions. Like a series of pools, the energy must flow easily between the centers for optimal health. Blocked or stagnant energy can produce adverse outcomes.

The chakra system can be found in the literature of many ancient societies. The first written record appears in the Vedas between 500 and 1500 BCE, capturing a much longer oral tradition, while evidence of their existence and importance can be found in ancient Egypt. Alabaster stone tablets as old as 3000 BCE recovered from the tombs of Pharaohs and priests have marked holes in which the seven sacred oils rested. These oils were connected to each of the seven main chakras. The chakras also appear in the Upanishads around 600 BCE and in the Yoga Sutras of Patanjali around 200 BCE.

The 10th-century text known as the Padaka-Pancaka provides readers with practices for working with each chakra energy center. And the Goraksha Shataka, also written in the 10th century, provides chakra meditation instructions. Much of the Western world was first introduced to the chakra system in the 1919 book, *The Serpent Power* by Englishman Arthur Avalon. The gift of modern technology and the insistence on visual proof for these centers has led to the research that links the chakras to the physical body. It is now clear the precise locations of these centers correspond to the seven major nerve ganglia in the body. All of these nerve clusters are also linked directly to the spinal column, which according to ancient texts, is the channel through which the energy can move freely between each chakra. Each chakra is associated with a color, sound, frequency, symbol, hand positions (*mudras*), and biological and psychological processes.

Studying the chakras can point you to areas that need attention and reveal techniques and practices that can support optimal chakra health. Many excellent books detail all the marvels of the seven main chakras. The following summary will give you a basic introduction to the chakras and how you can work with them to support your deepening embodiment.

The **ROOT CHAKRA**, known in Sanskrit as *Muladhara,* rests at the base of the spine (anal opening/tailbone). Its element is earth. It governs the adrenal glands, feet, legs, bones, lower intestine, and immune system. The base chakra helps us feel connected to the earth and our physical form. It supports our need for safety, certainty, and stability.

The **SACRAL CHAKRA**, known in Sanskrit as *Svadhisthana,* is about three inches above the root chakra, about where a woman's womb space is found. Its element is water. It governs the sex organs, lower vertebrae, pelvis, appendix, bladder, hips, and kidneys. It supports us in accessing our sensual and sexual pleasure. It inspires freedom, novelty, and adventure, as well as creativity.

The **SOLAR PLEXUS CHAKRA**, known in Sanskrit as *Manipura,* rests in the upper abdomen. Its element is fire. It governs the pancreas, upper intestines, stomach, abdomen, liver, spleen, gallbladder, and mid-spine. It supports us in accessing and using our personal power and provides us with the confidence and strength needed to carve out our individual path forward in life.

The **HEART CHAKRA**, known as *Anahata* in Sanskrit, is found in the center of the chest. It is located in the center of the chest. Its element is air. It governs the thymus, heart, pericardium, lungs, circulatory system, upper back, arm, shoulders, ribs, breasts, and diaphragm. It supports us in accessing self-love and love for others, as well as compassion, balance, and forgiveness.

The **THROAT CHAKRA**, known as *Vishuddha* in Sanskrit, is located in the pharyngeal plexus. Its element is sound. It governs the thyroid, neck, throat, trachea, mouth, esophagus, shoulders, arms, and hands. It helps us give and receive communication. It inspires authentic self-expression and living a life on purpose.

The **THIRD EYE CHAKRA**, known as *Ajna* in Sanskrit, is located in the center of the forehead between the eyebrows. Its element is light. It governs the pineal gland (master gland), endocrine system, brain, nervous system, eye, ears, and nose. It helps us access our intuition and understanding. It supports us in seeing clearly, especially things that are beyond the physical realm.

The **CROWN CHAKRA**, known as *Sahasrara* in Sanskrit, is located at the crown or top of the head, where our fontanelles (or soft spot) is when we are born. Its element is thought. It governs the pituitary gland, the muscular, skeletal, and nervous systems, the skin, and the cerebral cortex. It supports us in connecting with the Divine realm and assists us with spiritual growth and the meaning we bring to and get from life.

> ROOT: RED AMBER OIL
> SACRAL: MUSK OIL
> SOLAR: JASMINE OIL
> HEART: ROSE OIL
> THROAT: AMBER CASHMERE
> THIRD EYE: SANDALWOOD
> CROWN: BLUE LOTUS

There are three ways to work with the oils:

1. Anointing yourself on the skin. This could be done on the chakra point, on your wrists, or even under your nose.

2. Diffusing the oil into the air (sacred breathing).

3. Adding the oils to hot water and soaking in the bath (Sacred Bathing).

Daily use is ideal, but depending on your sensitivity, it may take some time to work up to using the oils every day. You can begin with one oil and then add a new one each week, or you can just jump in with all seven and see how it goes. The important thing is to pay attention to your body and what it is asking for. Back off if it feels like too much; add more if you are loving it. Sometimes an oil may smell off-putting at first. This is an indication that you may have too much or not enough balance in the corresponding chakra. I recommend using those oils at night on the bottoms of the feet. It can take some time, but the smell of the oil will begin to shift as you work with them.

If you are a healer, facilitator, coach, or lightworker, you will be well-served by having a daily practice with the oils because they can clear your energy body quickly.

For special areas of concern, growth, or in times when you want extra support, consider combining certain chakra oils in addition to your daily practice.

Think about how you want the chakras to work together. Here are some examples of how you can combine the oils together to create different outcomes:

- More powerful voice? Use 3 and 5
- More loving vision? Use 4 and 6
- Safety in sexual intimacy or with creativity? Use 1 and 2
- Clear vision of reality? Use 6 and 1
- Need protection when you speak? Use 7 and 5

Imagine bringing the energy from one chakra into the other as you anoint yourself with the combination. State your intention out loud.

Once these have been mastered, there is another level to explore. In my advanced work with my students, following the seven body chakras described above, we work with seven cosmic chakras located outside the body as described in ancient Egyptian and Vedic esoteric traditions.

Mastering Your Body's Polarity

"Trying to be a man, is a waste of a woman."
—Coco Chanel

In addition to working with the chakras, you will also want to become acquainted with your body's power poles. All living things are electromagnetic energy fields. In a truly physical sense, you are a magnet. You draw in energy and you push out energy, just like every living energy field. You can learn to connect with and direct this inflow and outflow, and better control the level of energy you feel and how it flows within your body.

Like all energy fields, the human body has two poles. One pole draws in and the other flows out. The "in" pole is often referred to as the feminine pole, and the "out" pole is referred to as the masculine pole. As you see pictured in the diagram below, the locations of each pole in a female-embodied person are opposite to how the poles sit in a male-embodied person.

The bottom pole (which sits in the pelvic bowl) is what energizes and charges the system. So for a woman, drawing energy in is a naturally energizing act, while sending energy out is a naturally energizing act for a man. Conversely, for a woman, sending energy out is a naturally draining act, while drawing energy in is a naturally draining act for a man. It helps me to think of having a battery sitting in my body.

As a woman, I have the negative pole (which draws in) to be sitting in my pelvis. I am bringing energy into my womb space and from there, I can pull it upward into my chest where it can flow out. Receiving is a woman's superpower. It's how she is able to transmute and create. It's how new life is seeded and how new realities are gestated—and created—in the sanctity of the womb.

For a man, he has the battery flipped so that he is drawing energy in through his heart and sending energy out through his pelvis. Taking action and being productive is his super-

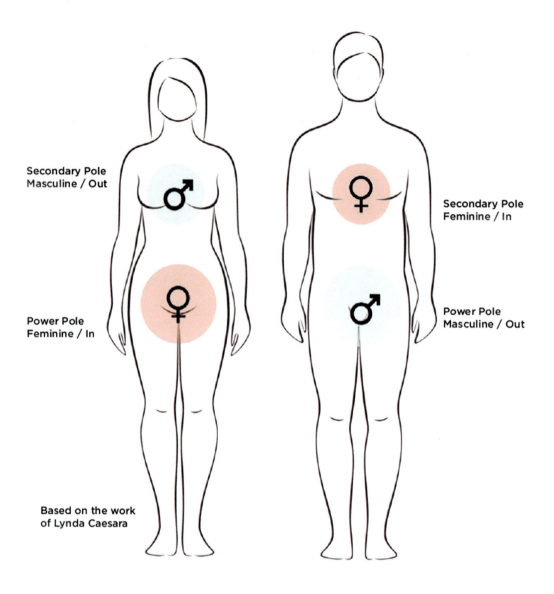

Based on the work of Lynda Caesara

power. Giving energy out is his strength. He creates with the use of his hands and feet, as well as his mind out in the open for all to see. Action and productivity charge him.

We are most vulnerable at the point where we are taking energy in. Women suffer tremendous trauma when they are violated sexually (where we receive in) because the trauma can shut us down and cut us off from our superpower. We are also more vulnerable to being overpowered, not just physically, but energetically when others try to control or manipulate us by attacking the solar plexus chakra. Men suffer tremendous trauma when they open their heart fully and are rejected or wounded. This kind of trauma can shut them down and cut them off from their softness, stealing their capacity to feel or receive love. A man's heart is as vulnerable as a woman's vagina. It is for this reason that many men have their hearts boarded up.

Proper breathing requires both inhaling and exhaling. Proper energy flow requires both receiving and giving. For us to be whole and complete, we need both of our poles (in/out, feminine/masculine) to be working properly. This creates a state of flow that allows us to magnetize to us that which we desire and repel away from us that which we don't. In addition, both men and women can use their masculine energy center to provide appropriate protection for their feminine energy center. And they can call on their feminine energy center to help them soften and surrender when connecting with and exchanging love with others.

Under the influence of patriarchy, particularly in the western world, the masculine form of energy output is favored, while feminine forms of energy are less admired, understood, or even acknowledged. For this reason, women and men alike are prone to over-favoring energy output. This has grave consequences for women if we try to emulate masculine power patterns, ignoring our need to receive and denying ourselves the full use of our superpower. The impact on emotional and sexual intimacy is enormous. Men too suffer in that they need nourishment and time to rest as well. The constant demand to stay strong and hard takes its toll on interpersonal relationships and makes sexual expression one-dimensional. Much of the disharmony between couples, and between men and women in general, could be solved by properly aligning ourselves. Maintaining polarity creates less static in the field. Like two negative magnets will repel each other, while opposites attract.

An energetically competent woman will then have her attention on her pelvis, completely owning her powerful receptive energy. As women, we must be comfortable standing in our receptive energy in order to not self-abandon. We balance this energy with active masculine energy in the heart. The good news is it's surprisingly easy for women to increase their feminine polarity.

It starts by just paying attention to our womb space. It doesn't matter whether you still have a physical womb, just place your hands over your low belly and breathe. Fill up the area behind your hands with slow deep breaths. Allow yourself to tune into the sensation you feel when you get the signal that you need to empty your bladder. Next, you can do a couple of Kegels. Just squeeze your pelvic floor muscles as though you are trying to stop the stream of urine. Now allow your hands to move down over the pubic mound. Allow your fingertips to gently rest on your clitoris. You can make micro-movements to wake up that area. As you feel the energy pooling, imagine drawing it deeper into your pelvic bowl. See the energy as light filling in the entirety of your pelvic area. Once that feels full, you can imagine drawing it up to your heart. As a woman, this where your energy moves outward.

As you allow the light to radiate out from your heart, see it falling like rain back down and refilling your pelvic bowl. In this way, you are running a full circuit through your body. Continue visualizing the energy moving like this for several minutes.

Doing this visualization practice daily will energize your body at a whole new level. If you don't feel anything just yet, give it some time. As you get more experience with it, you will be able to feel this potent energy instantaneously just by thinking about it. There are also essential oils that support the enhancement of your polarity. I work with the Divine Masculine and Divine Feminine blends made according to recipes found carved on the walls in the Egyptian temple of Dendera to enhance my polarities. Dendera was home to powerful anointing priestesses who used scent along with sound and many energy healing modalities.

As you master these practices, you will be able to skillfully manage your energy body and live tuned in and turned on! This is the quintessence of embodiment. Now we are ready to bring all of this together as we explore the Seven Queendoms and the path to self-sovereignty.

Part 3
The Seven Queendoms

It's time to wake up lovely. It's time to remember.

*The dark times are ending.
It's safe now. We can wake up.*

It's time to wake up lovely. It's time to remember.

*We are being called home.
And we are ready to remember.
To remember the vision that you are.*

*You are the Divine come to walk upon the Earth
To restore Peace, to embody Life*

*You are beautiful
A burning fire
A luscious body
A powerhouse of love*

Oh, sisters…
Stand firm upon the earth.
Open your feet and Breathe
Open your heart and Feel
Meet your soul and Remember

It's time to remember. It's time to come home.

You are whole and holy.
Now and forever.

The time has come to be seen.
We are ready. You are ready.

Be bold. Be free. Be wild. Be YOU.

Find your sisters and join hands.
For today we wake, Together.
Today we wake.
Together.

"*The only map of your right life is written on your soul at its most peaceful, and the only sure compass is your heart at its most open.*"

— Martha N. Beck

"*Your soul knows the geography of your destiny. Your soul alone has the map of your future, therefore you can trust this indirect, oblique side of yourself. If you do, it will take you where you need to go, but more important it will teach you a kindness of rhythm in your journey.*"

—John O'Donohue

CHAPTER 11
INTRODUCING THE SOUL MAP

It's time to bring together all of the concepts we have covered thus far so that we can create an action plan for creating a life we love. Let's start with a quick review of each of the elements that make up your SoulMap.

Thus far, we have learned that none of us escapes childhood without some form of wounding. We know that both family and society have contributed to our wounding. Without meaning to, we may have continued wounding ourselves by carrying on the dysfunctional behaviors we learned as children.

We have also learned that, while many wounds will heal of their own accord, some larger, deeper, and more toxic wounds will not heal without help. We have explored how wounds can actually become gifts and blessings, but only after they have healed. The challenge is to live from the scar, not the wound.

The scar has historical meaning that should not be forgotten, but it doesn't demand the spotlight. It represents a lesson, a teaching, and adaption, an overcoming. Its fresh skin, while no longer smooth, is filled with magic and medicine. It is not sore or painful to the touch. It is evidence of our victory over the past. And it has wisdom to guide our future.

Unlike the scar, the unresolved childhood wound is still filled with disease and toxins. It loves attention and seeks an audience. When touched, it causes pain. When squeezed, blood or pus spill forth, soiling all it contacts, spreading the toxicity to others, and wounding them as well. The wound exists for only one reason: to be healed. If we shy away from the work needed to tend to it, we will continue to live painful, poison-filled lives.

Our wounding resides not only in our psychology but also in our biology. So, we have to explore both our mental maps and our physical knowing. The body offers a direct route for finding the untreated hurts. Understanding how we hold and move energy within the body is one of the most powerful hacks for healing. It requires practice to sensitize yourself to the energy that is always running within you. Like an invisible river of life-force, there is a vast amount of energy moving within and between your cells and organs at the physical level, and between your chakras at the energy level. As you become adept at sensing and directing your life-force energy, your healing will happen at a much faster rate.

We have explored the healing salve of the Divine Feminine. We have gotten clear about the importance of connecting with and living from the source of our feminine sacredness within. The embodiment of our own sacred feminine sovereignty may be the most important healing act we could ever undertake—not only for ourselves, but for our entire human family and all of life on earth.

It is a calling of mythic proportions. And words cannot adequately convey my gratitude for having you on this soul-driven mission. Take a moment right now to drop into your womb-space and connect deeply with the treasures of feminine power. Feel the potent circle of sisters all across the globe waking up and leading the way with this work. Feel your womb, heart, and hands connecting with this luscious network of queens and priestesses all in service to what is emerging across our world now. This is soul-work at the highest level.

But it means nothing if it doesn't translate into deep and lasting change on the personal and communal level. The next step on the journey is to take all of these ribbons of love and knowledge and weave them into a bold new pattern. One that aligns with the value of love and is life-giving, life-sustaining, and life-enhancing.

To make this easier for myself and my students to apply to everyday life, I have created the SoulMap for Embodying Sacred Feminine Sovereignty. This map consists of seven distinct areas that all require attention and respect. I call them The Seven Queendoms. Each of these Queendoms is governed by a Queen Archetype who is accompanied by two Shadow Queens in need of healing.

As you work with each Queen to strengthen and heal each Queendom, you will find your life taking on a new shape. You will feel an increase in your personal power, your sense of inner peace, and your capacity to be present in your life in ways that have eluded you until now. Below is a preview of each Queendom that is discussed in detail in the next seven chapters.

The Seven Queendoms

The first Queendom is located in the root chakra and is ruled by The Grounded Queen. She holds the archetypal energy of the Earth Mother and she oversees everything related to Physical Sovereignty. Her goal is to provide a foundation of safety and security so that we can build a life free from fear. Her two shadow Queens are The Flighty Queen and the Frozen Queen.

The second Queendom is located in the sacral chakra and is ruled by The Passionate Queen. She holds the archetypal energy of the Lover and she oversees everything related to Sexual Sovereignty. Her goal is to harness the power of desire to increase life-force energy so that we can meet our needs free from guilt. Her two shadow Queens are The Stagnant Queen and the Siren Queen.

The third Queendom is located at the solar plexus chakra and is ruled by The Empowered Queen. She holds the archetypal energy of the Heroine/Warrior and she oversees everything related to Energetic Sovereignty. Her goal is to bring us into *right relationship* with our power so that we can be a bold stand for ourselves as sovereign beings free from shame. Her two shadow Queens are the Beheaded Queen and the Cut-Throat Queen.

The fourth Queendom is located in the heart chakra and is ruled by The Loving Queen. She holds the archetypal energy of the Healer and she oversees everything related to Emotional Sovereignty. Her goal is to help us have balance in our relationship with ourselves and others so that we can feel the beauty of love and the sting of loss without drowning in our grief. Her two shadow Queens are the Sacrificial Queen and the Solitary Queen.

The fifth Queendom is located in the throat chakra and is ruled by the Expressive Queen. She holds the archetypal energy of the Artist and she oversees all things related to Dharma (Sacred Purpose) Sovereignty. Her goal is to support us in living a life in active alignment with our soul's calling, to live life as sacred artwork free from lies and falsity. Her two shadow Queens are the Silent Queen and the Starring Queen.

The sixth Queendom is located in the third eye chakra (brow) chakra and is ruled by The Visionary Queen. She holds the archetypal energy of the Seer and she oversees all things related to Mental Sovereignty. Her goal is to keep our thinking free from illusion and allow us to access the vast pools of wisdom that reside within. Her two shadow Queens are the Foolish Queen and the Arrogant Queen.

 The seventh Queendom is located in the Crown chakra and is ruled by the Divine Queen. She holds the archetypal energy of the Goddess and oversees all things related to our Spiritual Sovereignty. Her goal is to facilitate the critical connection between our personality and our Higher Self/Soul so that we can live a meaningful life free from attachment. Her two shadow Queens are the Disembodied Queen and the Empty Queen.

Together these seven Queens form your Queens' Council. They have virtually every aspect of life covered and will provide you with gifts and tools unique to each Queendom. Their compassion and strength, their insight and their love will provide healing and grace. With their guidance and support, you can release the pain of the past and find a new way forward in embodied sacred feminine sovereignty.

CHAPTER 12
THE GROUNDED QUEEN

"And forget not that the earth delights to feel your bare feet and the winds long to play with your hair."

—Khalil Gibran

"Let us dedicate this new era to mothers around the world, and also to the mother of all mothers—Mother Earth. It is up to us to keep building bridges to bring the world closer together, and not destroy them to divide us further apart."

—Suzy Kassem

The Grounded Queen is the keeper of Safety. Her archetypal energy is the Earth Mother. She supports us in our physical connection to ourselves and the earth. Her domain is matter. And her cannon is Physical Sovereignty.

When we master our sense of Physical Sovereignty, we pay attention to our body's messaging. It shows up as goosebumps (God bumps/truth bumps) or raised hair on our neck, head, or arms. It shows up in the knot in our stomach or the ache in our back. It's in the precipitous drop in energy when certain people enter our space or when we face certain tasks. This is the Grounded Queen speaking in a physical form. She speaks to us through the cells, organs, limbs, and nervous system of our body. The signals are there if we are willing to listen. She is the early warning system, the canary in the coal mine, that lets us know when to remove ourselves from a dangerous place.

Being Physically Sovereign may be an unfamiliar experience for women who have been taught to ignore their body's needs and sensations. Similarly, if you experienced any form of physical and sexual abuse as a young child or even later in life, having a clear sense of safety in the world may elude you. If you had a difficult relationship with your birth mother, you might find it hard to connect with the fullness of the Grounded Queen's love. Indeed, if you struggled to feel safe growing up for any reason, you may find Physical Sovereignty challenging to embody. Like a neglected plant in the garden, we may not have a strong sense of our own deservedness. We might even wonder if we have the right to exist.

This Queen invites us to become committed to Physical Sovereignty and to stand our ground. She calls us to take personal responsibility for keeping ourselves safe now that we are adults. She helps us to pay attention to the red flags we see and feel in relationships. She guides us in making choices that honor our body and health. And she allows us to heal so that we become a safe place for ourselves, as well as for others.

The Grounded Queen's Challenge

The challenge we are called to overcome in the court of the Grounded Queen is fear. Fear is a natural response when our survival is threatened. The resulting physiological processes flood our body with hormones and chemicals that ready us for action. We snap to attention as we look for ways to escape the impending doom. Our focus turns outward as we seek to understand the threat and then formulate a plan. Our bodies go on high alert, and we may find ourselves feeling anxious or amped up. We may flip into hypervigilance and have a hard time settling or relaxing until we find a way to feel safe. If this is prolonged, after a time we may find it nearly impossible to turn off the body's fear response. Being on high-alert for sustained periods of time is detrimental to our health. Some people live this way indefinitely. To shift this, we must first acknowledge the fear we feel. This can be harder than it seems when we have adapted to it as a way of surviving. If we have been living with fear since infancy, it will feel normal. It's only when we have a nervous system reset and experience what the body feels like free from fear that we even register that another experience is possible.

The Grounded Queen's Gifts

The Grounded Queen offers us the deepest, most fundamental connection with our physical being. When we stand in our Physical Sovereignty, we know the power and importance of having a strong and healthy relationship with our body as the foundation of our life. No matter what our body looks like or how able it may or may not be, if we are embodying the power of the Grounded Queen, we treat it with loving care that channels the Earth Mother's love. The basis of all self-care is rooted in the Grounded Queen. Her gifts are nourishment and a sense of enoughness. We can most easily connect with this when we use the natural world as a source of medicine. Taking walks in nature, laying on the earth, and gardening are ways we can feel more connected to this Queen and her healing balm.

More than anything, the healing available to you with the Grounded Queen is her ability to support you in knowing your right to exist and have your needs met. It is only human shortcomings and the failures of our ego-driven social structures that fail to make sure basic needs are provided for all members of the human family. There is more than enough to go around, and if you have experienced anything less than that, it wasn't because you weren't worthy of it. Once you know this deep in your bones, it is far easier to align yourself energetically to receive that which you need and desire.

The Shadow Queens

When we are overcome with fear, we can find ourselves no longer grounded and seated on our throne. Rather we have shifted into shadow Queen territory. If we are facing too much fear and unable to connect with our roots, we can morph into the Flighty Queen. This shadow Queen leaves her body and disassociates. Like a flock of birds scattered by a loud noise, the Flighty Queen breaks her energy into fragments and moves it out the top of the head. Now it's like the lights are on but nobody's home.

This is a dangerous state. We are vulnerable when we are not present and awake in our own bodies. We might experience a higher degree of accidents, misunderstandings, abuse in relationships, even bullying. We might not be able to perform well at work. We could have trouble with money, not eat or drink enough, or avoid taking care of important life details. If we are in the Flighty Queen we aren't as reliable or trustworthy as we should be, not only for others but for ourselves. We might jump from thing to thing rather than stay focused and follow through. On the up-side, the Flighty Queen can find herself able to connect with super-natural or cosmic energies. But this, too, can prove dangerous. If she is unable to access the Grounded Queen to anchor herself on these out-of-body adventures, she will have a hard time discerning what is useful guidance and what is interference or trickster energy.

The second shadow Queen is the Frozen Queen. This Queen also appears as a reaction to fear. But rather than splitting and flying up and out, she digs in her heels. She freezes solid and can't be moved. While she may want to move, her fear has her locked in place. She may appear stubborn, resistant, and unbending. This shadow Queen refuses to bend or back down, even when she knows she should. Her stubbornness is a form of self-protection that can turn into self-sabotage. She often leaves a trail of broken relationships behind her as her hardness becomes unbearable to others. Job performance can suffer, and certainly intimacy is difficult. Seeking to connect with nature, experiencing the sun and a warming breeze can do wonders for this Queen.

Ultimately as adults we have to break out of the old patterns that we experienced in our youth. If we didn't have good models for selfcare, if we weren't cared for skillfully, if we were abused or neglected, embodying the Grounded Queen will take dedication and practice. We must have compassion for ourselves. And we must also commit to doing the work to shift these patterns. We are no longer the helpless child we once were. As adults, it's up to us now to create something different. We have the responsibility to create safety for ourselves, to take care of ourselves, and to meet our needs for physical safety. We are called to reclaim our body as the Temple it is.

A Personal Perspective: My Physical Sovereignty Map

For most of my adult life I actively ignored this form of self-sovereignty. No one in my family was particularly physical oriented. We sparred mentally, so other than raking leaves or shoveling snow, there wasn't much mastery for me to learn at home. As I grew up, I approached my life from a head space. I didn't eat particularly well or even enough. I went through sporadic fits of exercise—usually related to changing how I looked with the aim of getting what I wanted in a relationship. Still later I would exercise as a punishment for gaining weight. In those cases, I always ended up injuring myself. I developed food intolerances and environmental allergies that made breathing difficult—I always had a simultaneously stuffy and drippy nose. Finally, I did a fast and all my symptoms cleared. I made changes to my diet and found exercise I liked—walking, dancing, biking. But still to come was the work to actually learn to inhabit my body with my consciousness. I was always bumping into things—I am still kind of klutzy (took me years to admit that!).

Only in this last decade have I found my way into my body and learned how to listen to and learn from its infinite wisdom. Very often I get information from my body before an emotion is felt or a thought fully formed. Now I pay attention when I notice my jaw is clenching, or something just feels off in my gut. I am not perfect at it, but I am by far a safer place for me than I ever have been.

The Grounded Queen Writing Exercise: Taking Inventory

Consider, what is your Physical Sovereignty Map? Take some time to reflect on the questions below and write out a description of your own Physical Sovereignty Map.

As a baby, how you were fed, changed, bathed, kept warm, and allowed to sleep are all part of the operating instructions (agreements and behaviors) you were given around your body. Do you remember being held and hugged? Were you comforted with healthy physical touch? Were you deprived of touch? Did you experience beatings or spankings? Were you slapped, grabbed, or shaken? As you grew older, consider whether you were allowed to choose foods that you enjoyed. Were you gently encouraged to try new foods or if you were forced to eat certain foods you disliked? What were you taught about personal hygiene and selfcare in a loving, non-shaming way?

Allow yourself to think back over your school experiences. Did you feel safe in class? How was PE for you? Was it easy for you to participate in physical activity? Were you athletic with a capable, coordinated body? Or did you feel physically awkward and out of place? What about your health as a child? Did you get sick a lot? Were you hospitalized? Did you suffer any injuries? If so, how were injuries handled?

Use these questions to help to uncover what work might be waiting for you as you seek to embody the Grounded Queen within you. Write your thoughts below:

On a scale from 1—10 with 1 being the least and 10 being the most:

How safe was your family life growing up? ____

How well cared for were your needs? ____

How safe are you for yourself now? ____

How well do you care for your needs now? ____

THE GROUNDED QUEEN ENERGY PRACTICE: BECOMING ROOTED

The daily practice of grounding or rooting yourself is the best way you can help yourself avoid the two shadow queens. In this practice you will visualize yourself connected to the earth using the image of roots descending from your feet and tailbone into the heart of the earth and anchoring there. This gives you three anchor points—one coming from each foot, and one from your tailbone. Close your eyes now and imagine them in place. Feel the increase in stability you gain as you lock your roots into place deep within the earth. Once your roots are well connected, imagine sipping pure clean energy up through your roots from the heart of Mother Earth into your body. Allow that energy to pool in your pelvic bowl. As that energy enlivens you, say the following affirmations out loud:

It is safe for me to be in physical form. Mother Earth supports me and meets my needs.

My body is wise and worthy of love. I love my body and trust its wisdom.

It is safe to have my needs met. Abundance is everywhere. I am allowed to be cared for.

The Grounded Queen Anointing Oil: Red Amber

To enhance your experience of the energy practices and the writing exercises, apply the Red Amber Root Chakra Oil to your feet and tailbone for seven to twenty-one days in a row morning and night. Apply some to your wrists and even under your nose to smell the scent throughout the day, especially in moments that provoke anxiety or fear. This holy oil works as a homeopathic remedy to activate and enliven the root chakra. It balances and harmonizes the chakra's energetic expression. This helps you avoid being under or over expressed (and flipping into the shadow Queens) so that you can stay firmly rooted and on the throne of The Grounded Queen. All of the chakra oils are available on my website at RimaBonario.com.

Going Deeper

As you take this first powerful step on your journey into the Seven Queendoms by working with the Grounded Queen, it is important to set a baseline for yourself so that you can see what progress you are making. Every one of us was handed a set of experiences, messages, images, beliefs, and wounds around what it means (and doesn't mean) to be a woman. We have been defined, labeled, envisioned, controlled, informed, deformed, and reformed by external and patriarchal influences for most of our lives. Use the blank page provided to write words or draw images that help you access this external voice and what it has given rise to within the walls of your own being. What are you willing to release so that you may choose a new, and healthier vision for yourself and your life as a woman?

Continuing on with this inquiry, consider what you have been taught about being successful in the physical and material world. The usual definition of success focuses almost completely on having money and stuff. This is an external (masculine) experience full of doing and achieving. There is nothing wrong at all with using our masculine competencies to achieve great things in the material realm. But in order to properly balance ourselves and find deep satisfaction in life, we must also be sure we are including in our definition of success aspects and qualities that are based on an internal (feminine) experience. In the space below, list all the ways you have defined success in the past. Notice which seem to be focused on an external experience of life (doing) and which seem to be focused on an internal experience of life (being).

Now it's time to use your creative power to set forth an intention for what will fill the space you have just cleared. It is time to decide for yourself what you want to experience as you make space for a sovereign self-expression. As yourself this critical question: How do you want to feel, in your body, your heart, your mind, your soul? The following formula will help you to focus on your internal experience rather than focusing on external goals.

LIST OF ADJECTIVES	LIST OF OUTCOMES	LIST OF CLAIMS
I WANT TO BE/FEEL MORE:	*I WANT TO HAVE MORE:*	*BECAUSE I AM:*
luscious, juicy, soft, vibrant, alive, awake, joyful, surrendered, edgy, open, willing, wild, ready, safe, seen, held, embodied, gorgeous, happy, satisfied, content, settled, free, relaxed, calm, centered, engaged, fulfilled, empowered	romance, health, beauty, joy, love, sexual expression, freedom, aliveness, energy, vitality, self-connection, delight, sensuality, pleasure, love, rest, stillness, laughter, sweetness, light, connection	worthy, valuable, capable, loved, ready to BE, open to receive, willing to receive, able to say yes, a walking miracle, beautiful, whole, blessed, magnificent, courageous, loveable, allowed, deserving, aligned, an inspiration, worth it, ready, Divine

My deepest desire is to feel *(choose three adjectives)*

1.

2.

3.

so that I will experience *(choose two outcomes)*

1.

2.

in my life, because I am *(add one to three claims)*

1.

2.

3.

Once you have completed this sentence I invite you to make it into something beautiful, perhaps writing it out on a piece of colored card stock, maybe with a metallic gold pen. Then place it on your bathroom mirror so you can see it daily. Consider adopting it as a mantra or touchstone that can help you ground yourself and bring you back to your feminine focus when things get tense.

The Grounded Queen Summary Chart

Archetype: Earth Mother

Location: Muladhara (Meaning Root) Base Chakra—Tailbone

Element: Earth

Focus: Grounding, Nourishment, Trust, Prosperity, Abundance

Orientation: Self-preservation

Basic Right: To Be Here and Have Needs Met

Challenge: Fear

Gifts: Nourishment and Enoughness

Shadow Queens: The Flighty Queen (not enough) The Frozen Queen (too much)

Color: Red

Essential Oil: Red Amber

Stone: Red Jasper

Energy Practice: Dropping roots into the ground

Evidence: Embodiment, Being present in your body, Financial health, Physical health, Self-Care

Blessing: Gratitude for what we have and Earth Care: to honor and restore Mother Earth

CHAPTER 13
THE PASSIONATE QUEEN

"The light of the sacred prostitute penetrates to the heart of this darkness… she is the consecrated priestess, in the temple, spiritually receptive to the feminine power flowing through her from the Goddess, and at the same time joyously aware of the beauty and passion in her human body."

—Marion Woodman

The Passionate Queen is the keeper of Desire. Her archetypal energy is The Lover. She supports us in our sexuality and in our capacity to generate and create by activating our Life-Force energy. Her domain is union. And her cannon is Sexual Sovereignty.

When we master our Sexual Sovereignty, we are able to fully own our body and embrace the inherent right to have pleasure. Consider for a moment: Does the world believe that men exist for the primary purpose of providing pleasure and meeting the needs of women? It's not likely you answered affirmatively to that notion. But when you ponder whether the world sees women as primarily useful because they provide for the pleasure and needs of men, that feels truer. There is a toxic double standard when it comes to how we view male versus female sexual sovereignty. We understand ourselves as sexually sovereign beings whose sexuality and physical body exists for our own pleasure, rather than primarily to bring pleasure to someone else. It's not that we can't or won't exchange pleasure with another, it's that we don't see ourselves as existing primarily for *them* and *their needs.*

The patriarchal influences that lay at the foundation of the world's relationship to female sexual sovereignty have corrupted the sweetness that the ancients knew was the truth of our sexuality. Not only has this meant that women are not safe from unwanted sexual activity (be it violent or subtle coercion), but also that the open expression of female sexual desire, especially outside of marriage, is unacceptable. Only in the past several decades have women pushed back against these constraints and risked acknowledging themselves as sexual beings with the right to express themselves freely. Some fear that women who are overtly sexual put themselves in harm's way. But interestingly, without this correction, women are actually less safe. If women are pressured to hide their own desire and not speak or act freely on it, men can convince themselves "she wants it, but is just too shy to say so," and press forward without gaining consent. Until women regain their connection to their basic right to have pleasure on their own terms, they will continue to feel confused about whether they actually want or don't want the encounter.

When the feminine was demeaned and made subservient, we lost the sacredness of two equals coming together in the vulnerability and surrender of sexual union. We must all do the deep personal work needed to right this wrong. When the masculine was cut away from its twin energy of the feminine, a coarse and control-oriented form of sexual encounter gained traction. Sex became weaponized. While it could still be about reaching into the Divine Oneness by uniting bodies, hearts, and souls, it could also be about domination, power plays, and irresponsible pleasure seeking without regard for the impact on one's partner or, even one's own soul. This is not true sexual sovereignty, rather it is an abuse of our sexual power. And both men and women alike have suffered because of it. As women seek to find liberation and claim our right to be sexually sovereign, we would do well to avoid mimicking these sexually abusive ways of relating that lead only to emptiness and pain.

The Passionate Queen's Challenge

The challenge we are called to overcome in the Passionate Queen's Court is guilt. Our ability to open fully to the power of our desire is thwarted when we feel guilty for our yes or our no. In order to move past this block and begin embracing our sexually sovereignty, we will have to explore our inherited beliefs about sex and relationships. This Queen invites us to consciously examine these beliefs and intentionally choose which you wish to keep, change, or discard altogether. It means digging in and healing any past abuse or trauma, as well as being honest with yourself about your sexual history. It also means finding the core space of sacredness within your own sexuality.

Consider this guiding question: How are your sexual experiences and your desire for sex supporting you in living into your best self? Being sexually sovereign means you find your own form of sexy. You dress, move, connect, and express your sexuality freely and for your own pleasure. We've all felt that jolt of excitement when noticing, or being noticed by, an attractive person. But if we believe that that person is the source of this energy, we give our power over to them. In reality, the energy is produced within you, inside your sexual organs. It is YOUR response to their attractiveness or to their attention that creates this energy. It belongs to you. When you understand that the pleasure and energy you feel is coming from inside you, there is no need to feel guilty or indebted. You don't owe the energy to anyone. Free from guilt, the sexually sovereign woman is able to experience sexual attraction and sexual energy as an internal resource to be used toward her own unfolding, for her own creative projects, and for her own vitality, rather than something that has to be generated by, for, or exchanged with a sexual partner. Freedom from guilt also allows us as sexually sovereign women to joyfully engage in sexual activity when our body, mind, and heart are a 100% yes, and refrain when we feel a clear no, or even a nagging doubt, rather than ignore it.

Hopefully a growing number of younger women are free from this trap, but it remains to be seen how long it will actually take for centuries-old patriarchal ideas regarding sexuality to be expunged from our bodies, hearts, and psyches. We can all do our part but leaning into the work of practicing *right relationship* with our desire and our sexual energy. True sexual sovereignty means we are living in sexual integrity with ourselves and others.

THE PASSIONATE QUEEN'S GIFTS: DESIRE, LIFE-FORCE (SHAKTI), AND PLEASURE

This Queen offers us a whole new world when it comes to sexual expression, one that makes room for a fuller spectrum of sexuality. There is no fear or judgement of those who express their sexuality differently than we do because we see responsible sexual expression as sacred. Whether one is partnered or not, we have a right to generate and utilize the Life-Force Energy (or Shakti) that this Queen provides for us. According to Mantak Chia, a world-renowned Taoist Tantric Educator, it is this energy source that nourishes our soul.

Shakti is a Sanskrit word that literally means power. It is best understood as Life-Force energy rather than simply sexual energy. Shakti is also understood to be the female ability to connect with and unleash the divine energy present in our bodies. In Hinduism, Shakti is the female personification of the supreme deity, second to none, who is partnered with Lord Shiva, the masculine supreme deity, also second to none. We awaken our Shakti when we allow ourselves to feel desire and receive pleasure.

The Passionate Queen offers us desire as one of her most precious gifts. The word desire comes from the Latin word *desiderare,* and the phase *de sidere* is translated as "from the stars." So when we are connected to our desire, we are literally awaiting what the heavenly bodies will bring to us. Desire is linked with the feeling of enthusiasm. When we are expectantly enthusiastic about what is to come, we are engaging desire. The word enthusiasm comes from the Greek enthousiasmos, from enthousiazein which means, "be inspired," from entheos "inspired, possessed by a god," from en- "in" + theos "god." So when we enthusiastically move toward that which we desire, we are living in alignment with the very core of Life. We embrace our divine right to create Life and Life-Force. Desire is at the very heart of all creative acts in the Universe. We create responsibly and sustainably if we are coming from Soul. Our desire evokes more love and pleasure and less pain, not the other way around.

The Shadow Queens

There are two Shadow Queen expressions that get in the way of us being in *right relationship* with our sexual power. The first of these Queens is the Stagnant Queen. She is evoked when we have blocked our ability to receive, and the flow of our sexual energy is restricted. Like water that is trapped and unable to flow, our energy becomes stagnant, and we find ourselves unable to effectively generate that which we desire. The Stagnant Queen will make it impossible for our Grounded Queen to receive all she needs. Without the generative energy of your Shakti, it's very difficult to manifest the care that we have come to know we deserve by working with our Grounded Queen. The Stagnant Queen may have cut off her connection with her needs, wants, and desires out of guilt. She needs gentle, compassionate coaxing to risk the pain of opening up. If sexual trauma is part of your past, it's not unusual for the body to shut down or go numb. Having the support of a good therapist is an act of deep selfcare in moving toward sexual sovereignty.

Alternately the Siren Queen has her flow on high, so high it often flows unchecked out of her body and floods others. Leaking sexual energy contributes to the challenges we have in interpersonal relationships. This can be especially problematic if we are seeking to have our self-worth validated through our romantic and sexual relationships. The Siren Queen uses her sexuality as a weapon often seeking to lure in a sexual partner for her own gains. It matters not if their quarry is already in a committed relationship. That actually might make it more fun for her! She blows past others' boundaries wanting only what she sets her sights on. Control, not love or sacred connection, is at the core of her sexual expression. She wants to feel safe and guilt-free so she seeks to call all the shots. She often does this unconsciously, not realizing she is trying to protect herself. In the end, she causes herself the most pain by making poor choices and ignoring her own intuition. She ends up becoming her own abuser.

By leaning into the shadow work and energy work available to us, The Passionate Queen calls us home to a more loving and healthy relationship with our sexuality.

A Personal Perspective: My Sexual Sovereignty Map

My earliest sexual memory comes from age four. My six-year-old brother and I were playing at our friend Diane's house. Diane was about eight at the time. We were in her room and I remember her telling me to get on the bed next to her and pull down my panties while my brother was directed to stand at the end of the bed and pretend to take pictures of us. I knew it wasn't right and only pulled my panties down part way, but I still felt terribly ashamed afterward. I never told anyone. My brother and I never spoke of it.

This was the beginning of a pattern that took root and became like a dark and twisted tree growing from my vaginal and anal opening (root chakra) up through my womb (sacral chakra). The pattern held the message: sex is only okay if it's done in secret. This led to a distorted desire to have inappropriate relationships and an inability to maintain healthy relationships. I used my sexuality to try to entice men into loving me. In my 30's I found and joined Sex and Love Addicts Anonymous to help me stop this unhealthy pattern. I learned how to have better boundaries and greater self-respect. I became more discerning. But I also packed away a lot of my Shakti because I feared it. So while that kept me from being promiscuous, it also kept me from fully enjoying myself sexually with my husband.

I have lived in the Siren Queen and the Stagnant Queen, struggling with both too much and not enough Shakti. The Siren Queen brought chaos and drama to my life. The Stagnant Queen brought numbness and pain to my life. After seeing these patterns and how they were both branches of the same dark and twisted tree, I was able to do the healing work to remove it from within me. I replaced it with a gorgeous golden tree full of truth and light that allowed my sexual energy and power to move freely. I adopted the new message: sex belongs in the light of day where I and the Universe can rejoice in my pleasure.

This work had a profound impact on my capacity for sexual intimacy with my husband. The trick was to sink into my desire for my own pleasure, rather than seeing our love-making as something I did mostly for my partner. While this seemed selfish to my mind, it had the exact opposite effect. When in *right relationship*, the masculine sexual energy (giver) is in service to the feminine (receiver). It longs to please her and create safety so that she can surrender her mind and unleash the power of her body. And when that magic happens, it is the greatest moment of sexual fulfillment for the giver, as well as the receiver. When the polarity is strong between partners, the sexual energy expands exponentially. The masculine container becomes solid and safe, and the feminine moves into ecstatic states of surrender, which in turn bring the masculine into ecstasy.

We all have both masculine and feminine energy within, so this experience is possible when you are in sexual union with another regardless of sexual orientation. Couples of all sexual orientations can play with reversing the energy flow. Those in same-sex relationships often have more access to switching back and forth between being in one sexual energy or the other, unlike heterosexual couples who usually stay in the energy most closely linked to their sex. The key is to have strong polarity regardless of who is in giving mode and who is in receiving mode.

THE PASSIONATE QUEEN WRITING EXERCISE: TAKING INVENTORY

Sexual sovereignty may be even rarer than physical sovereignty. Consider in what ways you were or were not allowed to pursue pleasure as a child. What passions were allowed, and which ones were dismissed? How much guilt was present in your family up-brining. How much did religious attitudes such as piety, modesty, and purity color your understanding of your own sexuality and your sexual desires. How much autonomy did you have over your own body? Were you encouraged to have good personal boundaries in which you had some control over your personal space? If not, you may have been hugged, kissed, cuddled or tickled without being asked for your consent. Or perhaps you were made to hug or kiss someone you didn't want to.

Was yours a sex-positive household? Or was it never discussed? How did your mother's sexual expression influence your own? Did you follow along in the model she laid out for you or did you rebel against it and seek to find your own path forward? Did you find it challenging to own your sexual desires? Were you fearful that your sexual expression was "sinful," or would not be welcomed? When you consider what was presented to you as desirable, how did you rate? Did you find yourself wanting? Or were you one of the popular girls, often sought out and the object of affection and attention? How did the response of others shape your beliefs about yourself? What was your first sexual experience like? Did you have a good sense of your own no and your own yes? Did you honor your yes and know? Did you ever experience unwanted sexual contact? Were you ever sexually violated?

Just like with our beliefs and behaviors toward our body, our beliefs about ourselves as a sexual being are shaped by our experiences. Think of the millions of messages you took in from parents, teachers, peers, siblings, religious teachings, and the general cultural dialog about what sex is, what being sexy is, and what you should be, want, do or have related to sex. These are inherited messages, and most were added to your conditioning without your expressed consent.

Consider, what is your Sexual Sovereignty Map? Take some time to reflect on the questions above and write out a description of your own Sexual Sovereignty Map on the next page. Use these questions to help to uncover what work might be waiting for you as you seek to embody the Passionate Queen within you.

On a scale from 1 - 10 with 1 being the least and 10 being the most:

How open was your family about sexuality growing up? ____

How much were you encouraged to follow your desire? ____

How open are you to fulfilling your physical, sexual, and emotional desires now? ____

How healthy is your expression of desire now? ____

THE PASSIONATE QUEEN ENERGY PRACTICE: CONTAINING

The daily practice of creating a safe container for your life-force energy is a wonderful way to ensure that your Shakti will be available for your own vitality and enjoyment. Imagine that you are sitting in the center of an egg-shaped bubble that stretches about 12 inches above and below you and is about as wide as when your arms are fully open. This bubble is your auric field or your personal energy field. On the edge of this field is a membrane, and it is intelligent. Just like the membrane of a cell, it has a job to do in managing what goes in and what comes out.

When we don't have a solid energetic boundary to our personal energy field, we are often depleted as our energy is free to leak out. If we never learned good personal boundaries as a child, we may find that our bubble's edge is barely functioning. Conversely, we may have created a super thick wall to hide behind as a youngster in an attempt to feel safe. Sometimes we have a little of both. Maybe we wanted to withdraw from those people who hurt us, but we couldn't as they were the only source of love and resources. No matter your story, we all have an energy field, and every field has an edge.

In order for you to get the full benefit of your Life-Force energy, you want to be sure that the edge or your energy field is free from holes, tears, or dents. Take a moment to put your hands out all around you and make contact with your edge. Greet it and acknowledge its existence. If you can't feel anything at first, it's okay. Just imagine it. Notice if it has a color or an attitude of some kind. Is it thick and smooth or thin and bumpy? Imagine using your hands to smooth it out and thicken it up. Call on your life-force energy to make it glow and infuse it with strength. Imagine it like the glass walls of a greenhouse and you as a precious orchid sitting within it. Notice how the glass allows in sunlight but keeps out wind and rain. Notice how it keeps the heat from escaping so the orchid can flourish.

Because this membrane is intelligent, you can give it instructions and consciously direct how it operates. Up until this moment it may have picked up its operating instructions by osmosis from your parents or others in your life. Take a moment now to consciously choose how you want it to operate. Make it clear that no one else's energy should be inside your energy field. The space inside your bubble is for you and you alone. Ask it to help you from leaking your energy or upsets out on others. Notice how it is responding to these new instructions. Do you see a change in color, thickness, attitude/ can you feel it heating up or firming up? Now as you feel your Shakti nicely contained inside your new "greenhouse," say these statements out loud:

My energetic space is safe and secure. I can unleash my Shakti without guilt.

Life is pleasurable and I deserve to have pleasure in my life.

I embrace and celebrate my sexuality. My sexuality and sexual expression is sacred.

My hips open easily and I move my body gracefully and effortlessly.

Keep playing with this practice until you feel your edge is strong yet flexible. You can bring it in close when you want to be intimate, even all the way to your skin boundary, but just like you wouldn't inject someone else's DNA into your body, you want to keep others' energy outside of your energy field. Please be sure when working with energy healers that they understand their role is to inspire your energy field to heal itself and that you do not want any of their own personal energy to invade your private space.

THE PASSIONATE QUEEN ANOINTING OIL: MUSK

To enhance your experience of the energy practices and writing exercises, apply the Musk Sacral Chakra Oil to your abdomen and low back for seven to twenty-one days in a row, morning and night. Apply some to your wrists and even under your nose to smell the scent throughout the day, especially in moments that provoke guilt for taking care of yourself. This holy oil works as a homeopathic remedy to activate and enliven the sacral chakra. It balances and harmonizes the chakra's energetic expression. This helps you avoid being under or over expressed (and flipping into the shadow Queens) so that you can stay balanced and on the throne of The Passionate Queen. All of the chakra oils are available on my website at RimaBonario.com.

Going Deeper

The Passionate Queen's currency is Desire. It is through the energy of desire and the act of receiving that creation is completed and everything comes into form. This is a Universal Law. When we conceive of desire in this way, we are committed to desire as a holy catalyst. When you get very still and deeply connected, you can sense the Universe and its limitless nature of LOVE. At the level of soul, we see no conflict. Desire believes everyone is worthy of having what they want. As such, there is no need for guilt. But there is a catch. To have what we desire, we must be willing to receive. That sounds simple, but at the human level we really struggle with this. Most of us are not very good at receiving. Somewhere along the way we decided (or were told) that rather than receive, we should do something else. But know this: The Universe conspires (breathes) with you. The Universe aches to give to you.

Visit **TheSevenQueendoms.net/receiving** to access a free masterclass: *Understand and Dissolve The Six Blocks to Receiving*

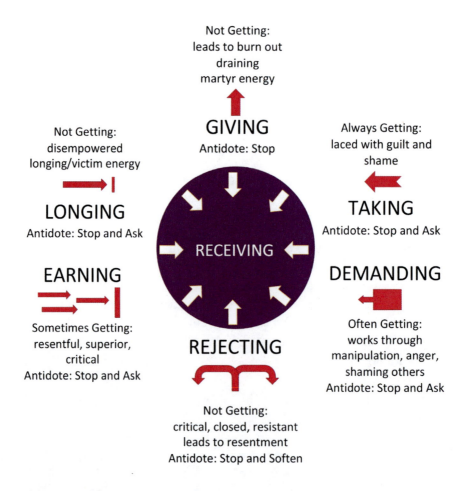

The Passionate Queen Summary Chart

Archetype: The Lover

Location: Svadhisthana (Meaning sweetness) Sacral Chakra—Low Abdomen/Womb

Element: Water

Focus: Emotions, Desire, Need, Movement, Pleasure, Sexual Connection

Orientation: Self-gratification

Basic Right: To Feel and Have Pleasure

Challenge: Guilt

Gifts: Desire, Life-Force (Shakti), and Pleasure

Shadow Queens: The Stagnant Queen (not enough) The Siren Queen (too much)

Color: Orange

Essential Oil: Musk

Gemstone: Carnelian

Energy Practice: Working with your auric field's edge

Evidence: Vibrancy, Aliveness. Being comfortable and safe in expressing desire and experiencing pleasure

Blessing: Permission to indulge and live life to the fullest

CHAPTER 14
THE EMPOWERED QUEEN

"Some women fear the fire. Some women simply become it."

—R.H. Sin

The Empowered Queen is the keeper of Power. Her archetypal energy is the Warrior or Heroine. She supports us in our energetic connection to our willpower and our sense of self. Her domain is action. And her cannon is Energetic Sovereignty.

When we master our Energetic Sovereignty, we are able to confidently embrace our power. We also know that we can exercise self-mastery and self-discipline at the deepest level of our being. We take responsibility for the experience of our energy that flows out from us and that which flows toward us. We carefully curate what is in our personal space. We know where to draw our boundaries physically and sexually. We feel capable of protecting and nurturing our energy body. We understand that our experience of life is filtered through our energy system and that how we show up energetically is every bit as important as our behaviors and words.

Being energetically sovereign and able to hold our power in *right relationship* is truly a high level of self-mastery. I would wager to say very few of us grew up with parents who were conscious about Energetic Sovereignty. Children tend to be more energetically aware/sensitive than adults. They often know a person isn't "right" without knowing why. If you were a keenly sensitive child, your parents may have found your insights and intuitions confusing or even scary. Because we are often forced into situations that run energetically counter to what humans need, we can dim our sensitivities just to survive.

Creating and enhancing your Energetic Sovereignty includes becoming aware of your energetic anatomy so that you can start to build a relationship with it. The chakra system we explored in chapter ten is a great place to start. You will also need to examine how you wield your power. Are you the kind of person who uses kindness and respect to access your personal power, or do you take the more typical tact of empowering yourself by consciously or unconsciously disempowering others? This is the accepted norm within the system of patriarchy, so don't judge yourself too harshly.

When we are energetically sovereign we do not need to use control tactics to feel safe. We don't seek "power over," but encourage others through "power with" as our model for leading. Remember, all gender expressions have access to both masculine and feminine energy. We can do so much more in life if we have mastered accessing and expressing all of our power. Women have a unique challenge with this in that we live in a world that almost exclusively recognizes masculine power patterns, which we may not be able to sustain as easily as our male embodied counterparts. In short, masculine energy is about productivity, action, order, and structure. While feminine energy is generative and flowing. It respects and honors rest and nurturance. It preferences community and collaboration versus individual efforts. As we seek to find more nurturing ways to be in relationship with ourselves and others, we will need to look critically at the ways of being we were handed by our families, as well as those offered by our societal institutions. This allows us to know ourselves better and therefore choose action that is in greater alignment with our aims as sovereign beings.

The Empowered Queen's Challenge

When we first begin to exercise our desire to live life on our terms, to make our own choices and to fulfill our needs, wants and desires, we can run into resistance. The subtle and not so subtle message can be one of shame: Shame on you for being so selfish. Don't go getting too big for your britches. How dare you think you are so powerful? These messages can often be followed by insults, put downs, and other demeaning language for the sole purpose of keeping us in our place, whatever that is. Or perhaps the shame we picked up on was less intentional. Like the mother who yells at her curious and oblivious toddler who wandered into the road. Out of fear for her safety, she sends the message that the child made a colossal mistake. The child can then form a negative association with exercising her will and following her curiosity which categorizes it as a dangerous or shameful act. As we talked about in chapters five and six, parents unwittingly create large and small traumas like this through their unskilled parenting tactics, especially if they don't know the importance of correcting the child's behavior versus criticizing the child.

A child raised with shaming doesn't see her behavior choice as a bad choice, rather she sees herself as a bad girl. This can push her to embrace the persona of The Bad Girl where she relishes the role of rebel, disrupter, and even destroyer. She may as well enjoy it if she's going to be treated like a bad girl, right? In this way she inoculates herself against the shaming comments of others because she's shameless. On the other hand, the child could internalize the shame in such a way as to create a very narrow path for herself. Now she has embraced the persona of The Good Girl. She seeks to walk the line of perfection so that she can avoid the pain of feeling shamed by those who would call her out. If these personas persist into adulthood, it's most likely that we have internalized the shaming voice and become our own perpetrators.

THE EMPOWERED QUEEN'S GIFTS: PRESENCE AND POWER

The Empowered Queen is one of the most potent places to work because power struggles are the most common causes of disharmony. This Queen gifts us the shining jewels of Presence and Power. When we embody the Empowered Queen, we use our power to bring harmony to our life and to the lives of those around us. It is our Presence that commands respect, rather than our ego that demands obedience. We seek to lead ourselves and others by creating space for all to contribute. We are building on the gifts of the previous two Queens. We are rooted in enoughness, grounded, and nourished. We are vibrant and alive with Shakti, and following our pleasure and desire. Now we can add personal power, informed action, and our will-power to the mix in order to enhance our influence. Most people think that power is about exerting control over others and our experiences. But the real key is to recognize our greatest, if not our only, point of power is over our internal domain. We can't control what happens in life, but we can control how we respond to it.

THE SHADOW QUEENS

If we have been bombarded with shame and self-doubt, it is more likely that we will find ourselves embodying the shadow Queens rather than the Empowered Queen. If we are uncomfortable owning our power and defending ourselves and our life, we can slide into The Beheaded Queen. As you might imagine, a Queen who has lost her head is unable to rule. She is stripped of her power and at the mercy of others. The Beheaded Queen has given her power away to others. She is not able to be present or powerful. Just imagine how pitiful she looks, standing there with her head tucked under her arm. It is impossible to take meaningful action from this place. Rather she is reduced to a victim state. She may become obsessed with finding who is responsible for her beheading. When she thinks she has found the responsible party, all of her energy goes into blaming them for her predicament. This further drains her and keeps her from managing her life. In reality, the Beheaded Queen needs only to look at her other hand to see the sword that cut her throat is her own. People don't take our power. We give it away.

Another shadow response to shame is to turn the sword on others. This is the way of the Cut-Throat Queen. She believes life is a zero-sum game. Someone is going to lose their head, and she's determined it won't be her. In her effort to protect herself, she may be quite liberal in her use of her sword. If she's not careful, she can harm those she loves beyond repair, and her life becomes one long bloodbath. Cut-Throat Queens often hook up with Beheaded Kings. And Beheaded Queens often fall for Cut-Throat Kings. Their sickness works together like the hook and eye of Velcro. The Cut-Throat Queen masquerades as powerful, but in reality, she feels insecure, small, and insignificant on the inside. Her fear of being found outdrives her desire to keep everyone away. Her use of energetic, verbal, and even physical violence is effective in that aim as people are wary of her. She suffers greatly from a lack of true intimacy and often believes that loyalty based on fear substitutes perfectly well for intimacy. But in time, this lie is exposed for what it is.

Personal Perspective: My Energetic Sovereignty Map

Being in *right relationship* with my personal power has been a life-long challenge. In many ways, I feel deeply empowered. Like that day I was determined to teach myself to ride a bike, falling down over and over, until I finally managed to beat the bike and bend it to my will. Somehow I created a persona for myself that said, "I can do it!" My mini-version of Rosie the Riveter, I guess. And while that determination served me well for many years, it also covered up a deep fear that it was not okay to need help. I developed the habit of trying to take care of everyone else's needs and feelings in an effort to feel safe. This carried over into my adult relationships in the form of co-dependency.

In my twenties, I perpetuated this dynamic by marrying a charming guy who turned out to be a drinker and a bully. His regular outbursts mirrored my experience in my family of origin. Just like I had learned to do as a child, I bent and shaped myself into ways that I hoped he wouldn't find offensive. I tried to shrink and be invisible as a way to stay safe. Have you ever done this? It's so painful, isn't it? I was lucky. I hit a turning point and realized that I had to get out. It took a huge amount of courage to leave that marriage. The fear of not being loved was so overwhelming at times that it seemed a small price to give my power over to someone else. In the end, though, the price is huge.

The Empowered Queen implores us to find the Heroine hiding within. She calls us higher into knowing our value and worth. And she demands that we let go of the shame that binds us to a fictional idea of ourselves as anything less than whole. Her message to us is loud and clear: You can be trusted with your power. I am so grateful for the path of healing I have walked because it has allowed me to help many others who have struggled with personal power. The freedom I feel is a sweet reward for the work it takes to release toxic shame.

THE EMPOWERED QUEEN WRITING EXERCISE: TAKING INVENTORY

When it comes to exercising your personal power, have you had significant challenges to overcome? Think back to your early years. How much autonomy were you given? How much space were you allowed? Did your parents encourage you to spread your wings, take chances, and make mistakes? Or were they always trying to pull you back, clip your wings, save you from yourself, or from the dangers of the world? The message we are often left with is that we can't trust others. Or worse, we can't trust ourselves. This may be doubly hard if we saw poor models of power, where power was used to wound, control, and manipulate. Did you consciously or unconsciously bury your power deep within because you didn't want to be like your raging mom or bully dad? Or perhaps you went the other route and embraced your inner assassin in a kill or be killed world. Or maybe you just gave up, believing nothing would change, so why bother trying.

Consider your relationships as they are today. Do you often find yourself in power struggles? Are you determined to be right at any cost? Are you determined to keep the peace at any cost? Do you know how to manage your energy body so that you can stay engaged and speak truth to power? Or do you boil over or shut down? Most people do fine most of the time, but there may be that one relationship, that one circumstance, where you struggle to maintain your personal power. Who or what is your nemesis?

Consider, what is your Energetic Sovereignty Map? Take some time to reflect on the questions above and write out a description of your own Energetic Sovereignty Map. Use these questions to help to uncover what work might be waiting for you as you seek to embody the Empowered Queen within you.

On a scale from 1 - 10, with 1 being the least and 10 being the most.

How much personal power and autonomy did you have in your family life growing up? _____

How much were you encouraged to think and decide things for yourself and act on your decisions? _____

How empowered do you feel in your everyday life right now? _____

How often do you find yourself boiling over or shutting down? _____

The Empowered Queen Energy Practice: Inhabiting your Core

This Queen is all about embracing your personal power. The energy practice that goes along with her is mastering your energetic core. When you are in your core, you are able to engage with the world. People can feel your intentions, your commitments, and your boundaries. They can feel you in residence. Your core is one of the most potent places that the Queen energy is felt. It's the seat of your sovereignty. Some people are naturally good at inhabiting their core, but many are not. Energy follows attention, so if you regularly exercise your core muscles, your physical strength can help you stay in your core. You can build strength with the plank exercise. Paying attention to your posture is also helpful. Opening the chest, rolling back the shoulders, and straightening your head is a good start. Think of the elegance and strength of a ballet dancer—male or female. That is what a powerful core looks like.

To build your core, begin by bringing your attention to the base of your skull where it meets your spine. Then in your mind's eye, trace your spine all the way down to your tailbone. Picture each of the cervical vertebrae, which start out fairly small in the neck, then the thoracic and lumbar vertebrae, which increase in size and strength as they snake their way toward the sacrum. Finally, at the very bottom, visualize the smallest of the vertebrae, the coccyx, and tailbone. Now imagine your spine growing, thickening and glowing with light that stretches from the skull through the entirety of the torso. I like to imagine the glow becoming a column of light that beams up through my head above me and down from my tailbone right into the earth. Like a powerful pole of light I can lean on, I feel it helping me to stand more erect. Next, tighten your stomach muscles and imagine yourself "sitting" back into yourself along the interior of your spine. When I connect with this feeling, it's like I can suddenly "feel" myself. I will often sigh or relax and spontaneously say, "There I am!" Once you feel yourself in core, say the following affirmations out loud:

I have the right to be me. I can act without shame.

I honor the power that is within me. I have the will to accomplish tasks easily and effortlessly.

I use the fire in my solar plexus chakra to burn away hesitation and doubt.

I complete what I commit to doing.

The Empowered Queen Anointing Oil: Jasmine

To enhance your experience of the energy practices and the writing exercises, apply the Jasmine Solar Plexus Chakra Oil to your solar plexus for seven to twenty-one days in a row, morning and night. Apply some to your wrists and even under your nose to smell the scent throughout the day, especially in moments when you need to stand in your power. This holy oil works as a homeopathic remedy to activate and enliven the solar plexus chakra. It balances and harmonizes the chakra's energetic expression. This helps you avoid being under or over-expressed (and flipping into the shadow Queens) so that you can stay clear and solid on the throne of The Empowered Queen. All of the chakra oils are available on my website at RimaBonario.com.

Going Deeper

In her classic book, *The Queen of My Self: Stepping into Sovereignty in Midlife,* Donna Henes lays out some rules for how the Queen operates. They fit nicely with the Empowered Queen. She defines four Attributes of Engagement which the Queen uses to support herself in accessing and activating her personal power. They are Self-Defense, Self-Discipline, Self-Devotion, and Self-Determination.

How is your capacity for Self-Defense?

Are you willing to defend your time, space, boundaries, priorities, preferences, ethics, needs, desires, safety, and sense of well-being? And can you defend them without becoming defensive, meaning not from a place of victimhood or complaining? Your sovereignty and self-defense needs to move from your center out, from the strength of your core. It is unassailable when it comes from a place of acceptance and ownership over your own thoughts, feelings, beliefs, and behaviors rather than an attempt to change someone else's behavior.

The Queen is En-Titled (she has a title). She confers that title upon herself. She doesn't wait for anyone else to do her coronation. She knows her own worth from her own efforts and accomplishments. This power is not about mastering others or having power over others. It's about mastering yourself and having power over yourself. It's about having and using your power to nurture and champion yourself. The Empowered Queen is here to help us cultivate the power to feed, heal, help, hear, change, mend, befriend, embrace, and love ourselves. Sometimes it means getting gut-level honest with ourselves about what is working and not working in our lives. Sometimes it means sharing that information with those in our sphere and asking for what we need to make it work again. It could also mean walking away from a job or a relationship that no longer works, especially if those involved are not receptive to our requests, or are unwilling or unable to meet our needs, wants, and desires.

When you are in your sovereignty and have sufficient self-defense, you have the power to take care of yourself on every level (even if you aren't exactly sure how it will happen). Once you own and accept this as your right and your responsibility, everything changes. You are no longer beholden to anyone or anything outside of yourself. You are no longer held hostage by or will tolerate situations that are bad for you, such as a dysfunctional partner, boss, job, or family member, financial troubles, lack of direction, etc. You find a way to improve your situation, even if you have to shift it inch by inch.

How is your capacity for Self-Discipline?

Having self-discipline means that you consciously curate your surroundings. Your life is like a museum, and you are hanging all the pieces that go in your art installation. You decide what gets into the space, what you will adorn your walls with, and what you won't allow. The Empowered Queen and her healthy sense of self invites you to curate your surroundings with what ignites your fire, your passion, your hope, and your soul. She asks you to curate your thoughts, words, and deeds. Notice I did not say curate your feelings. All feelings are welcome, all of you is allowed. Your feelings must be felt and metabolized. Then you are free to choose what to offer outwardly.

The Empowered Queen allows you to choose the best of the infinite possibilities within you. It's not uncommon to hear people say, "This is just how I am." Sometimes when working on a particularly stubborn pattern, we might decide that we cannot really change, but it is not true. If you seek the observer who is behind your sense of "I" in order to move past the structure of your old habits, you will see you have the power to access your infinite potential. Your personality is simply a set of habits. Inside of you is the infinite potential to be something entirely new. Self-discipline is the fuel needed to go the distance as you seek to release old habits and create new ones.

How is your capacity for Self-Devotion?

Are you devoted to yourself? Are you loyal to your Self, your soul, the beauty inside of you? At a minimum, are you at least as loyal and devoted to yourself as you are to others? If you aren't sure, consider the following questions:

- How do you devote time and attention to yourself (as opposed to your goals)?
- Are you always last on the list to be tended to, behind your job, your partner, your kids, your friends, and even your pets?
- Do you pay yourself first, making sure to put something in a separate savings account each month before you pay the bills? Even if it is just $20, money increases when it is bucketed.

- Do you heal yourself? Do you invest yourself? Or just distract yourself to avoid your inner life?
- Do you celebrate yourself? Do you feel gratitude toward yourself and your life lessons?

As you imagine what it would be like to treat yourself with active self-devotion, you might begin to get a sense of what is possible. Because the prize stallion is cared for with devotion, and he wins races and sires a new generation of champions. The Queen Bee starts out as a normal larva, and she is fed Royal Jelly by the entire hive so she can grow big and lay enough eggs to keep the hive vital. Nature understands the law of thriving. While it seems humans have forgotten, we can feel the truth in the pit of our stomach when we acknowledge the truth that when women thrive, the world thrives. So, what about it? Are you willing to do your part to insist on receiving what you need to thrive? That is how we change the world, by thriving so magnificently, we can't help but want that for everyone else—and we know what it will take to create that since we have created it for ourselves. The woman who is capable of self-devotion is a powerful woman indeed.

How is your capacity for Self-Determination?

Are you standing on your own two feet, meaning can you stand your ground when you are challenged? Are you planted, like an oak tree, rather than blowing in the wind like a leaf? Don't be a leaf.

Have a vision and move toward that vision. Embrace your decisions. Choose your direction. Follow through on the course of action you have chosen, even when it is difficult. That doesn't mean you can't change your mind, but you cannot be "talked out of" your mind. It is better to change your mind by moving toward something else, something more worthy, rather than to avoid something. If you identify and move towards safety instead of away from an abusive partner, where you land next will not be another abusive partner.

Self-determination helps you be unwavering in the other three areas of self-defense, self-discipline, and self-devotion. It makes possible the intention and attention needed for self-sovereignty and success. The Empowered Queen evokes self-determination so that she cannot be stopped or silenced.

When contemplating action, seek the counsel of all your Queens. And if you are concerned that your counsel might be polluted by your past conditioning, seek out a trusted mentor, advisor, or sister queen. Don't go to them expecting to get answers, but so they can point you in a direction or two for consideration. They can sit with you and keep you company as you seek and find your own answers. In reality, you know what you know, even if you don't know it yet. Get quiet and become willing to know the next right step. You don't have to have every step, leap, jump, or turn all mapped out. You just need a fixed point to move toward. Your feet will take you there once you set foot on the path.

Boundary Setting

You will most likely have to deal with the fallout from the people in your life once you start showing up in your personal power. It's no fun when we realize that our lack of self-defense, self-devotion, self-discipline, and self-determination has had the effect of training those around us to expect more from us than is healthy. If the changes are going to become permanent, you will have to survive the adjustment period. When you begin taking a stand for yourself and your needs, wants, and desires, it may cause confusion, hurt feelings, and frustration for your family. They may not understand why you are unwilling to over-function any longer. They may become frustrated, angry, and even resentful.

Depending on how your family communicates, you may want to have a conversation about what you are up to and even ask their support in your effort to change. I hope that they will indeed support you. But no matter how much they want to help, it is up to you to establish the new boundaries that are needed in order for things to change.

Here are a few things to keep in mind as you seek to put new boundaries in place:

- When you begin setting boundaries, you might feel afraid or ashamed. That is your old conditioning coming up, a younger part of you that is responding the way you did as a child. Remind that part of yourself that you are an adult now and it's okay for you to exercise your power.
- You cannot put new boundaries in place while simultaneously caring about someone else's feelings. Whatever they feel may be valid- disappointment, hurt, anger—but it is not your problem to manage.
- Let go of any guilt you may feel for not doing what others want you to do.
- If you aren't sure where a boundary needs to be set, pay attention to moments when you feel intense emotions such as anger or rage. Watch for times when you find yourself complaining or feeling stifled, threatened, or victimized as they will reveal places where boundaries need to be set and/or shadow work needs to be done.
- Complaining about something or trying to control another person's behavior is not setting a boundary. Boundaries are about defining what you will do, not about what you want others to do. It's best to make short, clear statements following this formula, "If you_____(i.e. don't come home before midnight), then I_____(i.e. will take your phone for two days.)"
- Follow through on your stated action boundary when it is crossed; otherwise, it's not a boundary. It's a fantasy.

- You don't have to be nice to people who aren't nice to you.
- You have a need, a right, and a responsibility to love, respect, and stand up for yourself.
- You are allowed to be who you are. You are allowed to live your own life harmlessly, regardless of how others respond.
- You are allowed to have privacy. You don't owe anyone an explanation or an inside look at your thoughts or your personal business. You get to decide what you do and don't want to share.
- You are the only one who gets to determine what you think and feel. You get to choose what actions you will take. No one else has the right to tell you what to think, feel, or do.
- You do not have to be perfect. You are allowed to make mistakes and not feel guilty.
- You are allowed to put up a boundary if people are speaking to you in a rude or disrespectful way. You have a right to tell them how you are experiencing them and ask them to stop. You are allowed to remove yourself from their presence and avoid them in the future if they choose to carry on.
- Be kind and gentle with yourself. You will set boundaries when you are ready and not a minute sooner.

Additional Empowering Practices

You can use the following practices as rescue remedies to connect with the Empowered Queen and help yourself increase your presence and power while eliminating shame:

- Set a small goal that can be accomplished before the day's end and follow through to complete it.
- Write a list of things you do that you don't enjoy. Choose one to delegate to someone else.
- Commit to a self-devotion practice, like sacred bathing, anointing with oils, or meditation, and set aside 10-30 minutes a day for seven days to pamper yourself. The act of doing all seven days, even if you don't want to, will build your sense of will and personal power.
- Clean or organize a space that you have let get messy.
- Reduce contact with or end the relationship with a person whose behavior often leaves you feeling drained, angry, afraid, or anxious.

Evidence of the Empowered Queen: Power and Presence

When you are embodying the Empowered Queen, you have access to a potent form of quiet confidence. You don't need to rattle your sword at every challenge. Rather you choose your battles wisely. The Empowered Queen energy seeks to lift up others as well as protect and care for herself. She is unafraid of success, nor does she step on or over people to achieve it. She will call out those who are bad actors, but she prefers to focus her energy on those who want to succeed with her. When she is challenged, she doesn't give her power away. Instead, she engages her core to stay connected to her power. She may choose to yield and stay or depart rather than bend or do battle. But the choice is made consciously once she has assessed her opponent's skills and level of madness. She is unlikely to engage in a battle that she knows she will lose unless it is for the purpose of making a principled stand. But even then, the Empowered Queen is in her power.

The Empowered Queen has worked at mastering her energy body. She has increased her capacity to hold larger amounts of energy, so she is less easily triggered. Consequently, she does not have much patience for dysfunction. She is quick to cut people loose who show themselves to be untrustworthy. She is not unkind, but she has no time for those who would hold her back. She has work to do in the world and the presence and power to do it.

The Empowered Queen's Blessing: Discernment

The Empowered Queen carries the sword of Truth which she uses to cut away what no longer serves. This allows us to reduce extraneous and superfluous people, places, energy, thoughts, and emotions. As an Empowered Queen, you can bless the world with this gift by modeling how to release old habits and attachments. Clearing away the junk is her superpower. She excels at reducing our need for more and more stuff in an effort to feel powerful. She knows that the never-ending pursuit of more possessions is actually a huge drain on our Life-Force. The blessing of the Empowered Queen is the discernment and the willingness to make tough decisions. You will bless the world by stepping into your power and leading the way!

The Empowered Queen Summary Chart

Archetype: The Warrior/Heroine

Location: Manipura (Meaning City of Jewels) Solar Plexus Chakra—Under the ribs

Element: Fire

Focus: Power, energy autonomy, individuation, will, self-esteem, proactivity

Orientation: Self-definition

Basic Right: To act and be a differentiates self, an individual

Challenge: Shame

Gifts: Power and Presence

Shadow Queens: Beheaded Queen (not enough) Cut-Throat Queen (too much)

Color: Yellow/Gold

Essential Oil: Jasmine

Gemstone: Tiger's Eye

Energy Practice: Core

Evidence: Living in Right relationship with power

Blessing: Discernment (Yes/No) and Releasing what no longer serves

CHAPTER 15
THE LOVING QUEEN

"Admit something:
Everyone you see, you say to them, 'Love me.'
Of course you do not do this out loud;
Otherwise, someone would call the cops.
Still though, think about this, this great pull in us to connect.
Why not become the one who lives with a full moon in each eye
That is always saying, with that sweet moon language,
What every other eye in this world is dying to hear."

—Hafiz (Translated by Daniel Ladinsky)

"If your heart is a volcano, how shall you expect flowers
to bloom in your hands?"

—Khalil Gibran

The Loving Queen is the keeper of Connection. Her archetypal energy is the Healer. She supports us in integrating opposites and finding balance. Her domain is healing. And her cannon is Emotional Sovereignty.

Emotions are the lifeblood of the human experience. Yet they are often the most misunderstood and harshly judged aspect of our humanity. We don't want to be overpowered by our emotions, but we can't ignore them either. Emotional Sovereignty allows us to master feeling deeply whatever is arising in any given moment. We can learn to stay present and vulnerable, and to be real with ourselves and others, without becoming abusive or sugar-coating our communications. As we move through our feelings to the other side we are no longer held hostage by them. When we develop Emotional Sovereignty, we find a freedom to express what's true without blame and judgement.

When we are in the habit of shutting down or off-loading our emotional content, we are out of *right relationship* with ourselves and we lose access to the power and energy of authentic emotional expression. Achieving Emotional Sovereignty requires that we understand what we learned about our emotions, and it means seeing the inner judgements we hold against ourselves and others when we are overwhelmed by emotion. Emotional Sovereignty invites compassion for ourselves and others knowing we are only living that which we have been taught. The good news is we can unlearn it. Emotional Sovereignty doesn't come from denying or capping emotion, but from being willing to dive deeply into what is present for us, be it rage, pain, grief, or sadness. If we don't feel it and move through it, it will consume us or others when it comes out sideways. I think we can all agree that none of us need any more scorched earth.

The reality is, to heal it we have to feel it. Emotional Sovereignty means slowing down and taking the time to get real with ourselves, down and dirty in the tears and the snot and the primal screams, so we can put an end to the war waging on our insides. It also means separating our feelings and metabolizing our emotional content from our behavior towards others. We are called to give it voice in a ritual container in a safe and structured way. This allows us to clear it and go on to act cleanly, speaking our truth and doing no harm.

THE LOVING QUEEN'S CHALLENGE

From the moment we are born, and even in utero, we are vulnerable to the whims of those we love and who love and care for us. This vulnerability continues as we develop our first crush and on into our teen years and beyond as we lean into loving another. With connection comes the risk of heartbreak. When we open ourselves to loving another we feel vulnerable. Mature love understands that relationship health is a function of acknowledging and respecting the mutual vulnerability inherent in choosing to love another. If your partner is not willing or able to join you in mutual vulnerability, you will have an uphill battle when it comes to creating a safe, intimate and loving partnership. Love and loss are two sides of the same coin. Whether the loss comes from a breakup or divorce or the death of a beloved, grief is the natural byproduct. Processing our feelings of loss is the challenge the Loving Queen invites us into.

The loss of a loved one or a relationship can be an isolating experience. Grief is a normal human response to loss, but it can become more than that if we hold it too closely and allow it to define us. Rather than be swallowed by grief, we can look to the active practice of mourning to help us mend our broken heart and let ourselves heal. We have all sorts of rituals to support us as we mourn. We hold funerals and wakes so that we can be surrounded by others. But we have lost touch with the deep knowing humans tend to do better when we mourn with others and the feeling of loss is shared. The act of mourning is different from the state of grief, which can sometimes swallow us. Mourning is an act that goes on for a period of time. It has a beginning, a middle, and an end.

Ancient cultures had dramatic community mourning rituals to help with the work of processing loss. Death wails are still practiced in indigenous tribes across the globe. These wails, also known as keening, were a common practice among the Irish and other Celtic tribes as they mourned their dead. The Catholic church repressed the practice claiming it was connected to paganism, and by the 1800's the practice fell out of favor. One of the oldest examples of communal mourning is the Western (Wailing) Wall in Jerusalem where Jews have gathered for centuries to mourn the destruction of their Temples during Roman rule.

Perhaps the most powerful example of communal expression is the Haka dance of New Zealand's Māori culture. It originated as a war dance offered before a battle for power or after a battle in honor of the fallen. The emotional dance is a primal human collective expression. Dancers move together, stamping feet, pounding chests, and moving arms and legs with vigorous motion. The dancers' faces express the intensity of emotions, with eyes wide, mouths open, and tongues extended at times. They blow air, growl and howl, and chant the words of the prayer/song with an unapologetic intensity. It is both beautiful and terrifying. And it is effective. The dance can be performed at celebrations such as marriages, as well as at funerals. I have been brought to tears more than once watching Hakas performed both in grief and in celebration. This is the point of a Haka, to evoke and release emotion for both the dancers and the community who watch.

In modern western culture, the protest march is often a form of communal mourning, one used by Americans and people across the globe after the death of George Floyd. The marching and chanting were a powerful way many people expressed and processed their fear, anger, and sorrow at the continuing discriminatory violence Black people and people of color face. The grief born of injustice can be particularly hard to resolve when there is no accountability. When we come together to share our grief, in large or small groups, and we use rituals that include movement and sound, we are able to more effectively process out the emotion and move forward toward solutions with greater ease. The body itself becomes the vehicle of healing.

The Loving Queen's Gifts: Balance and Connection

The Loving Queen is enthroned in the center of Seven Queendoms. She bridges the first three self-oriented Queendoms with the last three other-oriented Queendoms. This Queen helps us to focus on both loving ourselves and loving others. She offers us the gifts of connection and balance as we seek to be in relationship with ourselves and others. The human heart has a deep need for connection. Without it life is miserable and often unbearable. The Loving Queen shows us that love is a healing balm that works in all circumstances. When we ask the questions, "What would love do," and we follow through on that, the outcome is generally positive. The loving thing might include forgiving and making amends. Or it could mean setting strong boundaries or leaving. It isn't always easy to do, but choosing to be a channel for bringing more love into the environment is the gift and the responsibility of the Loving Queen. It is through the act of Love that we bring healing to ourselves and our world.

The Shadow Queens

Dealing with the vulnerability that we experience in relationships can be hard. Our relationships are imperfect because we are imperfect. And if we didn't have good models for how to navigate the moments of fear, doubt, disharmony, and hurt we can find ourselves off the throne of the Loving Queen and sliding into one of her shadow Queen expressions. If we have too much love for others and not enough love for ourselves, we become the Sacrificial Queen. Her biggest fear is feeling unloved and alone. She has forgotten that all the love she will ever need exists inside of her, and while it is wonderful to share that love with another, it is *she*, not they, who is the source of that love. Disconnected from the source of love within herself, she worries she is unlovable. This is a projection that comes from not adequately sourcing herself.

Deep down the Sacrificial Queen is withholding love from herself, so she believes others will do the same. In her fear, she downplays or ignores her own needs. Her strategy is to sacrifice everything for the object of her affection in hopes it will prove her worthiness or lovability and she will finally feel loveable and loved. But this earning of love is a trap. As long as she doesn't feel loving toward herself, or feel worthy of her own love, she will never be able to fully feel or accept the love offered to her by another. Once the love hormones wear off, doubt and fear will creep in, soon to be followed by criticism of her Beloved. She laments, "If you would just do this or say that I will feel loved by you." Again, this is a mirror of the way she feels about herself, most likely a hold-over from her unmet needs as a youth. But no matter the cause, lack of self-love is corrosive and eventually, it will destroy any trace of love and kindness in a relationship. As the relationship sours, the Sacrificial Queen blames her mate. She keeps a secret tally of all the wrongs she has endured as justification for her sorrow and misery. While her mate may in fact be behaving badly, the Sacrificial Queen decides seething silently is better than rocking the boat. She becomes bitter and resentful, and often engages in passive aggressive behaviors. She withholds love from the relationship. She is now the martyr and the victim. She feels superior and vindicated as she passes judgment on the failings of her mate.

The flip side of the Sacrificial Queen is the Solitary Queen. This Queen may see the inherent danger in loving another and she consciously or unconsciously chooses not to engage. She may think she is a Loving Queen, but in reality her heart is locked inside an inner tower and is not truly available for connection. This can happen slowly over time as mates become over-comfortable with each other and stop prioritizing the relationship. She may feel friendly and even fondness toward her mate, but she doesn't risk true connection by opening herself to the emotions she feels and the risk that deep loving requires. The Solitary Queen prefers to interact with others, as well as herself, from a "safe" distance. She can hide behind words, action, or thoughts, convincing herself that she is loving others, but deep down she knows she's faking it. She lives with a kind of free-floating anxiety wondering if or when she will be found out. This nagging sense that something isn't right keeps her from ever relaxing into love. From her high perch up in her tower, she must remain vigilant and on guard against any who might try to penetrate her inner sanctum. She puts up barriers to keep them out, becoming adept at creating moats, walls, thorny hedges and the like to stay safely isolated from love. But over time, this strategy will fail. The human heart is made for loving, and a life-long commitment to non-loving love is a tragedy that goes against nature. Life will continue to try breaking down these barriers. If she's lucky, the Solitary Queen will go weary of her fight. She may let her guard down, and love may plant a seed that has a chance to bloom.

A Personal Perspective: My Emotional Sovereignty Map

I was one of those "sensitive" children who often cried and took criticism hard. I could access deep feelings, but crying wasn't tolerated. Eventually my feelings emerged as anger—one of the only sanctioned emotions in my family. As a result, I became quite comfortable with anger. Having someone angry with me was certainly preferable to having them withdraw. As a parent, I also had a sensitive child. She would give me immediate feedback that my anger was scary and upsetting to her. What I didn't realize was that it was masking unfelt feelings of sadness and pools of unresolved grief.

Out of a desire to avoid passing on the wounds of my youth to my own child, I sought out ways to safely uncover and express the old emotional material trapped within me. Having developed a connection to my Soul helped me make a safe place for these old wounds to come forward. I began to dismantle these landmines that kept getting set off my daughter through therapy, shadow work, body-based processes, and forgiveness techniques. I allowed myself to deeply feel what I had been avoiding for much of my life. My angry outbursts are now few and far between.

Sometimes we are the target of our loved one's anger, bitterness, unforgiveness or resentment. If we spend enough time as a target, our hearts can become hardened and impenetrable, as a way to try to protect ourselves from the outbursts and emotional violence. Maybe we turn that violence on ourselves and become our own worst critic. I can say without a doubt that a lack of self-love is the most dangerous force in existence. It rots away everything good we have within us and leaves us empty and forlorn. Whether your inner critic is mild, medium, or bat-shit crazy, it's never too late to learn how to tolerate more love.

After my first marriage ended, my heart was so bruised and my confidence so shaken, I retreated into the life of the Solitary Queen for a number of years. As chance would have it, I found a kitten living next to a dumpster. I just couldn't leave her there, so I took her home and named her Iris. After a trip to the vet, I learned she was a he, and he, now renamed Cyrus, was in relatively good health. I had never lived with an animal before. We didn't have pets growing up. This little kitten and I formed quite the bond. His affection coaxed me out of my tower, softening my heart and preparing me to love again. Through the non-judgmental relationship we shared I began to open my heart once more, just in time to meet my beloved!

THE LOVING QUEEN WRITING EXERCISE: TAKING INVENTORY

The instructions we were given growing up for how we should handle our emotions may have been a bit more explicit than those we received around our bodies, our sexuality, and our personal power. But those instructions may be no less troubling. If you were lucky, your emotional upsets were met with soothing concern. Consider whether your emotional responses were accepted and validated before being soothed. Did you get a sense that your caregivers were comfortable with the emotion you expressed or was there pressure to not have your emotions? Did they want you to get over them quickly and be happy? Were only certain emotions allowed? Were you only heard if you turned up the volume on your emotional response or were you punished for increasing your emotional response?

Did you learn how to differentiate your emotional response from your behavior choices? Were you taught how to self-sooth or how to self-regulate in times of emotional stress?

Then there's the whole slew of things we learned indirectly by watching how others in our family expressed or didn't express their emotions. In addition to what we learned directly or indirectly from our families about acceptable emotional responses and behaviors, we took on messages from our friends, schools, places of worship and cultural references about emotion. The totality of these experiences creates the fabric of our emotional lives and underpins our behavioral choices.

Consider, what is your Emotional Sovereignty Map? Take some time to reflect on the questions above and write out a description of your own Emotional Sovereignty Map on the next page. Use these questions to help to uncover what work might be waiting for you as you seek to embody the Loving Queen within you.

On a scale from 1 - 10 with 1 being the least and 10 being the most:

How freely were emotions expressed growing up? ____

How well loved did you feel in your family? ____

How much love do you feel for yourself now? ____

How easily do you share love with others now? ____

THE LOVING QUEEN ENERGY PRACTICE: THE INNER FOUNTAIN

Begin by grounding and sending your roots into the earth as you learned with the Grounded Queen. Once you feel them connected into the earth, imagine drawing pure loving energy from the Earth Mother up into your pelvic bowl as though you are sipping a milkshake through a straw. As you feel the energy enter your pelvic bowl, allow it to begin pooling there. In a female body, this is where we receive energy. See the energy as light filling in the entirety of your pelvic area. Once that feels full, you can imagine drawing it up another level to your heart. In a female body, this where energy moves outward. Imagine a smaller chalice there and see it filling with this pure energy. Then allow the light to flow out from your heart. See it falling like rain back down and refilling your pelvic bowl. It should look like a double layered fountain. Bring the energy up and let it naturally spill back down and be caught in the larger pelvic bowl. In this way you are running a full circuit through your body. Continue visualizing the energy moving like this for several minutes. Allow that energy to cycle within you, say the following affirmations out loud:

My body holds an inexhaustible supply of energy and love.

I am worthy of love from myself and others.
I am allowed to keep some for myself and to give some away.

I commit to being gentle and kind to myself. I am loving toward myself and others.

I live in balance with others and with the earth. I create and live from harmony.

The Loving Queen Anointing Oil: Rose

To enhance your experience of the energy practices and the writing exercises, apply the Rose Heart Chakra Oil to your heart area for seven to twenty-one days in a row morning and night. Apply some to your wrists and even under your nose to smell the scent throughout the day, especially in moments that you desire greater balance, connection, and love. This holy oil works as a homeopathic remedy to activate and open the heart chakra. It balances and harmonizes the chakra's energetic expression. This helps you avoid being under or over expressed (and flipping into the shadow Queens) so that you can stay firmly connected to the throne of The Loving Queen. All of the chakra oils are available on my website at RimaBonario.com.

Going Deeper

The act of loving is incomplete without appropriate boundaries. We talked about boundaries in the domain of the Empowered Queen through the lens of owning our power. But if we don't consider them in relation to how we love others, we are offering a form of love that isn't healthy. Traditionally pink or red is the color we imagine when thinking about the heart, but the Loving Queen sits in the heart chakra, which is associated with the color green. The green color is associated with personal love and human romantic attachments. Perhaps this is why jealousy is seen as the color green. Being overly attached is a form of possessive love. To become possessed by another or to want to possess another is unhealthy. Finding the right balance is essential. The pink color is associated with Universal love (the High Heart Chakra). It is the form of absolute love that sees the Divine perfection in each moment and each person. Sometimes that kind of love is best given from afar when the human (green) form of love is not able to be offered in a healthy way.

To activate the full power of The Loving Queen, we can use the portals of Acceptance, Balance, and Forgiveness.

Acceptance

In order to properly use our capacity to love, we must first see clearly and accept what is in front of us. If we are not telling ourselves the truth or refusing to accept the current reality of our relationships with others and ourselves, we can't know how best to love. Take a moment to reflect on what aspects of your relationships you have been unable or unwilling to see, what reality have you been unwilling or unable to accept? Accepting something doesn't mean that you condone it and therefore are stuck with it. It means you are aware of and not resisting *what is*. Once you know *what is*, you can then determine what may need to shift. You can call upon the power of The Loving Queen and the heart chakra to support you in making that shift in the most loving way possible, including setting boundaries as needed. To manifest the change, you will need to be able to imagine it without triggering internal resistance to having it. This is why we must cultivate acceptance as the energy of non-resistance. As manifesting maven and purveyor of feminine magic Elizabeth Pervis says,

> *"Desire + Absence of Resistance = Manifestation"*

This is the same formula to use if you wish to call in a new love for your life. First you will need to clear away any vestiges of old relationships. You can use sage, paolo santo, florida water, rose water, or incense like Frankincense and Myrrh to cleanse your home of the energy of past lovers. You can also clear your body with these same tools, and/or take a ritual bath with essential oils like Frankincense and Myrrh to clear your body and energy field. Next imagine doing a womb and yoni clearing so that any energies from past lovers are no longer left unattended within you. Imagine them melting away and clearing out. Next clear your home of photos, knick knacks and other reminders of past lovers. Make sure to remove any of his or her possessions from your home. Empty your phone of photos, text messages, and voicemails to make room for your new beloved. Clear your car and the property around your home too if that feels appropriate.

Now that you have cleared away the old, it's time to make space for your new beloved. Have an empty drawer in the bathroom and an open rack in the closet. Make sure there is room in the bed for a partner and both sides of the bed can be accessed. Have room for another car in the garage if possible. You can even purchase nice sheets and update your underwear as a signal to the Universe that you are prepared for a new beloved. Do all these things with a happy and expectant heart. If you start to fret about how or when your beloved will show up, take a few deep breaths and remember that s/he is already with you in Universe time. There is only time and space between you both now. And eventually that will cease to exist, and you will be together.

BALANCE

As you look at what is in your life and your current and/or past relationships, take inventory of the level of balance you see present. Do you do the majority of the giving or the receiving? Do you do the lion's share of the emotional work? Are you saddled with all the care-taking tasks, or the earning tasks, or the day-to-day tasks? Notice how much you expect of yourself and your partner around these things. Look closely at how you were raised and whether you were indoctrinated into the thinking that says a good wife or mother does XYZ; a good person, a good girl, is XYZ. Is that contributing to imbalance in your life?

Are you giving yourself adequate time for selfcare? What do these old messages have to say about selfcare? Did you have a parent who was selfish and neglected their parenting in favor of themselves? If so, you may have decided you don't want to be like that and have swung the pendulum too far in the other direction. Were you the oldest of many, becoming a surrogate mom when you were still a child? You may have been taught that your needs aren't valid so that you could care for your siblings. Perhaps you had an addict for a parent who demanded to stay in the center of family life. Or maybe you had a parent who nullified his or her own needs and became the family's martyr, constantly over-giving, so much so that they were bitter and resentful much of the time. Perhaps you were groomed to be the same way. Do you have a "cross on wheels" that you drag around with you as you over-give, propping up the favorable view of yourself as "the unselfish one," or "the good one?"

When we are seeking emotional sovereignty, we have to untie these knotty spots within us that can have us using acts of love in manipulative ways. Bringing balance into giving and receiving is one of the keys to avoiding manipulations.

Forgiveness

This brings us to the final focus of forgiveness. We are not perfect. Others are not perfect. We will all make mistakes and occasionally engage in manipulations to get what we want. As we seek to remain in emotional sovereignty we have to notice when we are carrying around unforgiveness in our heart. That can be unforgiveness toward ourselves as well as toward others. Because we are human and imperfect, loving people means we will get hurt. This is unavoidable. We will be disappointed, and we will disappoint others.

In my family we like to say, rupture happens, and we all seek to make repairs as soon as we are able. Without forgiveness, our hearts close down. And that interferes with our ability to love, and that means to love ourselves as well. But rushing to forgive isn't effective either. With big hurts, we must do the work of trying and convicting those who we wish to forgive before offering that forgiveness. It's about acknowledging the gap between what we needed and what was given and how that gap hurt or damaged us or the relationship. Once that damage (or debt) has been seen, then it can actually be forgiven. The slate cannot be wiped clean before the debt has been recorded. This is why there are four parts to a real apology:

1. I am sorry for … (acknowledging the wrong-doing or gap)
2. It was wrong because … (acknowledging the damage)
3. In the future, I will … (resolving to change behavior in a specific way)
4. [Name], will you forgive me? … (Asking for forgiveness allows the other to clear)

If we have free-floating hurt, sometimes we need to simply forgive life for the hardships we have suffered. Especially in times like this when there is such a huge reckoning taking place for the many ills and crimes that have been committed by humanity in general. It can also be useful to "forgive life" when we experience the unthinkable, like the death of a loved one. We know death is part of the game of life, but that doesn't make it any easier to move past the hurt and loneliness we feel. Sometimes we just need to try and convict life for its brutality. We can find relief in naming how hard it can be to do this thing called being human. And once we have convicted life, we can forgive it to once again be free to find the joy and love life holds.

While forgiveness is essential to all healthy relationships, one cannot go on and on forgiving someone for the same transgression, especially if they show no signs that they care about the impact of their behavior and put in no effort to stop it. When you have people in your life that repeatedly show they are unable to change hurtful behaviors, you may need to assess whether it is intolerable, and the relationship needs to end. This can be difficult. It can feel like we are choosing between loving ourselves and loving another. But tolerating abusive behavior not only hurts you, it hurts them. By allowing it, you are participating in the very unfortunate experience of a soul damaging itself by damaging others.

When you feel angry it can be a sign that a boundary violation has occurred. Making difficult choices and setting boundaries is not easy. Otherwise, you'd have done it already. You will know when you know. You will set a boundary when you are really ready to do so and not a moment before. And when you are ready, keep in mind that you cannot simultaneously set a boundary with another and take care of their feelings. If you aren't ready to follow through, then don't set that as a boundary. Find something smaller you can stick to. And remember to call on The Loving Queen and the principle of Universal Love when you are really stuck. You can turn things over to the Divine, minute by minute, hour by hour, day by day.

Additional Connecting Practices

If you are finding yourself drowning in grief, feeling resentful alone, unloved, or isolated, try some of these as rescue remedies suggestions for returning to the open heart of the Loving Queen:

- Chanting alone or with others is a powerful practice for opening the heart.
- Attend a Kirtan, live is best, but recorded Kirtan music on YouTube or a Virtual Kirtan will work too.
- Listen to a heart sutra chant on YouTube or other streaming platform.
- Play with your pet or visit pet shelters and make some furry friends.
- Do some deep breathing on your own or have a facilitated breathwork session.
- Do a few heart-opening yoga poses (asanas) such as reverse plank, warrior 1, camel, and cobra.

Evidence of the Loving Queen: Responsible Love

When the heart chakra is balanced and open, you'll feel deeply connected. You may notice the harmonious exchange of energy with all that is around you, and feel a deep appreciation of beauty. When there's a blockage in the heart chakra, you may have difficulty relating with others, and experience excessive jealousy, codependency, or being closed down and withdrawn. You know you are embodying the Loving Queen when your inner and outer voice is supportive. If you hear yourself constantly criticizing others, there's a very high chance that, whether you admit it or not, you are equally hard on yourself. The Loving Queen is able to love in balance, meaning she is equally skilled at loving herself and others. She doesn't hide in her tower out of fear of connection, nor does she ignore herself and her own needs to prove she is worthy or good enough. She has mastered the skill of consciously choosing when and how to preference her own needs over the needs of others. She isn't perfect and that's okay. She treats herself and others kindly, even when things go wrong. Her main goal is to bring harmony into her interactions. So she is willing to admit when she's made a mistake. She is also willing to ask for what she needs when attempting to restore a broken connection. She loves responsibly.

The Loving Queen's Blessing: Forgiveness and Reconciliation

The Loving Queen offers two very potent blessings for the world: Forgiveness and reconciliation. We all grew up with imperfect care-givers and we ourselves are imperfect. The reality is no matter how hard we try to avoid it, we will at times act in ways that rupture our relationships. When the connection is bruised or broken, there's precious little value in seeking to place blame. It is a better use of our time to determine how to move forward. But we can't rush into premature forgiveness by sweeping our emotions under the rug. In order to offer true reconciliation, there must first be an accounting of the experience. Ron Kraybill's Cycle of Reconciliation, which has been built on and adapted by myself and others, is a reliable way forward after there has been a rupture. It follows several steps that must be completed in order so that the relationship can be repaired and returned to harmony. Once we have successfully navigated all of the steps, including negotiating any changes requested by either party, we can safely and honestly offer forgiveness and/or make amends and relationship harmony is restored.

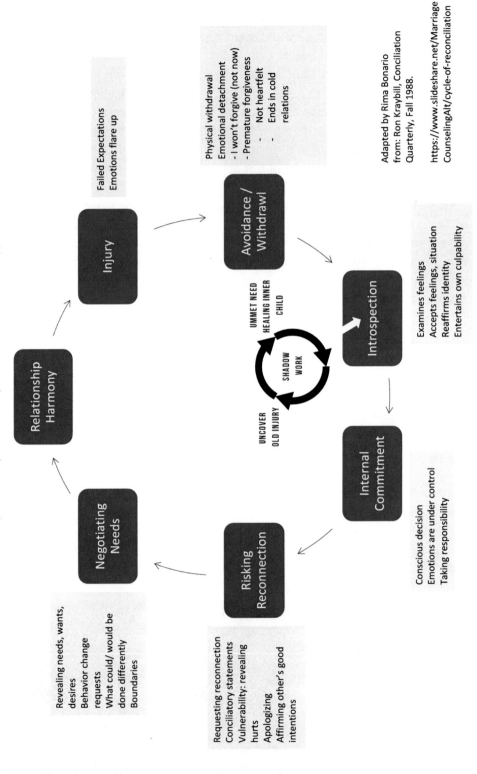

The Loving Queen Summary Chart

Archetype: The Warrior/Heroine

Location: Anahata (meaning unhurt, unstruck, unbeaten) Heart Chakra - Chest

Element: Air

Focus: Love, Balance, Self-love, Relationships

Orientation: Self-acceptance, Acceptance of others

Basic Right: To love and be loved

Challenge: Grief

Gifts: Connection and Balance

Shadow Queens: Queens: The Solitary Queen (not enough) The Sacrificial Queen (too much)

Color: Green

Essential Oil: Rose

Gemstone: Rose Quartz

Energy Practice: Golden Figure 8/Infinity Loop

Evidence: Balanced and responsibly loving relationships with self and others

Blessing: Forgiveness and Reconciliation

Chapter 16
The Expressive Queen

"For women, then, poetry is not a luxury. It is a vital necessity of our existence. It forms the quality of the light within which we predicate our hopes and dreams toward survival and change, first made into language, then into idea, then into more tangible action."

—Audre Lorde

The Expressive Queen is the keeper of Purpose. Her archetypal energy is the Artist. She supports us in living out our soul purpose by offering our creativity and our gifts to the world. Her domain is creative self-expression. And her cannon is Dharma Sovereignty.

The word Dharma is found in both Hinduism and Buddhism. It refers to the deep truth and cosmic law that underlies right behavior and social order. It also means conforming to or living out one's duty or nature. When we master Dharma sovereignty we have a profound sense of who we have come here to be. We connect with the deepest form of ourselves that feels clear and vibrationally uncluttered: Our Soul Essence. Forming a relationship with our Soul Essence requires a commitment to truth. We must be willing to tell ourselves the truth about who we are before we can express ourselves authentically with others. Leaning into this work can be challenging as we have often formed false ideas of who we are supposed to be in the world. Sometimes we adopt the Essence of others in an effort to survive. The Expressive Queen finds her own unique voice and shares it with the world.

The concept of Dharma can sometimes be confused with fate. But it is not really about hemming us into a single life-path. Rather it helps us acknowledge who we are at our core so that we can align with it. For example, it is the Dharma of fire to be hot. Asking fire to not be hot makes no sense. The Expressive Queen wants to know what befits us. Is our Dharma to be nurturing, strong, or bubbly? Are we here to lead, teach, or heal? Is our purpose to beautify, inspire, or protect? The Expressive Queen invites you to find your deepest truth and live from it.

While our Dharma is not a job or career, it is possible to have our chosen profession align with our Dharma. For example, I believe teaching is a key aspect of my self-expression. At every level of my education, I found myself "teaching" things to my friends and fellow students. My first formal career was as a middle school teacher. When I left teaching for corporate work, I really enjoyed leading training courses. Even when I am invited to give a Sunday sermon or a short talk, I can't help but offer some sort of teaching rather than just an inspiring message. It is my truest expression to serve in this way. It fills me with delight, and I feel aligned and on purpose.

Finding alignment requires that we have the courage to tell ourselves and others the truth about who we are, at the deepest level. Only in this way can we discover what befits us. What is it that calls to you over and over? What nags at you, or hides below the surface waiting for your attention? What are you as yet unwilling to acknowledge and say out loud? We must reclaim our voice if we were silenced or told to keep secrets growing up. And we must be gentle with ourselves as we seek to find and use our voice. Sometimes our first attempts to speak up and find our path are messy and embarrassing. But we must persist in the work to find, speak, and hear our truth.

THE EXPRESSIVE QUEEN'S CHALLENGE

The greatest threat to our authentic self-expression is lying. First and foremost, we cannot lie to ourselves. If we are unwilling to admit to ourselves what we most deeply desire to create and express in the world, we have no chance of creating a fulfilling life. Lying is a complete misuse of the Expressive Queen's power. We must hold ourselves accountable whether we are intentionally misleading another or simply allowing them to think something is true when we know it isn't. It is impossible to create a life that is in alignment with your Dharma when you are not being true to yourself. If we grew up in a family that lacked integrity, you may have to work at changing the habit of hiding or little-white-lying in order to feel safe or save face. Speaking the truth may be hard, but in the end it's always worth it. As the saying goes, if you try to avoid conflict by not telling the truth, the war you start will be with yourself.

Hearing lies is just as challenging for this Queen. In order to be successful in living authentically, you will need to surround yourself with others who are also committed to authenticity and truth. Consider paying attention to what people do as well as what they say. If their actions contradict their words, that's important information. Do they follow through and keep their word? If not, it is perfectly okay for you to limit contact with them, or even remove them from your life. The Expressive Queen needs to create and live in a clear and clean frequency, one that is free from misinformation. Be mindful of the quality of information you allow into your awareness. Seek sources that are trustworthy. If you feel yourself getting sucked into wild theories that are shocking and hard to believe, you might want to put the brakes on and step away. It could be hard to believe for a reason. It's often useful to "borrow perspective" from someone you admire and trust who thinks a bit differently from you, or even several people.

Avoid gossip and trash talking, and avoid listening to others who gossip or talk trash. It's a huge energy drain, and it takes precious energy away from what you could be creating. Seek to use your voice to create more beauty and harmony in the world. Be inspiring and uplifting. But also be willing to take a stand against injustice. It can be scary to speak truth to power, but it needs to be done. Try bringing the energy of the Empowered Queen and the softness of the Loving Queen together to support your Expressive Queen so she shares powerfully and from the heart.

The Expressive Queen's Gifts

As we learn to speak our truth and offer ourselves in the world, we are able to cultivate an authentic and impactful presence. The Expressive Queen powers our presence so that we can make a real difference in the world. Our life and how we live it become a work of art. We are artists and the medium we work in is Life. When we embrace the Expressive Queen our creativity and artistry makes the world a better place. We add value because we are intrinsically valuable and therefore our truest expression is a potent contribution. Our voice is needed, our presence is required. These are the gifts that await us as we integrate and embody this Queen.

The Shadow Queens

If we were not shown good models of communication or encouraged to trust in the power of our own voice as children, we may struggle with being self-expressed. We can find ourselves sliding into The Silent Queen, who swallows her words and her dreams rather than taking the risk of speaking out and being rebuffed in some way. The Silent Queen can be a killer queen. She can be ruthless in her self-criticism, insisting that your words and plans are worthless. She often serves up rounds of shame and embarrassment after you do decide to speak, forever pointing out ways you could have said it better. She isn't trying to offer constructive criticism, rather her goal is to silence you altogether. She is really just a terrified shadow pattern that wants to keep you safe, but the cost for this safety is your very Soul. Do not make this deal.

Even if you struggle at first to find skillful ways to share your emotions, thoughts, and beliefs, it's better to try and stumble as you gain skill than to retreat into a fake representation of who you really are. Happiness cannot be found in such a shrunken version of you. Try giving the Silent Queen practice at expressing in safe ways. Picking up an artistic hobby can be a game-changer for her. Take a class or teach yourself. But be prepared for pushback. The Silent Queen will try all her usual tactics to shut down your creative expression. Meet her criticism with a cordial, "Thank you for sharing." And then go on about your work. You may need to remind her that you and she are safe and it's okay to use your voice. The more you move through her fear and create anyway, the less afraid she will be.

Alternately, you might find yourself inhabiting the Starring Queen. This Queen has too much energy for expression. She is in such high need of being seen that she often inadvertently takes up all the space in the room. It's all about her. Conversations with her feel more like a monologue than a dialogue. She generally listens only long enough to find something that sparks her interest and then she turns the conversation toward herself. Mostly she is just trying to be relatable and generous in offering the stories and insights she thinks are entertaining or interesting. But her motivation is coming from old wounds. She lacks the presence of the Expressive Queen, so she loses touch with those around her. The Starring Queen's need for affirmation and attention shifts a conversation into a performance. Now she is on the stage and everyone else is her audience. There is no way that authentic connection and self-expression can occur at such a distance because the vulnerability needed to create intimacy requires proximity and mutual exchange. Ultimately, the stage is a lonely place. The Starring Queen needs to come down from her stage and create for herself rather than for the audience she believes holds the key to her happiness. True happiness comes from self-appreciation and self-value not from living a performative life.

A Personal Perspective: My Dharma Sovereignty Map

I can remember as a teenager getting exciting and speaking loudly—the way many Italians do. Despite the fact that my family did this all the time, my dad would on occasion rebuke me for it, saying, "Tone it down!" He used to make this little motion with his hand like he was reaching for a radio volume dial and seeking to quiet me. It was demeaning, offensive, and stifling. My stomach would knot up, I would catch my breath and stop speaking (and breathing!). Tears often sprang to my eyes; my throat would close down. This display of emotion often resulted in a secondary rebuke to not be so emotional, and my shame would be complete. It was painful, both physically and emotionally. You know that searing pain that can happen in your throat at times of great emotion? That's your glottis, the area in your throat that allows you to inhale air without allowing food to come along for the ride. The painful sensation, or "lump in the throat," happens when we need to both swallow tears and breathe. The glottis is trying to stay open as you cry, but it keeps being forced closed as you swallow, causing a painful tension in the throat muscles. This pain is a clear signal that we have something important to say, and the act of saying it is challenging us. It means there is deep emotion attached to our words and our experience. We need to pause and take time to really listen to what it is that we need to say. What Truth is rising to the surface?

In this case, my truth was that being told to be quiet was painful. It seemed like an arbitrary requirement that I alone had to meet, since everyone else was allowed to yell as loud and as often as they wanted, or so it seemed to me. Over time, I found myself less likely to speak up. This actually made things worse, as I would hold back until I couldn't any longer, and then my emotions would erupt in very damaging ways. I struggled to know how to be heard in my family. I alternated between seeking out and wanting attention and trying to shrink myself so I could stay out of sight. The anxiety I felt infected my peer relationships as well. It showed up in every place where I had the opportunity to engage in creative self-expression.

For example, it took me years to find a way of dressing that felt deeply my own. I was terrified of standing out, although I desperately wanted to be seen. I was drawn to artsy types who dressed wildly and decorated their homes with vibrant colors and eclectic art. I had a deep need to feel accepted and liked, so rather than allowing my own artistry to come through, I always opted for what I saw others wearing that looked cool. But somehow it never looked cool on me. It's obvious now that I was trying to wear other people's clothes and rock their look, rather than looking within to find and rock my own look. Working with the Expressive Queen helped me find my own style, and my own voice. Not only did I forge new roads in my appearance, but I took my own path in my career, creating a business based on what interested me and matched my Dharma. Working with The Expressive Queen is the reason I now love what I do. I am no longer working in mis-matched jobs or wearing mis-matched clothes trying to emulate what others are doing. I have found and followed my own path. And it is such a JOY!

THE EXPRESSIVE QUEEN WRITING EXERCISE: TAKING INVENTORY

This Queen functions best when she has the confidence to speak and live in truth. Consider your early years. How did your family communicate? Were conversions easy and fun, or fraught with drama? Did you feel you had to hide things from your family? Did your family have a lot of secrets? Were you expected to lie to protect others? Were you lied to? Could you trust those around you to follow through and keep their word? How much BS was in the air? Was your voice honored and encouraged? Were you allowed to express yourself creatively in art, clothing, your room's decor, your choice of classes, your friends?

Were your dreams and goals encouraged? Was your natural curiosity nurtured? Or were you directed to play with certain toys and study certain subjects? How about others in your life? Did you see those around you pursuing their dreams or were they giving their Life Force energy over to things that had to be done, rather than searching for the fit that aligned with their truest calling in life? Serving in your true calling is one of the highest expressions of your voice. When your Dharma is dismissed, ignored, or silenced, it can stunt your ability to speak up and block the sense that it is okay or safe to speak up and tell the truth. It can send the message that you are not understood and will not be heard. It can translate into the belief that you don't matter.

Consider, what is your Dharma Sovereignty Map? Take some time to reflect on the questions below and write out a description of your own Dharma Sovereignty Map. Use the questions to help to uncover what work might be waiting for you as you seek to embody the Expressive Queen within you.

On a scale from 1 - 10 with 1 being the least and 10 being the most:

How safe was it to speak up when growing up? ____

How often were loving words used to provide correction and inspire growth? ____

How easy do you find it to use your voice and share your creativity now? ____

How comfortable and confident are you in moving toward your dreams and goals? ____

THE EXPRESSIVE QUEEN ENERGY PRACTICE: ME/NOT ME

The daily practice of clearing your energy field and removing outside influences will support you in activating the power of this Queen. This is the practice of visualizing moving anything that is not YOU out of your body and auric space and calling back to you any and all parts of you that have been consciously or unconsciously left elsewhere (outside of your auric field). Begin by imagining a light source tuned to the frequency of your name scanning your auric field and body from the top down. Every time it hesitates or hits a block of some kind you've uncovered something that is not you. Imagine it melting, vaporizing, disappearing in some way. If you know where it belongs, send it there. Otherwise let Mother Earth have it. She will transmute and reuse the energy. Continue scanning all the way down your body and beyond to about a foot below your feet. Keep sending out anything that is not you. Once the space inside you is clear, imagine calling home or magnetizing to you any and all parts of you, aspects of your attention, or energy that are not currently inside your body or auric field. As they feel the pull, visualize them gently returning back to you from wherever they are now. As they come home, your unique vibrational frequency will become stronger. Notice how it feels to be filled up with you and only you. As that frequency increases, say the following affirmations out loud:

I release any and all cords, ties, bonds, and agreements made by me or others under false pretenses.

I love being authentically me. I express myself and my desires and dreams clearly.

My body and field are mine alone and inhabited solely by me.

I make time for my creative expression. Creativity flows in and through me.

*My voice is necessary. I deserve to speak and hear the truth.
My Dharma is a gift to the world.*

The Expressive Queen Anointing Oil: Amber Cashmere

To enhance your experience of the energy practices and the writing exercises, apply the Amber Cashmere Throat Chakra Oil to your throat for seven to twenty-one days in a row morning and night. Apply some to your wrists and even under your nose to smell the scent throughout the day, especially in moments when you want to communicate effectively and express yourself. This holy oil works as a homeopathic remedy to open and activate your voice and the throat chakra. It balances and harmonizes the chakra's energetic expression. This helps you avoid being under or over expressed (and flipping into the shadow Queens) so that you can stay connected to the throne of The Expressive Queen. All of the chakra oils are available on my website at RimaBonario.com.

Going Deeper

When you want to understand how and why you hide things from yourself, look at how your family trained you. Were there secrets to be kept, lies told? Was it safe to be honest?

Look at what patriarchy tells us about the role of women, what women are "supposed" to want, to be, how they are to behave. What of this has been unconsciously rooted within you without your expressed permission? Imagine it leaving you now. Allow it to be replaced with a fresh, blank canvass that you can fill however you like—without consequence, without shame or guilt. What would you put on that canvass?

To help you get started answer these questions:

- Who would I be without my role as _____? (Mother, wife, daughter, teacher, employee, rescuer, good girl, mediator, etc.)
- What is my soul mission? What am I here to BE, to exemplify, to model, or offer to the world?
- What is helping me and what is stopping me from living my highest, soul-level dharma?
- What excites me the most and what scares me the most about living at my highest, soul-level dharma?
- What is the next smallest step I can take to move in the direction of my soul calling?

When you are looking to create your life be mindful of whether the desire to create is soul-driven or ego-driven. So how can we tell the difference?

The ego speaks like this:

Wow, Sarah got a Lexus. It's pretty cool. I need a raise, or a better paying job. This one stinks. Maybe I could stop by the mall and get that Coach bag I've had my eye on or find some new shoes.

Our soul speaks like this:

Do I really want more stuff for my closet? Will that really fulfill me? I have always wanted to plant a vegetable garden (or tap dance, play guitar, write, sing). I love to have fun, to travel (or to ski, or sky-dive, swim). I love to help people. I'd love to teach art or dance. I've always wanted to…

The ego again:

You can't do that. You're too old (or too young, too this, too that). Besides you'll never make any money doing that. And what would so and so think if I took up glass blowing? Who has time for that anyway? I have too much to do. Oh no, here comes the boss…

It's this type of negative mind-rant that keeps us from acting on the dreams we have or distracts us by pulling us toward "stuff" that promises joy but can never deliver. If ego is in charge, what we do is driven by externals. We give our power over to what we think people think about us. We define ourselves from the outside in. We have an idea of who we think we are based on what we want others to think we are. Embodying the Expressive Queen means we are committed to defining ourselves from the inside out.

Additional Expression Practices

If you are needing to free up the energy in your voice or discern you way through misinformation, you can use the following practices as rescue remedies to bring yourself back into the Expressive Queen:

- Use a powerful mantra or chant to move energy such as, "Om," "HamSa," "Om Mani Padme Hum," "I am that I AM,"
- Speak and write words of gratitude
- Drink pure water and stay hydrated
- Spend time in silence
- Sing a favorite song
- Make a powerful statement of truth

Evidence of the Expressive Queen

When you are embodying the Expressive Queen, you feel as though you are heading in the right direction. You may still get nudges to change direction, maybe even make a U-turn, but you have confidence that you are following your Soul's guidance. As such you find it fun and exciting to live authentically. You enjoy dressing in a way that brings you pleasure and living in a home decorated in a style you love. You are able to use your voice and speak up as needed. You are so well-connected to your own truth that you don't tolerate lies and falseness from others or yourself. While it may not always be easy to speak your truth, you know that there really is no other choice. When you embody this Queen, you have a regular practice of clearing your body and energy field so that you remain free from others' energy. This allows you to inhabit and offer your purest, most uncluttered self-expression, and the world is all the better for it!

The Expressive Queen's Blessing: Service and Generosity

Of all the Queens, the Expressive Queen most directly blesses others by generously offering herself as a gift to the world. By committing to live authentically and in alignment with her Dharma, she is capable of being of service with just her presence. But even more than that, this Queen creates a world that works for all by offering her time, talent, and treasure in support of causes that she believes in. The Sovereign acknowledges it rests with her to take care of the realm. And while we can't solve all of the world's problems, The Expressive Queen is willing to do what she can, where she is, with what she has to make life better for all. Speaking up in the face of injustice, working to help those less fortunate, fighting for public policy that leaves no one out, these are all hallmarks of this Queen's blessings.

The Expressive Queen Summary Chart

Archetype: The Seer or Oracle

Location: Vishudha (meaning especially pure) Throat Chakra - Pharyngeal Plexus

Element: Sound

Focus: Listening, Resonance, Finding Your Voice

Orientation: Self-expression

Basic Right: To Speak and Hear Truth

Challenge: Lies

Gifts: Creative Presence

Shadow Queens: Silent Queen (not enough) Starring Queen (too much)

Color: Sky Blue

Essential Oil: Amber Cashmere

Gemstone: Sodalite

Energy Practice: Me-Not Me/Clearing

Evidence: Speaking your truth and following your Soul's guidance to live authentically

Blessing: Service and Generosity, giving of your time and energy to a cause you believe in

CHAPTER 17
THE VISIONARY QUEEN

*"Another world is not only possible, she is on her way.
On a quiet day, I can hear her breathing."*

—Arundhati Roy

The Visionary Queen is the keeper of Wisdom. Her archetypal energy is The Seer or Oracle. She supports us in opening our intuitive and holistic ways of seeing. Her domain is clarity. And her cannon is Mental Sovereignty.

When we have wounds related to our thinking and our accomplishments as young children, we can often take on the idea that we are incapable or in some way not good enough. We may feel a low-grade or acute fear of appearing foolish or stupid and struggle when faced with learning new things or when we make a mistake. Mental sovereignty means we are conscious of the wounds of our youth that lead us to taking on false beliefs about ourselves and the world. With that awareness comes the possibility of catching these false beliefs in the moment and reframing them into a more accurate truth, a truth born of wholeness and our right to live, to succeed, to enjoy, and to love and be loved.

Clear thinking doesn't just come from the mind. It comes from the heart and the gut working in tandem with the mind. In other words, there is an alignment between the directions coming from your body, heart and mind. There is congruence between the information present in your emotional and physical being, and the conscious thoughts you are having. This is often described as feeling a 100% YES! in your system. Clear thinking can be an instantaneous intuitive knowing or it can come over time, like a long and slow mulling that reveals a solid answer. Having clear vision feels smooth, not choppy or crunchy inside.

It's not uncommon to get antsy waiting for the clarity to show up, but a mentally sovereign person is willing to wait. Mental sovereignty means learning to tolerate ambiguity in yourself and others. Eventually, you will receive an answer. One very common hallmark of clear thinking is the energy for action that accompanies it. Once the way forward can be seen, we feel excited and maybe even compelled to act on it, even if it is only the next smallest step forward. In fact, most clear thinking only offers the next one or two action steps because it is aware that new information will be revealed once those steps are taken. Mental sovereignty includes a healthy component of trust, something that is easier when your thoughts have been confirmed by your body, heart, and soul.

The Visionary Queen's Challenge

The Visionary Queen's task is to guard against being blinded by illusion. She must be careful not to allow her wounds to color all she sees. This means she is willing to hold her perceptions lightly. By committing to see from her truest self, she is able to avoid the trap of believing her own stories. The wisdom of the Visionary Queen and her powerful capacity to self-reflect allows her to recognize when her judgment is clouded by past hurts. She takes her time to think through her perspective rather than rushing into action. When the dust has been kicked up by inner or outer conflict, she waits for it to settle so that she can see clearly what is real.

The stories from the past are like photographs hanging on the walls of our home. Some are favorites, we return to them again and again. They may be joyful scenes or horrific scenes. But unlike Mary Poppins, our magic isn't in jumping into the scene before us and bringing it to life again. Our magic is in staying in the present moment. There is an indigenous saying that reminds us we can never step into the same river twice. That is to say, the water is constantly moving so when you return to your favorite spot on the riverbank, you will step off into completely different water. The river of time works the same way. The photos on the walls of our mind and heart are of moments in time that no longer exists anywhere but in their frames. They are now just illusions. To see clearly what is in front of us, to be able to respond to the world freely, with wisdom and insight, we have to let go of the images that captured something that has long ago ceased to exist.

The skill to differentiate between what is real and what is imaginary is more important than ever as we find ourselves bombarded with a dizzying array of opinions. If you didn't experience honesty and transparency in your family dynamic, it might be hard to trust your powers of perception. Part of the healing process we face is to shift from seeing ourselves and our life solely in the context of our individual life expression. The Visionary Queen invites us into a view of the world that is larger than any one person. Our story, while personal, is also transpersonal. If we can only see what's happening through the ego's lens, we will miss locating ourselves in the larger story of humanity's unfolding. We are part of the Universe evolving itself through us. It takes the power of the Visionary Queen to lift us high enough to see this bigger picture and therefore be freed from the illusion we encounter when seeing only half the story.

The Visionary Queen's Gifts

It is through the Visionary Queen's gifts of wisdom and insight that we can rise above our mundane view of our life and grasp that greater meaning awaiting us there. By looking out beyond that attachment to the material realm, we find a new level of information that is available to us. We can call on our intuitive capacities that reach up into that which is unseen, that which can only be felt and understood in the language of the Soul, to support us in assessing and understanding of the events in our lives. The Visionary Queen breaks us out of our prison of pain by reframing the past in a broader context so that we can wrench from it all the learning and transcendent implications it holds, while releasing the wounding it was wrapped in. The ultimate healing occurs when we can see the way our trauma has served us, if only to help us to know what we no longer want in our lives. Every "opportunity for growth" becomes precious, thereby neutralizing the hold it may have had over our ability to move with speed and focus on our happiness. If we are willing to put the work in, we will be rewarded with a whole new series of scenes that feature joyful, authentic, and whole versions of ourselves.

The Shadow Queens

If we were not supported in accessing the wisdom and insight available in The Visionary Queen, we may instead slip into the Foolish Queen. The Foolish Queen cares not for the power of reasoning and thinking. She is impulsive and impatient. She throws caution to the wind and runs without care into the roadway of her life. It usually doesn't take long before she is run over by someone or something she didn't see coming. In some cases, this may reinforce her inner judgement that she is stupid. If she was raised to believe that she couldn't manage her way out of a paper bag, she may have given up trying. If she's lucky, she might recognize her error of failing to check to see if it was safe before proceeding. But rather than using it to help herself, she may use it to berate herself. In other cases, she may just brush it off, denying her part in the collision, choosing instead to chalk it up to bad behavior on the part of another. She might even rage at them and push them away. But if it happens again, and again, like a Groundhog Day nightmare, she will soon find herself feeling alone and powerless in a world that seems determined to run her over. The path of the Foolish Queen is one of zero responsibility. Ultimately she will find herself at the mercy of others since she has opted not to take any responsibility for thinking her way through the challenges and solving the dilemmas that life offers.

On the flip side, the Arrogant Queen believes that she always knows best. She feels confident in her skills and lacks trust in others. This might be for good reason if she was surrounded by harmful people growing up. To compensate, the Arrogant Queen becomes over-responsible. She has an out-sized notion of her power and believes herself to be the most competent, or the only competent, person around. She consciously or unconsciously trains others to let her handle everything. When she finally grows tired of the burden, she calls on a feeling of superiority to take the sting out of her resentment. The Arrogant Queen can be an intellectual snob. She might use her intelligence as a weapon to cut others down and make herself look better. Beyond healthy mental competition, she must be the victor or else. This is rooted in the fear of being hurt, so she seeks to dominate and control through her mental acuity.

A Personal Perspective: My Mental Sovereignty Map

In my family growing up, having a sharp mind was prized above all else. I learned that in order to be safe I had to be smart. Having a super-smart older brother only made my drive to achieve all the more vigorous. Believing I could figure things out and solve problems was a way I told myself I could be safe. I got really, really good at finding creative ways to solve problems. To be sure developing that skill served me. But like all childhood adaptive behaviors it came with a price.

Some of my biggest revelations on my healing journey were seeing that several of my blind spots came from a false sense of my own power and brilliance. I took on this belief under the high expectations of my professor father. While I am powerful and brilliant, like all people I have my limits. I need help from time to time. A healthy life includes being able to see when I reach the edge of my ability and ask for help. It's also important to hold our gifts with humility, something I couldn't manage for years not out of malice but out of blindness.

Having worked with The Visionary Queen, I am aware that there was a time when I came off as a know-it-all for years, not making room for others' input or perspective as that somehow felt dangerous. For me, it was priority number one to never appear stupid. Making a mistake was completely unacceptable. This kind of harsh thinking cut me off from my ability to feel compassion for myself and others. I was super self-critical and critical of others too. It wasn't until I began giving myself the permission to question the assumptions and adaptations I took on as a child that I could see how I had distorted my gift and turned it into a weapon. I also struggled with judgment, particularly of those who seemed they were too materialistic, or too beautiful, or too shallow. It was all just a reflection of my own insecurities which were hidden deep beneath the surface.

My criticism didn't stop there. For most of my life I have struggled to turn off a nasty voice that is constantly comparing my physical appearance to other women. At the time I had no idea that I was dealing with body dysmorphia and unable to accurately assess my body shape and size. My vision was literally distorted when it came to seeing myself. I have always been fairly petite, but I have a serious bubble butt. Once, my dad off-handedly said I had my grandmother Borsotti's butt. She was quite a large woman, probably 225lbs and just over 5' tall. I was mortified. I came to the conclusion that I must be horrifically fat. Another time he commented that he was shocked at how big my nose was when I was born. A third time he announced that all good dancers had long legs. He was talking about Debbie Reynold on TV, not me. But the words sunk in. Even though I loved to dance, I quit my dance classes after that. I concluded my legs were just too short for me to be good, so it seemed smarter to just have my Saturdays back instead of wasting my time.

My efforts to make peace with my body eventually lead me to explore the healing art of Tantra. By learning to see myself through the eyes of self-love in the practice of Tantra, I am able to manage my body dysmorphia. I'll never forget the first time I could really see myself clearly in a mirror. The illusion that I had been living with lifted and I was amazed at what I saw. I was stunned by how beautiful I am and how seriously fabulous my body is. While the dysmorphia can return if I am stressed or feeling disconnected from myself and my beloved, it's never as bad as it used to be. Even more importantly, I know it's a false view when it arises, so it no longer sets off my inner critic. I have learned to call on the Visionary Queen to help me see clearly. She has become one of my greatest allies, guiding me faithfully every day in living a life based on clear vision and wisdom.

The Visionary Queen Writing Exercise: Taking Inventory

We all want mental clarity. It's what Western culture tends to value most. Of the seven areas of sovereignty, mental sovereignty (how we think and what we think) may be the most consciously manipulated during our upbringing. As children we are told hundreds perhaps even thousands of times each day what we should think about ourselves, others, and the world. In subtle and not so subtle ways, our caregivers, authority figures and cultural influences all strive to impress their point of view upon us. It matters not whether that view is authentically ours. Our schools, religious institutions, the advertising industry, our peers and foes all seek to influence and shape our beliefs about ourselves and the world. This often clouds our vision and leaves us feeling confused or detached from our own inner knowing.

Consider your informal and formal education. Were you encouraged to think independently and to question what you were taught so that you could discover for yourself? Or were you treated like a blank slate upon which others wrote the truth? Were you allowed to disagree or voice an alternate viewpoint? Or were you expected to fall in line? Were you encouraged to trust your intuition, or did caregivers and authority figures insist that they were the only ones who could see things clearly? Seeing past the illusions that have been thrust upon us and then taken in as our own is a critical step if we are to access our mental sovereignty.

Consider, what is your Mental Sovereignty Map? Take some time to reflect on the questions above and write out a description of your own Mental Sovereignty Map. Use these questions to help to uncover what work might be waiting for you as you seek to embody the Visionary Queen within you.

On a scale from 1 - 10 with 1 being the least and 10 being the most:

How much did your family respect your thoughts and opinions growing up? ____

How much room was made for differing opinions? ____

How confident do you feel about your ability to solve problems now? ____

How connected are you to your intuition now? ____

THE VISIONARY QUEEN ENERGY PRACTICE: CHAKRA MEDITATION

The daily practice of connecting with the chakra system, and especially the third-eye chakra, can go a long way toward restoring and preserving a clear view of yourself. By balancing and connecting all of your body's energy centers you will have access to a more holistic understanding of life. Use this chakra meditation and visualization to access this holistic viewpoint. Start by visualizing a ruby red orb at the base of your spine, imagine the sphere spinning, then glowing and radiating red light out into your body and auric field. Breathe deeply and imagine this red light soothing and healing your body, mind and soul. When you are ready, visualize moving up to the sacral chakra and connect with its vibrant orange orb. See it spinning and then glowing and radiating orange light out into your body and auric field. Breathe deeply and imagine this orange light soothing and healing your body, mind and soul. When ready, move up to the bright yellow orb in the solar plexus, then the verdant green orb in the heart, the sky-blue sphere in the throat, the deep indigo orb in the third eye, and the brilliant violet orb in crown. After opening and balancing all these chakras, allow them to connect with and communicate with each other. As you feel peace and calm coming over you, say the following affirmations out loud:

I am open to the wisdom and insight that resides within me.

I see myself and the world with clarity.

I create and manifest my vision for my life.

I trust myself to see what needs to be seen.

The Visionary Queen Anointing Oil: Sandalwood

To enhance your experience of the energy practices and the writing exercises, apply the Sandalwood Chakra Oil to third-eye (brow) for seven to twenty-one days in a row morning and night. Apply some to your wrists and even under your nose to smell the scent throughout the day, especially in moments when you are feeling unclear or confused. This holy oil works as a homeopathic remedy to activate and enliven the third eye chakra. It balances and harmonizes the chakra's energetic expression. This helps you avoid being under or over expressed (and flipping into the shadow Queens) so that you can stay firmly rooted and on the throne of The Visionary Queen. All of the chakra oils are available on my website at RimaBonario.com.

Going Deeper

Cultivating the power to reframe life's painful experiences and use them for your benefit may be one of the best gifts I have ever given myself. One of my favorite bible stories is the story of Joseph and his Coat of Many Colors. In the story his horrible brothers sell him off as a slave. He is taken to Egypt where eventually he earns his freedom. Things go wrong again, and he ends up in prison. While imprisoned he has a dream showing that Egypt will face a terrible famine. He sees how the Pharaoh can act to save his people from the famine. The Pharoah gets wind of this and enacts the suggestions saving his people. Joseph becomes the Pharaoh's main advisor after that lives a cushy life in the royal palace. In time, his father and brothers show up begging for food as their people have suffered greatly in the famine. They do not recognize Joseph, who hangs back to see if his brothers have grown into better people. Once he is satisfied he reveals himself. The brothers repent and ask his forgiveness, which he grants. Astonished, the brothers ask how his heart can grant such forgiveness after being so terribly wronged. Joseph replies, "What you meant for evil, God meant for good."

Like Joseph, I believe that at any moment in our lives no matter how painful, we can find meaning and even joy. Viktor Frankl's powerful book *Man's Search for Meaning* cemented this belief for me. I read his book in my World Religions class at age fifteen, and it changed me at depth. Frankl was an Austrian neurologist-psychiatrist and a Jew who was interned at Auschwitz. As a survivor of the horrors of the holocaust, he writes in vivid detail about his experience as a prisoner of the Nazi's in that concentration camp. As I read the heart-breaking realities he and others faced, I was riveted by how he managed to find hope and love in that awful place. He shared how they found ways to take responsibility for their daily experience of life, to cultivate a private pool of inner peace within themselves. With great effort and care, they sought out evidence of beauty in nature and art. This practice allowed those lucky enough to survive to emerge with their souls intact. He lays down a path that anyone can use to move through times of great suffering and overcome even the most unimaginable circumstances. This is the re-frame of all re-frames. From age fifteen on, I thought if Frankl and others in his book could do that at Auschwitz, I surely could too.

Later in life I built on this understanding. I found that it was meaning, not happiness, that was the basis of joy for me. I came to see it as a kind of paradox: you don't have to be happy to be joyful. Joy and happiness are two very different things. Happiness is dependent on circumstances. We are happy when we get a bonus, or when that person who caught our eye says yes to an invitation to lunch, or when we get the job we interviewed for. These externally driven moments of happiness are fleeting. They are pleasing to the ego and its quest for achievement. But notice what happens once we've spent the money, married our crush, or worked at the job. More often than not, in time our mind turns to the next thing we want in order to be happy. We want more money, a better partner, another job.

Joy on the other hand is not based on external circumstances. It is not dependent on the actions of another person, or luck, or even you. Joy just is. When faced with moments of deep pain, it helps us to see the gifts that will emerge from the sorrow. This is not to say we should not feel that sorrow deeply. True maturity comes when we are able to feel both joy and pain at the same time.

I experienced this about six months after Tobias and I were married. Since I was already thirty-four when we married, we began trying to get pregnant right away. It just so happened that right about that time an incredible career opportunity opened up for me. The position would allow me to have my work life and my spiritual life become intertwined—one of my most authentic desires. While it was a position of greater authority, it was likely to be less stressful as the scope of the organization was significantly smaller than where I was working. Perhaps most importantly, I felt it would allow greater flexibility for our family after the baby came if I was pregnant. I interviewed for and was offered the position. It meant leaving a job that I loved and a tight-knit work family I cherished, but it was just too great an opportunity to pass up.

While I had no legal obligation to inform my potential new employer that there was a possibility I was pregnant, I felt I had a moral obligation to do so as the position was one of executive leadership. I made a doctor's appointment and found out that we had our wish, and I was indeed a few weeks pregnant. My husband and I were thrilled!

When I shared the news with my potential employer the response was so affirming. They knew I was right for the position and welcomed me whole-heartedly. I gave my notice knowing that the change would better support our new family in the long run. Christmas was just a week away, so we decided to tell our families with notes under the tree written from the baby. Everyone was excited as it would be the first grand baby on both sides. Within another week we learned that we were pregnant with twins. More excitement! A week after that, I had what's called a missed miscarriage. That means the embryos stopped developing. There was no heartbeat, no sign of life, nothing that should be there at 8 weeks.

That weekend, supported by the strength and courage of my loving husband, I went through a medically induced, physically intense mini-labor. It was a painful experience, physically and emotionally. People don't talk too much about the kind of loss you experience with a miscarriage. It's such an intimate loss. While I had begun developing a relationship with the growing lives within me, no one else "knew" my babies. Not even my husband shared the bond that had begun growing between us. Even as early in the pregnancy as this loss came, I felt profound sadness.

And yet, within days, I also began to see the gifts that were being bestowed upon me. I was showered with love and blessings from everywhere. My friends surrounded me with love. Co-workers and friends from my soon-to-be-ex employer reached out in love. Flowers and prayers came from my soon-to-be employer. My brother, sister, and parents were incredibly loving and supportive; a true gift considering at that time relations were often quite strained in our family. My new in-laws' compassionate response gave me great confidence in our growing relationship. And my husband, well, he was absolutely amazing. The depth of his loving kindness during those days and weeks still moves me. Even my cat seemed to be extra loving toward me. These were experiences I treasured in the midst of the sorrow.

I also knew that, had I not been pregnant, I might not have investigated the job opportunity that presented itself or had the courage to let go of a great position to step into something even better. My ability to look past the painful circumstances allowed me to experience joy and gratitude for the good in my life, while still grieving deeply for my loss.

The Visionary Queen invites us to raise our eyes up from the ground and look past what is happening at the individual level to see what is happening at the transpersonal or mythic level. It's there where we can often find something that helps us make sense out of nonsensical situations. We see ourselves as embedded in a larger story and that allows us to transform our personal stories into transpersonal stories as we understand the work we do. We come to realize the healing that happens is for more than any one individual, it is for all of us. If a woman has wounding associated with her mother, she can see this break reflected in the dismissal degradation of the Archetypal Mother. It reflects the Great Mother Wound we all share. As she chooses to heal her issues with her mother at the individual level, she brings healing at the Archetypal level as well. From an esoteric and visionary perspective, we are myth in form, therefore what we heal makes a far bigger impact than we might imagine.

This healing work is not about ignoring or pretending we aren't suffering and full of sorrow. It's about knowing that the sorrow isn't all there is. Mr. Rogers famously shared his mother's advice during times of communal catastrophe. As a young boy she helped him with his fear by saying, "Look for the helpers. There are always helpers."

No matter what we choose to look for, we will find it. The Visionary Queen invites us to master the skill of looking for and finding joy, especially in times of great suffering. This is the ultimate act of rebellion when faced with oppression, to refuse to have your spirit broken, to remain capable of finding joy. The more we practice finding joy, the more we discover that it is everywhere. When you decide to find joy, joy begins to find you.

Additional Visionary Practices

If you are struggling with clearing your vision and directing your thoughts, you can use the following practices as rescue remedies to bring yourself back into the embrace of the Visionary Queen:

- Get out into the sunlight and let it warm your face.
- Journal about a childhood story and reframe it in a way that feels freeing.
- Hum or chant the sound "OM."
- Set a single intention each day for three days and work to accomplish each one.
- Write a letter to yourself and forgive yourself for something that you did in the past.

Evidence of the Visionary Queen

You know you have embodied the Visionary Queen when you recognize that life is one long healing adventure. You have become familiar with the process of uncovering your life's conditioning and masterful at reframing and releasing its hold on you. You have acknowledged the events of the past and sought out healing. You see yourself clearly both your brilliance and your limitations. You understand how to direct your thoughts so that you create from a place of clarity. Embodying the Visionary Queen means seeing past the mundane world and recognizing the mythic context and the call to operate simultaneously in both domains. You seek out the inner wisdom and spiritual insight that resides within. You live more and more in alignment with your Soul Essence. And you love finding joy in the most interesting and unlikely places.

The Visionary Queen's Blessing: Clarity and Vision

The world is in dire need of this Queen's blessings. We are living through a time of unprecedented misinformation. There has been an erosion of trust in our institutions. The internet has become the wild west of our day, with every manner of expression and "lawlessness" going on unchecked because it happens online and not in real life. But as we've seen, what happens online doesn't stay online. Cyber bullying of children that has led to suicide. All-encompassing conspiracy theories have led to political violence and insurrection. Reality feels less solid with each passing day. We are in need of a new vision for our human family, one that lifts us beyond the impulse of individual survival into the imperative of collective survival. The Visionary Queen and her access to both the mundane and mythical realms can re-cast the meaning of life. She can point to the act of consciously evolving Life itself through our individual and collective expressions. And when she joins forces with the Divine Queen as the basis for Reality, a new world can't be too far behind.

The Visionary Queen Summary Chart

Archetype: The Seer or Oracle

Location: Carotid Plexus (Brow)

Element: Light

Focus: Recognition, Intuition, Insight, Dreams, Visions

Orientation: Self-reflection

Basic Right: To See

Challenge: Illusion

Gifts: Wisdom and Insight

Shadow Queens: Foolish Queen (not enough) Arrogant Queen (too much)

Color: Indigo

Essential Oil: Sandalwood

Gemstone: Lapis

Energy Practice: Chakra Meditation

Evidence: The ability to see both the mundane and mythic perspective, to re-frame challenges and find joy

Blessing: Truth and Understanding

CHAPTER 18
THE DIVINE QUEEN

"Who is She? She is your power, your Feminine source.
Big Mama. The Goddess. The Great Mystery.
The web-weaver. The life force.
The first time, the twentieth time, you may not
recognize her. Or pretend not to hear.
As she fills your body with ripples of terror and delight.
But when she calls you will know you've been called.
Then it is up to you to decide if you will answer."

—Lucy H. Pearce, Burning Woman

The Divine Queen is the keeper of Mystery and Magic. Her archetypal energy is The Goddess. She supports us in our connection to the Divine. Her domain is Spirit. And her cannon is Spiritual Sovereignty.

When we master spiritual sovereignty, we have a vibrant and deeply personal spiritual experience of life. We may choose a particular set of religious beliefs to augment or deepen our personal experiences, or we may choose to keep things simpler. The perennial wisdom at the core of every major spiritual path is where we find the way of the mystic—direct experience with the Divine rather than dogma—and the joy and gifts of spiritual sovereignty.

The answers we seek are found within. When we connect with and receive guidance from our Soul or Higher Self, life is filled with meaning, mystery, and magic.

Spiritual sovereignty is all about embracing the gnosis (inner knowing of universal truth) that sits in the mystical center of all great religious traditions. Think of it as the hub in the center of the wheel and the various religious traditions as the spokes. It doesn't mean giving up your particular path, but it does mean allowing yourself to think critically about that path and any aspects or teachings that seek to keep you oppressed and disconnected from the Divine in you. It means giving yourself permission to use your inner compass and your inner connection with Spirit to guide your life. Coming to value your inner compass and your personal connection to Spirit, requires focusing your attention there more than on any external voice. It means carving your own path straight through the world's bullshit to the Source point within you.

We are all sorcerers and sorceresses. The question is where are we sourcing from? The only sustainable source is within because it is within that our connection to Spirit resides—that which is I Am or that which We Are. Here is where we come face-to-face with the deepest, truest version of our Self—our SoulSelf. Living from this place changes everything. Our lives are no longer our own, and that is just fine, more than fine. All of life becomes a prayer offered in devotion to the unfolding mystery operating in, through, and as us.

The Divine Queen's Challenge

In order to live fully in the wisdom and grace of the Divine Queen, we have to be wary of our attachments. According to the Buddha, all suffering comes from an inability to detach from our expectations of life. Consequently, we get attached to our idea of who we are or think we should be. We have attachments to who we want others to be. We have attachments to the way we want the world to be. We have expectations of every area of life to be a certain way. And when these expectations aren't met, we suffer. The Divine Queen simply doesn't have room to come into our lives if we are clinging too tightly to what we believe life should be like. Having a relationship with the Divine means being open to the mystery. We may never know why things turn out very differently than we hoped for, but if we can call on the power of the Visionary Queen to remind us that we might not be seeing things clearly, that small wondering can create a space for the love of the Divine Queen to show up for us.

The Divine Queen's Gifts

Being human can be wondrous and delightful. It can also be really tough. Life is a mixed bag and no matter how deeply we do our practices to keep us grounded and connected. There will be times when we lose our shizzle and come undone. It is in these moments when the Divine Queen's loving embrace is the most luscious and loving medicine. She brings with her Divine Grace, allowing us to find and feel compassion for ourselves and others. She whispers to our hearts that Love will carry the day, especially when it doesn't look like it will. She reminds us to look within and lean into the mystery and magic of the Divine Feminine path we have been walking. In her arms we find all we need to rest, to wait, to restore ourselves, and then to move forward once again.

THE SHADOW QUEENS

It is possible to have too much of a good thing. Even with the energy of the Divine Queen we can hit the space of diminishing returns when we forget that the whole point of knowing her is to bring her presence squarely and palpably into our own bodies. Too much emphasis on expanding our consciousness up and out will lead to the Disembodied Queen. This Queen may feel blissed out and high on Love, but she is completely ineffective where it matters most in the arena of human affairs. Her favorite pastime is spiritual bypassing when it comes to doing her own work and spiritual shaming when it comes to others. Because she disowns her own human nature, she can't stand to see humanness in others. She performs her spirituality and says all the right things, but in reality she avoids responsibility for her own growth like the plague.

If she's operating in a traditional religious expression, you may find her on several committees at her synagogue or church. She never misses a worship service. But her heart is hard and her words uncharitable. She's content to leave things, "in God's hands," without realizing she owns a pair of God's hands. If she's more spiritual than religious, you may find her compulsively attending pujas, kirtans, yoga classes and spiritual workshops. She never stops long enough to integrate any of the teachings, rather she's just seeking to maintain her spiritual high. In her mind, the mundane world isn't worth much and she prefers to hang out only in feel-good land. This Queen uses her privilege to shield her from the everyday work of Sovereign Service. And so, like all the other shadow Queens, she is really an un-sovereign. As you seek to bring the Divine Queen more fully into your life and expand your awareness into the mystical realms, take care not to banish your connection to and compassion for your own and others humanity.

On the flipside, Empty Queen is trapped into a two-dimensional understanding of life. She can't connect with anything other than what she can touch. Her life-focus is on her own carnal comforts. The right shoes, the right car, these are the things that bring her comfort. And in the end they are no comfort at all. The house, the boat, the jewelry can all be lost in an instant, leaving behind the gaping hole they tried to fill. This Queen is often in danger of succumbing to substance abuse. Any friend of Bill W. who has worked their way through a 12-step recovery program understands addiction as primarily a spiritual disease. The spiritual void that is at the heart of all addictions usually has its root in unresolved trauma and an attempt to find relief from the pain they cause. Whether its sex, shopping, work, or drugs and alcohol, the relief is temporary, and the addict eventually feels the Empty Queen taking up residence inside her. Because grace is ever-present, it's never too late for healing to happen. But the farther we go down the rabbit hole of looking for a physical solution to a spiritual problem, the harder it is to find to find your way home.

A Personal Perspective: My Physical Sovereignty Map

Whether you still practice the faith tradition of your childhood, or you have moved on to something new, or to nothing at all, we cannot escape the call of our Soul to come home to ourselves. Maybe you feel you have this department well in hand. Or maybe you feel lost. Ultimately we have to forge our own unique relationship with what we think of as the Divine. Whatever is true for us, The Divine Queen comes to us to re-awaken to the truth of our being, and we are lost no more.

After getting divorced I struggled with finding a way to continue on with my Catholic faith. The divorced Catholic is like a stitch out of time. I had fallen out of attending Sunday mass, and the holidays were particularly rough that first year as a newly divorced woman. I didn't want to attend the extended family gatherings and face my cousins and their perfectly beautiful families. I had already skipped Thanksgiving and Christmas was dragging me under. I always enjoyed mass at Christmas time, with its uplifting message of hope at the birth of baby Jesus so I decided to go to midnight mass. I chose the chapel at the University of St. Thomas near where I was living. I reasoned that since it served college students, perhaps the priest's message would be more relatable than the ones about the sin of abortion and the need to not beat your wife. Unfortunately, I was treated to a history lesson rather than a hopeful message.

The Bible reading and the priest's homily dryly catalogued the line of Jesus' ancestors. There were only three women mentioned in the entire list. Two were considered whores, and the other had a virgin birth. Not very relatable. To make matters worse, the entire line, except for Mary, came from Joseph's family, who, according to the Good Book, wasn't even Jesus' birth father. In this telling Mary, it appeared, was just a convenient vessel in a man's world. It was the last straw for me. After that I abandoned the Catholic church as an institution, but not my love of the saints and mystics or the core of Jesus' message. I eventually found my way to Unity, which offered me a more relevant version of Christianity that was also open to the spiritual truths found across all religions. I cried my way through the first two months of service as I found myself welcomed into a deeply loving relationship with God. I learned I was loved no matter my mistakes and that I could grow into the Divine being that I was.

This church became a powerful spiritual home for me. It was listening to Rev. Howard Caesar's series on The Four Agreements that led me to my oneness moment. It was where I met and married my husband. It was the new employer I moved to when I was pregnant with Sophia, taking on the role of Executive Director. My time there healed my spiritual wounding beyond what I thought was possible. It was as much a learning center as a church, and we hosted an incredible lineup of speakers. I had the honor of meeting and studying with Deepak Chopra, Wayne Dyer, Julia Cameron, Oriah Mountain Dreamer, Marianne Williamson, Joe Dispenza, and eventually Don Miguel Ruiz. But just as impactful for me were the many lesser-known teachers who came to present workshops and classes.

In one of those workshops, I learned of a new creation story. In this story it was said that humans were here to give our souls an experience of contrast (meaning life in 3D, the physical or manifest realm), which I had heard and resonated with. But the part that was new to me explained that we were supposed to arrive here with full awareness and memory of our true nature as a Divine Soul.

Instead, something went wrong. Now we are stuck here in a crazy funhouse with strange mirrors that give us a distorted image of ourselves with no sense of our true identity to anchor us. My Whole body tingled with "truth-bumps" as I listened. The takeaway for me was this:

Our Soul connection is our birthright.

This was meant to be an adventure, challenging but fun as we were meant to be consciously connected with our truest self! Without that connection it can feel like flying blind. While I might not be able to replicate the fullest connection we were meant to have according to this story, I was already well on the way to hooking up some kind of hack. Doing the work to actively connect with my Soul has provided me with what I can only describe as an internal guidance system—like a GPS from my Soul. I have a direct connection to Divine Guidance now. I am so grateful that my Divine Queen operates from this powerful connection.

Every day the Divine Queen is calling us home to the deepest parts of ourselves. But sometimes it may seem like that voice feels far, far away. Some days it can feel as though we will never find peace or grow into what we hoped our lives would be. Instead, we may come to believe that we have to settle. Settle for less joy, for watered down love, for unspoken and unlived dreams, for the pain of dysfunctional relationships and unsatisfying sex, or the lack of the basic human right to feel safe in our own skin!

The Divine Queen is here to say, "NO, my beloved! You do not have to settle anymore!"

And the best part is, if we make an effort to connect deeply with her, she will show us exactly how we can shift ourselves and our lives so that we are thriving rather than surviving, so that we laugh often, love openly, and live authentically.

THE DIVINE QUEEN WRITING EXERCISE: TAKING INVENTORY

Spiritual sovereignty is all about your soul connection. It is the fundamental knowing and owning of your Soul Essence, that part of you that is one with the Divine, the Source of Life, the Mystery. It is often the most hard-won of the seven sovereignties because humans have done so much forgetting and worked so hard to obscure this Truth.

Think back on your early years. In what ways was your magnificence hidden from you? Were your religious experiences uplifting or shaming? How did they play out once you got home? Were the values you heard at your house of worship consistently followed? How much hypocrisy did you see? Did you sense as a youngster that something bigger had to exist? Many young children report having had deeply spiritual and even psychic experiences only to find them waved off by adults. Were you one of those children? Or have you felt lost and adrift as long as you can remember?

Was spirituality and religion treated as hogwash or cultish beliefs? Or was it a safe place for you? Did your family give their power away to religious leaders and doctrine? Or was there room for questioning? What happened when something came up in the family that was at odds with your faith tradition's teachings? Was their shame, betrayal, choosing the teachings over the family? Was your faith experience the cornerstone of your success, the barrier to your happiness, or something in between? What is your connection with something greater than yourself like now?

Consider, what is your Spiritual Sovereignty Map? Take some time to reflect on the questions above and write out a description of your own Spiritual Sovereignty Map. Use these questions to help to uncover what work might be waiting for you as you seek to embody the Divine Queen within you.

On a scale from 1 - 10 with 1 being the least and 10 being the most:

How important was having a spiritual life growing up? ____

How much room was there for you to explore your own path? ____

How connected do you feel with your Soul and/or the Divine now? ____

How satisfied are you with your spiritual life? ____

THE DIVINE QUEEN ENERGY PRACTICE: SOUL CONNECTION

The daily practice of connecting to your Soul Essence can be extremely rewarding. There are an infinite number of ways to make this connection including meditation, contemplation, using prayer beads or traditional prayer, or chanting and singing. I like to make it physical by imagining capturing my Soul in my hands and bringing her into my body. There is a Native American practice I like that invites us to imagine that there is a unique sunray that belongs only to us. Within that ray is our Soul's unique frequency. To do this practice stand with your feet shoulder width apart and drop into your womb and heart. Set the intention of connecting to your Soul. You may already feel that connection, or you may feel nothing at all. Either is okay. Next bring your attention to the sunlight streaming onto the planet. Tune into your unique ray that is on its way to you now. Stretch your arms out and bring up over your head. As your hands get closer, imagine capturing your unique sun's ray between them. Holding it between your hands, slowly lower your hands all the way to your abdomen while imagining that ray is entering your body and moving down through all of your chakra centers. Tune into how the unique frequency that belongs to you is organizing and harmonizing the energies within your chakras, your body, and your auric field. Allow yourself to enjoy this pleasant sensation. When you are ready, say the following affirmations out loud:

I am a walking expression of the Divine and Divinity resides within me.

I take time to connect with my Soul Essence and my unique frequency.

I receive guidance quickly and easily and live a life of never-ending Grace.

Every moment is filled with untold magic and mystery and I see the Divine inner wisdom at play in all things.

The Divine Queen Anointing Oil: Blue Lotus

To enhance your experience of the energy practices and the writing exercises, apply the Blue Lotus Chakra Oil to the top of your head for seven to twenty-one days in a row morning and night. Blue Lotus oils is one of the most treasured oils of the ancient Egyptians. It won't take much as this sacred oil is quite strong. Apply some to your wrists and even under your nose to smell the scent throughout the day, especially in moments that when you feel disconnected from your Soul Essence. This scent is quite strong so just use a tiny dab. This holy oil works as a homeopathic remedy to activate and enliven the crown chakra. It balances and harmonizes the chakra's energetic expression. This helps you avoid being under or over expressed (and flipping into the shadow Queens) so that you can stay firmly connected to the Divine Queen. All of the chakra oils are available on my website at **RimaBonario.com**.

Going Deeper

The Divine Queen often appears to us in times of need. Sometimes she disguises herself so that we can hear her message. Back before I knew anything about the feminine aspects of the Divine, she showed up as a softer, more embodied version of what I called God. I had long since given up the idea that the Divine had any kind of gender. I saw it more like Source energy. I hadn't really considered what it might be like to embody such an energy. And even though it was obviously genderless to me, I still called it by the name I learned as a child. Regardless of how she clothed herself, I can look back now and see it was an early visit from the Divine Feminine version of Source.

On this particular day in 2001, I was deep in the throes of yet another pity party. Two years previously, I had left my marriage and begun to do deep healing work of figuring out exactly who I was and what I wanted from life. Even after two years of therapy and the support of a couple of 12-step recovery programs, I was no closer to happiness. I was a divorced early 30-something who had just ended another romance in a string of ridiculous relationships. And it seemed as though I was destined to continue repeating the same lessons over and over again. When was I going to grow up? When was I going to get a life? When, when, when? I was emotionally and physically exhausted.

Lying on my bed that day, it seemed that I was a perpetual student in the school of hard knocks. I was nonplussed. Hadn't I earned my PhD by now? And just when and why did I enroll in this school anyway? I had heard that maybe our souls choose these lessons before we are born for some higher purpose. I was ruminating on this idea and wondering what on earth (or heaven) my soul must have been thinking when another thought occurred to me. What if we weren't in some big Earth School at all? What if life was more like summer camp than Pain U? Maybe we come here for a while to learn some new skills, have some fun, meet some other cool souls and then head back home when the summer is over. If true, it made sense that we might have summer romance heart breaks, or endure teasing, bug bites, and scraped knees.

Well, I thought, if life was like some spiritual summer camp, it appeared I hadn't landed at some cushy camp in upstate New York. No, my life-camp seemed more like an episode out of the reality show *Survivor*. A low wail emerged from deep within me as tears sprang to my eyes. "Okay, okay enough already, I want to come home! Now! This isn't any fun anymore!" I yelled as my tears turned into sobs. After the crying stopped I laid there feeling emptier and more alone than ever.

Then, in a flash, my awareness shifted, and something began to rise to the surface. It was as though I remembered something very important about my true nature. All at once I could see that my soul was cut from Divine cloth, and so in the deepest part of me, I was Divine too. For just a moment it was as though I was inside God's head (not that God really had a head) and I knew that God was tired. 14 billion years of creation was a lot of work and The Creator was in need of a vacation. How better to get away from it all than by taking up residence in billions of small pieces in amnesiac humans on planet Earth? If this startling thought was true, it could only mean one thing: I'm God on Vacation!

It was a shocking line of thinking at that time in my life, one that pushed right up against my Catholic upbringing. I had no knowledge of the Divine Queen that resides within me at the time. It was literally coming from some part of me that I had no idea existed, something that was beyond the bounds of what I thought of as "me" and "my mind." But it rang so true that in my heart of hearts I just knew it was right.

Oh my, I thought, here I was on vacation from all that responsibility, and I was blowing my time off on all this petty garbage and relationship drama. At that moment I resolved to start enjoying my vacation. I had called out for help and gotten an answer that was worth really living for. I was now in it not just to survive, but to thrive. I committed to creating a new life for myself, one that was fun, enjoyable, relaxing, interesting, and adventurous - in short, a life that had all of the qualities that I would expect from a vacation. And I was up for the challenge of living *sacred* instead of living *scared*.

But it wasn't as simple as just resolving to change. As I crossed the threshold into my new life and ran straight into a brick wall, a wall many years in the making. I could see how I had become attached to my past woundedness. It was part of my identity, so I kept drawing situations and circumstances into my life that mirrored that woundedness. I could see how by staying stuck, by hanging on to my identity as a victim, I was now victimizing myself. But the price of keeping my victim and martyr status intact had simply gotten too high. I knew I had to find a new identity. It took strength and courage to see clearly when needed to change and become open to new possibilities. With the help of some amazing teachers, and a tenacious inner spirit for the first time in my adult life, I felt a taste of inner freedom. While I wasn't completely free from every limiting idea of who I thought I was. I was free enough to begin exploring more deeply who I was once letting go of the victim/martyr identity.

Who was I really? What were my likes and dislikes? If I was having a Divine Vacation then I certainly had the freedom and flexibility to decide whether I would like to go cruising, sailing, surfing, dancing, sky-diving, or anything else under the sun. It was a time of true self-discovery. Two decades before it had a name, I basically sought to "Marie Kondo" my life!

Marie Kondo is a Japanese organization expert who took the world by storm with her Konmari method: a suggestion that we can eliminate a lot of the junk in our homes just by asking whether a particular belonging "sparks joy" and releasing it if not. I didn't have the benefit of her language, but I was determined to examine my life and keep only what brought me joy. At this point on the journey, I got stuck. If you have tried Konmari you know it can be shocking to see how much mediocrity we surround ourselves with, and my life was no exception.

I unleashed a lot of dormant creativity. I made collages. I took up salsa dancing. I ate exotic food. I studied world religions. I listened, I learned, I lived. The freedom to explore all that this marvelous world has to offer without the past fears and judgments that had held me back was exhilarating. It was a rich and exciting time.

With this freedom came new responsibilities. Since I was God on Vacation, I couldn't blame the external world for the quality of my inner life, I alone was responsible for whether I was feeling pain or joy. I could see it was up to me, guided by my connection to the Sacred within me, to create a life based on what was real and true. I wanted an authentic life that I could live without a moment's hesitation, without fear, without doubt, and I was willing to make it happen. Nearly two decades later I am living the life I had envisioned that day, seeking to embody the Divine Queen on a daily basis. It's a work in progress for sure. And a labor of love that I am honored to fulfill.

Additional Connecting Practices

If you are overcome disembodied and blissed out or empty an unable to connect with your Soul, consider these rescue remedy practices to bring you back to the Divine Queen:

- Take a walk in nature and allow yourself to feel awe for the beauty of creation.
- Look up guided meditations on YouTube and play one or two.
- Have a conversation with your Divine Queen. Tell her what you need and ask for her help.

- Draw inspiration from the life of a saint, prophet or spiritual teacher.
- Spend time with a baby, there's nothing like new life to restore one's faith in the miracle of life.

Evidence of the Divine Queen

When you are embodying the Divine Queen, you feel connected to your Soul. While you may not hear or see anything unusual, you will have a sense that you are not alone. You will experience life as an interconnected set of overlapping energy fields. And as such information can be rapidly transmitted from where it is to where you are. In this way you can get answers and information that you need very quickly in what feel like miraculous ways. Life will take on a higher meaning and every day takes on an air of sacredness. You may find it much easier to commit to and follow through on your devotional and spiritual practices. Living in communion with the Divine feels fun and natural. And while you have greater compassion and empathy for those who suffer, including yourself, you also understand the bigger picture at play. As philosopher and author Ken Wilber says, "It hurts more but bothers you less." Consequently, you are able to take action and be of loving support to those in need because you aren't paralyzed or overwhelmed by the sheer volume of human suffering. You find practical ways to help others to experience a bit of heavenly on earth.

The Divine Queen's Blessing: Transmitting Light and Love

As you make progress embodying the energy of the Divine Queen, you will become capable of transmitting the light and love of the Divine. Your presence will be filled with more than just your own positive energy, it will be imbued with the radiant love that comes from the Divine Feminine Source in the Ground of Being. You may even feel how this energy activates your heart and womb. I often feel a welling up or tingling in my body. With love and intention, you will be able to create a coherent field through the vibration and frequency of love. Others who come into your presence will feel calm and content. And as a bonus, you will feel a kind of bliss and joy that exists completely outside of circumstance. Not only will this enhance your good feelings, but it can have very positive effects on your emotional, physical, and mental health.

The Divine Queen Summary Chart

Archetype: The Goddess

Location: Cerebral Cortex (Crown)

Element: Thought

Focus: Union with Higher Power/Divinity

Orientation: Self-knowledge

Basic Right: To Know and to Learn

Challenge: Attachment

Gifts: Life-Force (Shakti) and Pleasure

Shadow Queens: Empty Queen (not enough) Bliss-Ninny Queen (too much)

Color: Violet

Essential Oil: Blue Lotus

Gemstone: Amethyst

Energy Practice: Soul Connection/Unique Sunray

Evidence: Regular guidance and connection with Spirit and Soul

Blessing: Transmitting Light and Love

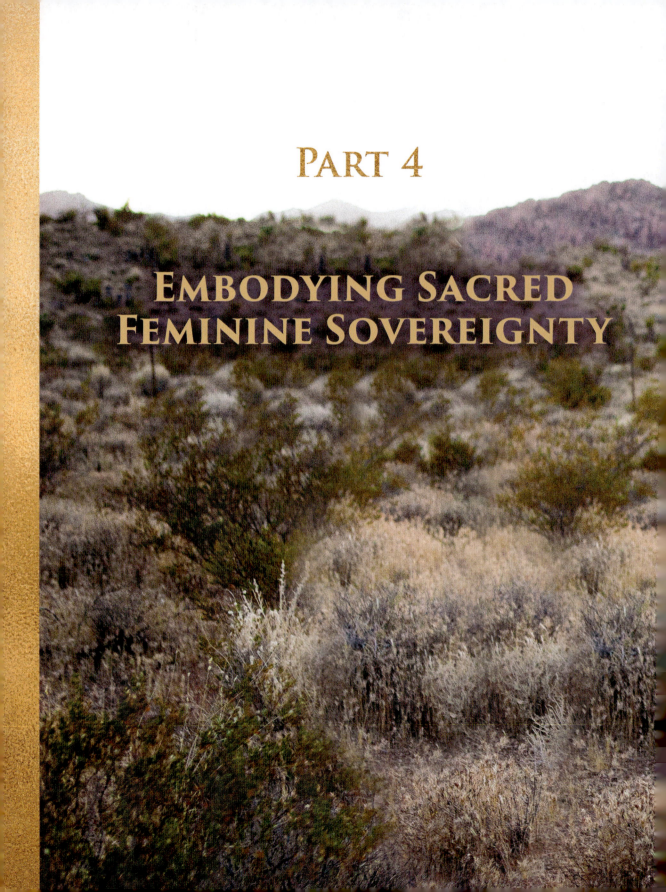

Part 4

Embodying Sacred Feminine Sovereignty

"It is time my child.

It is you.
You are She.
You are Me.
There's no one left to wait for...
Let us begin."

If you close your eyes for a moment, and slow your breath, perhaps you will feel her arms around you, maybe like the feathers of wings, they will caress you.

If you quiet your mind for a moment and still your thoughts, perhaps you will hear her words inside your mind, maybe like rain nourishing parched earth.

If you open your heart for a moment, letting go of fear and doubt, perhaps you will know She is within you, maybe always has been, loving you forever.

So what now?
This is the hard part: Integration

Working with the energy of the Divine Feminine to live as the Sovereign of your Life is like nothing we humans usually deal with. Her currency isn't in driving with single minded focus, although She isn't opposed to you using that tool on her behalf.

*She prefers to dance Her way to Her destination. Her desire is to create art while
She creates life.
And now she has come for YOU, my dear Queen.*

She is asking you now to climb the stairs of the dais before you. To notice the hands of those who have come to help you ascend. Look around and see the audience of many helpers who have been there to support you, and will continue to be as you rule. Approach your throne, dear Queen. Notice how it looks. Notice what you feel.

No matter what it is, the time has come to turn and face the room. And firmly plant your seat on the throne of your life.

*Deep breath now.
You can do this.
Yes, my love. You belong here.
We have all been waiting for you to arrive.*

Listen, my love. Your Queen's Council has gathered before you and they are speaking to you now:

All Hail to Her Majesty!

Breathe it in. You are HOME!

"To darkness are they doomed who worship only the body, and to greater darkness are they who worship only the spirit."

—The Upanishads

CHAPTER 19
Maintaining Your Sovereignty

Now that you have met the seven Queens of your council, it's all about integration and maintenance through devotional practice. Maintaining sovereignty is like taking vitamins, it requires daily intentional action. Accessing your Queendoms and living from your Soul-Map requires commitment and presence.

Much of what ails the world is a kind of laziness about being conscious. humans have a tendency to seek out the path of least resistance. That can look like grabbing a bottle of wine and the TV remote. We check out or medicate rather than being present to ourselves and our lives. Perhaps it would be more generous to say it's a kind of safety mechanism rather than laziness. The habit of numbing out and going unconscious can look very different from person to person. Here is a small list of ways people can check out:

- Overwork, being over-scheduled
- Food: over-eating or depriving oneself
- Not getting enough sleep
- Being codependent—caring more about other people's behaviors/emotional state than your own
- Pursuing sexual connections or other forms of pleasure to the point of losing oneself
- Excessive self-criticism
- Outraging over things beyond your control
- Hyper focus on materialism, stuff, money, etc.
- Self-isolating
- Social media scrolling or trolling

I believe that we use these behaviors to cope with the inner trauma we experience when we lose connection with our sovereignty. This can happen in childhood if we don't have a safe environment in which to express ourselves. Of course, abuse steals our sense of sovereignty. But even well-intentioned caregivers can dampen our sense of self-sovereignty by encouraging us to live a life that makes them feel comfortable rather than helping us discover what brings us alive and joyfully connects us to our soul.

I spent the next three days recovering physically, all the while berating myself mercilessly. It started out as a lament for having let this kid push me too hard. Next it was a barrage of insults about how weak and feeble I was physically and mentally. Finally, it concluded with the sinkhole of unworthiness. I was going to be pudgy and alone forever and I just needed to accept my fate. I just wasn't worthy of love, support, a healthy body, or a relationship. It was painful on so many levels. I continued paying for that gym membership for a decade and rarely used it. I was most definitely not in my sovereignty.

Fast forward about twenty years and I tried going back to the gym. My husband had begun working out heavily. He suggested we get a family membership to Lifetime Fitness. By this time, I had been to some nice spas and had fallen in love with eucalyptus steam rooms. This gym had one, so I agreed. We would go together as a family once or twice a week. But it didn't become my own until I created a way of stepping into it that was mine and mine alone. I decided to dress in workout clothes first thing in the morning on Monday, Wednesday, and Friday and after dropping my daughter at school I would head straight to the gym. I told myself I only needed to walk on the treadmill for 20 minutes and do some yoga moves, then I could sit in the steam room for twenty minutes. It was the right balance of effort and reward for me in the beginning so that I looked forward to going.

After a couple of weeks, I started walking thirty minutes. Sometimes I would watch a TV show on my phone and walk for an hour, always followed by my yoga exercises and then 20 minutes in the steam room. Eventually, I was drawn back to the weight machines and started working out my lower body. In about three month, my body shape changed considerably. But what was most important was the change in how I approached working out. It had become a devotional practice versus a punishment for not being fit enough, skinny enough, or desirable enough. My relationship with my practice was first and foremost about rewarding myself with a luxurious steam room during the harsh Kansas winters. I was completely in my sovereignty. And I loved it.

But a funny thing happened. They were offering free fitness tests at the gym. My husband got one and he thought I should too. They took fat measurements with calipers, ran me on a treadmill, and had me stretch over a reassuring tape. The report came back saying, among other things that I can't recall, my body age was three years older than my actual age. Instantly, I stopped feeling like what I was doing was enough. The old urge to push myself showed up. I hired a fitness instructor to teach me how to use kettlebells, thinking that this was my chance to finally get really fit, to be able to actually build muscles that could be seen by others. My husband was getting shredded, and I wanted some of that for me. I didn't have the awareness to understand that what had been a loving devotional practice was now shifting into another punishment-driven activity rooted in not feeling good enough. It only took two lessons for me to injure myself with the kettlebells because, obviously, punishment yields pain. I damaged my back badly enough that I wasn't able to continue with the devotional practice that had worked so well for me. And once again I felt like a failure. I had fallen into the trap of giving away my sovereignty once again.

I know now that what works best for me in physical, mental, emotional, and spiritual practice is a gentle, authentic approach that brings me joy. If it doesn't bring me joy to do it, I listen carefully and think long and hard about saying yes. Sometimes the joy isn't immediate. Still, if the slog to get to the payoff is too harsh, I know better than to force myself to go ahead with it. I must always move at my own pace.

To this day, my daughter and husband crush it at the gym. They love it and it brings them both so much joy. I will on occasion participate in a way that works for me, but I must always be on guard for the subtle pressure to keep up out of a desire to connect with them and be part of their joy. This is a life-long effort for me. One that I have come to see as an integral part of my daily devotional practice.

Being committed to discerning what is and isn't for me is a powerful practice. Paying attention to the signals within is hard work when we have been trained for years to ignore our own knowing and reach instead for what others want from us and for us. The key for me was to give up the pressure of trying to be sovereign all the time and instead focus on catching myself when I was off the path and gently make the shift back into my sovereignty.

One day a young monk arrived at the hidden monastery where a guru of legend lived. He was determined to ask the question that had burned within him. When they came face to face the young monk said, "Master, please tell me the secret you have that keeps you so centered." The guru laughed and his eyes sparkled as he replied, "Never centered! Always moving back to center."

There is no such thing as staying in our sovereignty 24-7. It's not fix-o-dent and forget it! Sovereignty is about awareness. Awareness is the oldest and best friend we have. It is the one un-changeable thing: all else changes. And it is the most reliable thing we have. If you are going to embody your Queen energy, you must cultivate a relationship with your awareness. The breath is the second most reliable thing we have. Use the breath to help you move energy and find answers. Pause, breathe, and the awareness will follow.

Stay present in your body and be gentle, but also be a warrior. Gentle energy is good. Warrior energy is good. There is no set strategy to know which to be when. A sovereign life requires that we engage, that we stay awake. You will know when to be gentle and when to be a warrior if you lean into life and engage with the moment.

To do that you will need to stay awake. But here's the thing: you will fall asleep. Pay attention to yourself and others and notice when you and they go to sleep. Then wake up! Again and again. Be there for yourself. Be there for others. One great way to do this is to ask yourself what is worth staying awake for. Find out what it is that you value most and what are you willing to endure or give up to get more of it.

The ultimate goal is to be both awake *and* relaxed. It's a paradox, really. Lean in to living the paradox of being and becoming. When you have access to all seven of the Queen archetypes you can be grounded, creative, empowered, loving, expressive, intuitive, and guided in any given moment, or even all at the same time. But it requires that we surrender to the practice of loving ourselves.

> *It is the devotional act of loving ourselves that is our practice.*

In devotional practice we experience ourselves as love through such surrendered actions as dance, meditation, prayer, anointing with oils, sacred bathing, or yoga. The form is not as important as the devotional act itself. Practice is about surrendering to something bigger than ourselves, which might not always feel immediately good. I don't always enjoy doing my banking, but when my books are balanced, my house is clean, and there's food in the fridge, I feel peaceful and responsible, which brings me great joy.

The devotion is both to me and to something larger. Whether you call that God, Goddess, The Universe, or Spirit is unimportant. As you offer time attuned to That Which Is, what you will find with a great thrill is That Which Is you, too! Therefore, all devotional practices of self-loving and self-care, if done consciously, are ultimately a deep form of devotion to the Divine.

When I love myself fiercely and make room for what my body needs, even for what it wants, I am healthier, happier, and more impactful. I deeply desire a more gentle, healthy, and loving world. So my first and most profound task is to create a gentle, healthy, and loving environment for myself, my body, and my family.

I teach my students who struggle with a devotional self-care practice to start by committing to seven minutes of self-care. These small, super-doses of self-care seem more manageable when you are first working to develop a devotional practice. My two favorite devotional practices right now are sacred bathing and anointing myself with sacred oils. Almost every morning, I start my day with a 20–40-minute hot bath. I add Myrrh, Frankincense and Golden Water oils to my bath water and then I either put on a guided meditation, inspiring music, or sit in silence. It's a luxurious experience and it's been a life-changing practice for me. I enter my day feeling so nourished and well-loved.

The following pages offer you 77 ideas for seven-minutes of self-care. See which ones call to you. It's worth the effort to find what works for you. Remember: the form is unimportant. It is the act of self-love which is the devotional practice.

1. Drink a cup of hot water with lemon first thing in the morning.
2. Take a 10-15 minute walk around the block.
3. Meditate or pray to connect with your Soul after waking before looking at any devices.

4. Lay out in your backyard (on the earth if possible) for 5-15 minutes.
5. Make a doctor's appointment that you have been putting off.
6. Schedule a massage.
7. Ask for a hug.
8. Set a timer for twenty minutes and read a fictional (even trashy!) novel.
9. Listen to an uplifting podcast from your favorite spiritual teacher.
10. Put on some uplifting music you like and move your body for 5 minutes.
11. Change into something more comfortable, or if you hang out in sweats all the time, put on something that makes you feel sexy.
12. Cuddle with a pet or a person for ten minutes to get some oxytocin going.
13. Take your car through the carwash.
14. Drink cool water with lemon throughout the day.
15. Eat a piece of fruit slowly, paying close attention to how it tastes.
16. Schedule a tea, coffee, or lunch date with a girlfriend.
17. Take 5 slow, deeps breaths.
18. Turn the phone off for 30 minutes to an hour (and put it out of reach) while focus on completing a task that has been nagging at you.
19. Place your hands on any part of you that feels achy or emotional and say, "I love you."
20. File your nails.
21. Give yourself a foot massage, or book one with a professional.
22. Do a mud mask or give yourself a facial.
23. Take a warm bath with Epsom salts and your favorite essential oil.
24. Shake out your hands for 30 seconds to move some energy—it works!
25. Yawn and/or take some big sighing breaths with sound.
26. Do a few jumps to enliven yourself.
27. Eat something healthy and delicious.
28. Call a friend you haven't spoken to in a while.
29. Dab essential oil on wrists and temples (lavender for calming, peppermint/orange for energy).

30. Do your favorite craft or art project.
31. Take a 20-minute nap.
32. Go to bed 15 minutes earlier than you normally do.
33. Avoid all screen time for 1 hour before bed.
34. Light a candle and make a wish, hold the feeling of its completion for seventeen seconds.
35. Turn the lights down low after 8 p.m.
36. Do 2-3 yoga poses or gentle stretches on the floor.
37. Listen to soothing music for five minutes.
38. Dedicate a place in your home to your spiritual life and decorate it accordingly. This could be as simple as a single shelf in your bookcase or as big as a spare bedroom.
39. Put a pillow behind you on your office chair to make it more comfortable.
40. Go through your underwear drawer and toss out any old ones.
41. Buy yourself a plant or flowers, or bring some in from your yard.
42. Make a list of 8 things you are grateful for.
43. Massage your earlobes and ears for 60 seconds.
44. Skip the alcohol or sugar for a day or two, or a week or two.
45. Make an appointment to see a financial advisor.
46. Get a physical or visit a naturopath for a health assessment.
47. Rest your eyes for 5 minutes.
48. Use the alarm feature on your phone to set up several chimes throughout your day to remind you to stand and stretch, drink water, or eat a healthy snack as you work.
49. Lay in bed on Saturday or Sunday morning for an extra hour or more just resting.
50. Delete something from your calendar.
51. Color a page from an adult coloring book.
52. Sit quietly and watch a fire burn (in a fireplace or outdoor fire pit, or even on YouTube).
53. Touch something soft, or rub it against your cheek, and really enjoy the sensation.

54. Gently squeeze and massage the area between your eyebrows for 2 minutes.
55. Put a post-it note on your mirror with a loving message for yourself.
56. Join a circle of women for connection (book club, coaching circle, walking group).
57. Diffuse some essential oils in a diffuser while you work.
58. Roll on a foam roller for 1-3 minutes to loosen tight back muscles.
59. Take a probiotic to help your digestion.
60. Tell someone you love them (it could be you!)
61. Try out a new restaurant.
62. Drink a smoothie or fresh pressed juice.
63. Hire a service like Molly Maid to clean your house for you (just once or ongoing).
64. Hang a key and purse hook by the door you use most so you always know where they are.
65. Add something beautiful to your, office, altar or prayer corner.
66. Eat a meal by candlelight.
67. Sit under a tree or under the stars for 10 minutes and soak in the energy of nature.
68. Buy a new pillow (or decorative pillow) for your bed.
69. Pull a card from an oracle card deck.
70. Journal for 5 minutes about your dreams for the future.
71. Put soft socks or slippers on your feet and enjoy the softness.
72. Leave the radio off while driving and focus on finding beauty in your surroundings.
73. Find (or print) a happy picture of yourself as a child and put it where you can see it.
74. Pick up an unfinished book you'd like to finish and read a chapter.
75. Give yourself permission to throw out foods you have that you know aren't healthy.
76. Delete or unfollow/unfriend someone who has been aggravating you on social media.
77. Light a candle that smells good.

"*Women, if the soul of the nation is to be saved,
I believe you must become its soul.*"

—Coretta Scott King

CHAPTER 20
SOVEREIGNTY IN ACTION

Loving ourselves deeply is just the first step on the journey to embodying sacred feminine sovereignty. As we seek to ever-more perfectly fulfill that task, the call to bring that love into the world won't wait for us to be perfect. The devotional self-practice must sooner rather than later turn outward, less it get twisted into thinking love of the self is all there is.

You have a role to play in the larger world. And the world is waiting for exactly you, exactly now. If you are raring to go, that's wonderful. If you are feeling anxious or scared, that's wonderful too. No matter what, the Goddess is standing here, right beside you, waiting for you to take that first step outward. With a never-ending supply of love, the Divine Feminine holds you now, loves you now, launches you now into your future.

It will take patience and initiative.

It will take action and rest.

It will take commitment and surrender.

They say what is within the cup is what pours out: if you bump a coffee cup, coffee spills out. If you bump a teacup, tea spills out. So if there is hate inside, hate will spill out. If there is anger inside, anger spills out. If there is peace inside, peace spills out. So naturally you want to cultivate peace within you. But like tea or coffee, it is meant to be drunk and Life desires to drink its fill of you. Whether or not you are ready, it will have you.

STAYING COOL BUT NOT CLOSED

If your peace only persists because you choose not to engage with the world, then all you have done is altered your mood. You have not actually done the work to arrive at inner peace. If you do not do the practices that contribute to lasting inner peace, you will have to edit your life to maintain your good mood. That is an exhausting and lonely road.

The only kind of inner-peace worth having is the kind that comes from being with what is real and emerging, to allow it in, the joy and the grief, the desire and the fear, to break yourself open so you can feel all the feels, and then find a way to come back to center.

When you are real, when you are willing to make mistakes as you carve a new way forward, you are showing up strong and taking a stand for a new way of being.

The world is messy. People are messy. I am messy. You are messy. Life is not a Disney movie. If our good mood requires it to be so, then we are never going to find the peace and joy we really want. Worse than that, it sets up a sort of zero-sum game: It's either my peace of mind or yours. If hearing about your pain, your plight, or your illness interrupts my peace of mind, then I will shut you out so I can stay "peaceful."

But the Queen cannot do this. She knows that she can't sit back and let it work itself out. She must make choices that consider the whole. She must lead. We must lead.

If being asked to wear a face covering makes me feel afraid, or controlled, or inconvenienced, I will say no in order to maintain my inner peace. If examining my conscious or unconscious beliefs about the way our cultural and institutional systems disempower or treat BIPOC and LGBTQ+ people differently makes me uncomfortable, I will avoid it in the name of peace. But this is not peace.

If my inner peace is that fragile, I don't actually have inner peace. I am just in a good mood. And we all know how easily those can come and go. The conclusion is this for me: I must be devoted to my self-care while at the same time be devoted to the care and concern of others. They must go hand-in-hand. The simple truth is this: *I do not have to choose.*

That is perhaps the greatest lie that has been told to humans throughout time. You must choose between what is good for you and what is good for others. You get yours. They will get theirs. But as we are coming to see, this is a fantasy.

How do you divide up the air? "I'll take mine clean, you can have yours dirty." How do we chop up the sea so I can keep mine from rising and allow yours to fend for itself? How do we build barriers to keep hate from infecting the data streams that flow invisibly between homes and nations? It is impossible. There just aren't enough walls, towers, or armies to keep part of the world safe while the rest languishes. I hear some are seeking to move to Mars. Colonists throughout time have sought their fortunes across the miles, but eventually the chickens come home to roost. There is no escaping it. Wherever we go, there we are.

In truth, we are completely interconnected. Justice for others is justice for me. Health for others is health for me. Safety for all is the way forward. So I will give all I have, do what I can with what I have, to help us all live better. Starting with myself and moving outward. For I am my brothers' and sisters' keeper. And the keeper of myself...

As we watch around us and see governments, businesses, families across the globe adjust to the shifting sands of early 21st century life, it's obvious we are collectively asking the question, "How shall we live together?"

We are being asked, "What kind of world do I want?" and "How much dysfunction am I willing to tolerate?" Perhaps even more importantly, "What am I willing to sacrifice to bring an end to that I don't wish to tolerate any longer?"

The Queen knows there are no easy answers to these questions, but they must be asked, and the answers pondered. Not so that we can solve it all in the snap of our fingers, but so that, at first, we can imagine a new world, and new way. If we can dream it, we can be it. And then we can bring it into being.

We can start with the small steps we take to be loving and joyful as often as possible. But that isn't enough. We have to use our *No,* as well as our *Yes!* We are in a time of reckoning and the Queen will do her duty to take an active role in the yes's and no's that must be spoken. Spiritual by-passing may want you to ignore wrongdoing so that you can keep a "high vibe." If you are unmoved by the callousness and carelessness of human existence in certain parts of the world, toward certain peoples, then you are not in high vibe mode, you are in escape mode.

But a word of caution as we head into the fray. The Queen doesn't trade in outrage-fueled "call-out culture" that thrives on the gossip mills of social media and virally shares suspicions of individuals in take-down style without knowing the full story. She looks for deliberate and fair-minded ways to hold people and institutions accountable for their errors, without ejecting from the tribe unless truly warranted.

These are the milestones a Queen looks for when there is a need for accountability:

- Acknowledgment of harm
- Sincere remorse and regret
- Honest interest in what would be better
- Willingness to seek support and remedies for growth
- Amends made and changed behavior that is sustained over time
- Celebration of a soul re-membered unto itself and welcoming them back into the community

Whether it is within our own hearts and families we do this work, or on a larger scale, it must be done. We can no longer turn the other way when otherwise good people do harm:

- In our homes
- In our schools
- In our neighborhoods and towns
- In our places of work
- In our places of worship
- In our systems of governance and our public spaces

It is our duty to take a stand. Yet, I can't deny that part of me hates that. Part of me recoils from that duty, that call. Truth be told, I just want to live a peaceful life, focus on expanding the love and bliss I have worked so hard to cultivate over the last few years, enjoy my family and friends, and take some cool vacations once in a while. But I also know that all of my work to make my life as amazing as it is, has to have meaning outside of just my personal gratification. It has to *serve*.

THE QUEEN IN ACTION

In my efforts to reconcile these sometimes-conflicting parts of myself, my Divine Queen has given me some instructions that have proven invaluable to me over the last several years. Perhaps they will be helpful to you.

My Beloved Rima, thank you for heeding the call… the call to love, serve, protect, and evolve all which you hold dear. Thank you for not hiding or playing small, for not worrying about what others think, and for taking aligned action.

As you step forward into the fray, may these thoughts nurture and sustain you:

1. Give your Life-Force to causes you care about, but make sure you are actively keeping some for yourself.
2. If you are going to be successful, then you must do more than give some and keep some, you must also actively work to increase your Life-Force energy through your practices so you have more and more to share.
3. Look within for your marching orders. What stirs you deeply is the best place to get a window into the yearnings of your heart (not what outrages everyone in your Facebook feed) Get quiet. Listen for what is yours to do. And do that.
4. Check your motives at each and every turn. Sometimes they won't be perfect, and you'll go forward anyway (with that call, donation, boycott, protest, or post). But never forget you are a fallible human living in a world populated by other fallible humans. Stay humble.
5. Also stay brave. You won't always get it right when you use your voice, but if you are doing 3 & 4, you are most likely going to do good. And when you cause harm unintentionally, be brave enough to clean it up.
6. Pay attention to your body and your energy. Take breaks if you are starting to feel it taking a toll. Sitting by is also stressful so seek the balance that allows you to take guided action without depleting yourself. Use the practices you know to keep yourself whole in the midst of deep fragmentation. Do them with Purpose and Passion.

7. Connect with your support system, a friend, a loved one, someone who you can decompress with, someone who is willing to hold you as you cry when it feels hopeless and cheer you on when you feel empowered and activated.
8. Take breaks when you need them. Yes, this bears repeating. You are no good to anyone if you are dried up and crunchy or waterlogged from constant grief. You get to be joyful. In fact, you MUST take time to find moments of joy in the face of joylessness, even knowing that pain and misery may just be a news cast away.
9. Love this world with all your heart. Love the plants, the stars, the sun and the moon, the oceans and forests, the two-legged, four-legged, no-legged and winged ones, AND the crazy fucked-up humans that you share this reality with. LOVE like your life depends on it—because it does.
10. Ask for help from and trust in the Divine. The creative matrix that gave birth to form did so out of the energy you call LOVE and as such it has, at its core, an evolutionary perspective. While the evolutionary trajectory you are on may be a mystery to you, work daily to tap into it and have faith in it. It will not abandon you.

So just what is it that is ours to do when we are facing problems of epic proportion?

I really admire those people who know in their bones they are here to help humanity in the most practical of ways. It's like they showed up on earth with the guts and grit necessary to step into the breach. I have served alongside some of the most courageous and visionary people who have dedicated themselves to these kinds of actions. They are our first responders, health care workers, and teachers. They staff and lead social service agencies and emergency services. They are the ones who save our asses over and over in times of tragedy. They are the "fingers in the dike" kind of people.

Perhaps you know the legend of the boy from the Netherlands who saved his people with his quick thinking and sheer determination. With most of his country below sea level, he knew well how important the many dams, also known as dikes, that populate the countryside are in keeping the people and animals safe from deadly floods. This particular boy spotted a small crack in a dam. He knew that he couldn't leave and get help because the force of the water would cause the crack to widen and the dam would eventually break, killing many people. He takes the only action he can and puts his finger in the crack to hold back the water. He takes personal responsibility and, despite the cold weather, stays there all night until an adult comes to find him and is able to fix the crack.

I am blessed to know some amazing women who, like the little Dutch boy, or really more like Joan of Arc, suit up and show up in the trenches, ready to hold back water and armies alike. They are the helpers after the storms. They are the visionaries that try to prevent the worst disasters, or at least properly prepare for them. They have the gift of sight, and often lead the charge to adjust in the face of a coming catastrophe long before us regular folk can see the writing on the wall.

If my friends are any indication, I can say unequivocally these folks are tired. They need reinforcements. They need rest. They need support. They need us to make choices that make their work easier, not harder. If you are feeling called to be trained to help at this level, know that you are needed. It's been heartening to see that in a world facing a global health crisis, 2020 saw an 18% increase in the number of applications to medical schools. Dubbed "the Faucci Effect," the Association of American Medical Colleges (AAMC) says an increase of this size is unprecedented. This news gives me great hope.

But take heart if you aren't likely to be heading off to medical school, signing up for the police academy, or running for local office. There is a swim lane for everyone. It's just a matter of finding yours and going for it!

Taking time in quiet space can help, so can trying something and seeing how it goes. You don't have to find your service work on the first try. In fact, it may take several attempts to discover your true calling. Even in times of lockdown you can add your Life-Force to the family cauldron.

If you feel overwhelmed with how to use your gifts to help reshape the world in a more fair and just way, try starting closer to home. Here are some things that might spur your knowing as to what is yours to do to heal yourself, your loved ones, humanity, all living creatures and the Earth herself:

If you are a **Lover of Dance**, put on some music and move your body. Sweat your prayers for wholeness and health, for a fairer and more just world. Spin and twirl and wake up your Shakti. Use your intention to radiate it outward and share your Life-Force energy with all who need it.

If you are a **Space Whisperer** who loves to make things beautiful, make an altar, mesa, or sacred space in your home. It doesn't matter if you have never done it before. Just collect a few beautiful items and with intention arrange them in a sacred place and put your prayers for healing and love into the space.

If you are a **Sacred Shaman**, get out your sage, your rattle, your drum. Shake and beat and burn the negativity out of our collective space. Help us release that which no longer serves.

If you are an **Oil Priestess** like me, get out your oils. Your Young Living oils, your doTERRA oils, your homemade or hand-crafted oils, or the oils you purchase from me. Anoint yourself as you feel led. Take them outside and anoint the earth. Diffuse them into the air (you can use a pot on the stove) and bathe with them. Let their sacred medicine flood over and through you and out into the world.

If you are a **Goddess of Art**, get out your paints, colored pens, scissors, and tape. Enter the Temple of your Soul and bring forth images and artwork that heals through love. Let your creativity be a love-note to all LIFE.

If you are an **Oracle, a Channel, a Seer**, get out your cards, your tools of divination, your pendulums, and your intuitive powers. Bring forth messages of love, guidance, and hope. Tell us what you see.

If you are a **Mistress of the Word**, open your journal and let your words flow forth unchecked by the inner critic, free flowing from your heart on to the page. Write us poems of love and healing, and never forget that in the beginning there was the Word.

If you are a **Sacred Singer of Songs**, let us hear your voice rising up to the heavens now. Bless us with your sweet sounds of Love as you send healing vibrations into the airwaves for all to feel.

If you are a **Holy Music Maker**, pick up your instrument and play. Play us sweet music that uplifts and heals, the music of the soul to carry us home to each other.

If you are a **Protector and Lover of Nature**, plant something, work with the land, your hands in the soil, sending love and light into all of Life as you cultivate beauty in nature.

If you are a **Sacred Parent to a Beloved Child,** love your sweet ones fiercely. Allow them to pull forth from you the most powerful love on the planet—that of the Creator's love for its creation. Radiate that love out to all of creation.

When you serve with the deepest of intent to love and heal the world, what you do is sacred and holy. Find your passion and give it to the world. You are medicine incarnate and we are hungry for you, dear Queen.

It's crunch time sisters. So let's find a few other Queens to join up with and make it a party!

"Love turns work into rest."
—Teresa of Avila

Chapter 21
Finding Sisterhood

When I was young, I was never one of the IT girls or in the popular crowd. I could hang out with them, but I also hung out with the nerds, the outcasts, and the in-betweeners. I was a floater.

As an adult, I still enjoy a wide range of friends. I really like people and I like gathering them in groups. In my home in Kansas, we used to throw lots of parties. There was nothing I liked more than the sound of laughter and the hum of conversation I heard when we had company. But even in my own home I rarely deeply connected with my guests. Instead, I flitted and floated from group to group, checking in to see that everyone had food and drink and was having a good time.

Eventually I began to long for a different kind of connection with my friends: one that was more deep than wide. For over a decade, I had the privilege of leading small groups focused on transformation, and I wanted more of that in my life. But I also wanted something else. I didn't know what it was until I went to a week-long women's retreat in the mountains of Montana. It was there I saw up-close and personal what had been missing for me: Sacred Sisterhood.

What I experienced was life-altering. I had been to many co-gender retreats that were transformative, but none seemed to stick with me like my week with the women in the wilds of Montana, and the wilds of our hearts. There is little else like the power of small groups to transform. Something magical happens in the space between souls. You know, where two or more are gathered…

It's not just a biblical truth, it's scientific. Research shows that our brains and minds develop "resonance" between them. Any time we are in proximity with others, we tune in to one another and our brains sync up as we share energy and information. This is especially powerful when the focus of our time with others is on surfacing and healing unhealthy beliefs that no longer serve us.

I have heard many people say that small group work has resolved issues which years of therapy seemed unable to address. Many of the originating emotional experiences which form the basis of our belief systems happen before our long-term memory is active. Those pre-verbal or pre-narrative experiences are stored as implicit memories and are not easily accessed. We can't process in therapy what we can't explicitly recall.

Bonnie Badenoch and Paul Cox describe this phenomenon in their paper, *Integrating Interpersonal Neurobiology with Group Psychotherapy* published by International Journal of Group Psychotherapy. Their research shows definitely that circles can offer a potent opportunity for healing because there is a high likelihood that one person's trigger will mirror implicit triggers for others in the group. When women sit in circle and share their personal stories of sorrow and triumph, we may hear experiences specific to being female that can serve to surface implicit memories in us. When these often-hidden memories are accessed with vividness, they become available for transformation.

Badenoch and Cox also note that a circle can become "an empathy-rich environment for holding the pain and fear that emerges." Being seen and held in a compassionate way by our sisters creates an attunement which helps us to repair wounded circuits of regulation for both the women receiving and giving care. Over time, the circle members' compassionate state of mind is internalized by each member's body, nervous system, and brain. According to Badenoch and Cox, with repeated exposure to the group, this can create a "permanent representation" or an "inner community" which can be accessed even outside of the circle. The harmony within the circle becomes grounded and circles that are highly attuned automatically shift into a calm, empathetic, holding state of mind, when one member is experiencing a trigger.

But in reality it goes much deeper than brain science. What I experienced in Montana and in many other circles since then is the power of The Pack. One of my teachers called this out explicitly when she said that The Wild Woman as an archetype is a pack animal. On her own, she appears crazy, but in community she is powerful.

Please take a moment to breathe that in.

How often have you felt crazy or ashamed of your inner longings, your inner wild woman? Have you ever wished you could chuck your whole life and run off to live in the forest, or by the beach, or in the mountains? Have you ever wondered if you were broken to feel such a primal discontentment even though you have so much you love, your family, partner, career, home, etc.? Is there, in the farthest corners of your soul, a lonely ache for something more? Do you float around on the surface of your relationships like I did missing out on the kind of connection that can sustain you in dark times?

Having a supportive circle of women in your life takes courage and commitment. Courage because they won't settle for anything less than all of you, the wild, wacky, whining, snarling, snot-nosed siren. They want all of you because that's where the medicine is. It takes commitment because opening ourselves up and exposing our vulnerabilities is only possible when a sacred and safe bond is formed between sisters. That doesn't mean that there aren't struggles or breakdown in sacred circles. There most definitely are. But a safe circle is one that has enough leadership and experience within it to facilitate healing when breaches come.

If you have never sat in sisterhood before, I urge you to find a circle holder who is running a program that interests you and take the plunge. You can also call your own circle if you prefer. I have done exactly that when I didn't know where to find what I wanted. But be warned. If you call the circle, you will be leading it by default, and eventually that many wear on you. Even though I usually am teaching 2-4 circles at any given time, I myself sit in 2-4 circles where I am only a participant. I do so because I need the Magic of The Pack. I need places where I can let it all hang out, my insecurities, my fears, my longings, and my shame. Having a fresh flow of sunlight shining on my shadowy insides is essential for my well-being. And it gets a large chunk of my time and money to provide myself with the nourishment that only my sisters can offer.

In the beginning of my time in circle I must admit that I worried about looking like I had myself together. I hadn't yet experienced the gift of being vulnerable and deeply seen. I often found myself wanting to share all my hard won-wisdom and sometimes ended up coaching others. Sometimes that was welcome, other times it was not. But eventually I let that bullshit go and I claimed my right to be there for myself. I am so happy now to take advantage of the gift of sisterhood to "out" myself, to lay bare the dark places needing light and the tender spots needing love.

Yet even as I pour myself out, I can do so from a sovereign place. My intention is not to dump all my drama on the group, but to own my experience, stand in the cleansing fire and be witnessed as I burn away what no longer serves. It may look the same to the uninitiated, but spilling outward so that space can be made for healing feels very different to both the spiller and the circle than a dumping. When we spill out our hearts, those in witness feel honored by your trust and in awe of your courage. When we dump our drama, many in the circle may end up feeling slimed or used.

No matter how amazing your circle and/or facilitators are, keep your Queens handy. Stay sovereign. Don't give away your power. And at the same time lean in and surrender to the love that the circle has for you, even as they hold the space knowing you will find your way home. If you notice lots of fixing others during circle time, or sisters showing up expecting to be fixed, that is a red flag. The best circles are ones which hold the perspective that no one is broken; we are all inherently whole. We just sometimes lose our way or outgrow our current circumstances and need support in releasing what no longer works as we shift toward a new, more aligned expression.

Some circles may last a lifetime, others will come and go. Be aware that when you outgrow your tribe, the impulse may arise to want your circle to change and shift along with you. But that wouldn't be fair to those coming up behind you who need the circle just as it is. My suggestion is to resist this impulse. Don't try to "evolve" a group for your own benefit. It is thankless work and will almost certainly not be welcome. Plus, it is likely to steal your gratitude for what you have learned from the circle turning it into resentment that it won't grow with you. Rather than do that, why not just notice when it is time to depart and make a graceful exit. Alternately, the tribe may simply expel you as you grow beyond it and lose resonance. Try not to take it personally.

Some of your sisters may wish to hold you in and keep you from moving on. Don't let them if you know it's time to go. You may feel a wide range of emotions as you consider leaving, including sadness and grief. Give yourself the time you need to feel all the feelings that come with growing and moving on. And as much as possible, celebrate the beauty and joy you found while being part of the circle.

There is one caveat to this. If you are in the habit of leaving relationships the moment they become uncomfortable, then think deeply about why you feel called to move on. If the impulse to leave is about moving away from something that is challenging rather than moving on to something that is calling to you, consider taking time to try to work through it first. Of course, if there is clear abuse happening, you are wise to exit immediately. But if it's just your garden variety discomfort, speak up about it in the circle. Lean into your sisterhood. Ask for what you need and be willing to receive it.

If the impulse to leave is coming from being drawn to a new level of expression for your soul, and you can depart with a grateful heart as you expand toward the next level of learning, then by all means go for it. But again, take your time. Check in to make sure you have received all the wisdom the circle holds and that you are not just floating from group to group in order to stay at the surface level.

You aren't going to do it perfectly. Neither will your circles. But I believe with every fiber of my being that circles of women will save us from ourselves, and from the devastation inflicted by the patriarchy run amok. Individually it is very difficult for the feminine to challenge masculine structures and come out of it intact, but together we are a force to be reckoned with. And having sisters who will hold our feet to the fire, and hold our hands and hearts when we are troubled, ensures we will be a force for good.

"Love turns work into rest."
—Teresa of Avila

CHAPTER 22

REMEMBER TO REST

Here we are at the final chapter with the last nugget of wisdom I have to offer you. I left it for last not because it is unimportant, but because it is so important that I wanted it to be the last thing on your mind. As you continue on your journey of enfoldment, remember to rest!

When you are operating in the realm of the Feminine, how you do your work is even more important than the work you do. How you live, love, breathe, create, produce, and give birth IS the work. It can be physically, emotionally, mentally and even spiritually exhausting to evolve at the speed these times are requiring. Awakening, embracing, and embodying the Queen is no small feat. Take time to rest and allow for integration. If you are feeling tired, listen to your body. Sleep more. Take power-naps in the daytime. Try not to stay up so late. A tired and bleary person cannot be fully conscious. The evolutionary process of becoming Queen is a growth process, and just as children grow when they sleep, so do you and me. You will not be able to sustain yourself if you are cutting your own rest short in favor of others.

Rest is sacred, so claim it!

This is your birthright: Holy Rest.

And yet, the Queen has a realm to run. She cannot abdicate her role as sovereign. So how do we effectively run our lives *and* channel the calm and clear nature of a true Queen? How do we luxuriate in our majesty *and* still tend to what is important? The Queen knows a secret: Holy Rest is more than sleep. It's feeling spaciousness in your entire being.

Transformation is a body-mind-soul experience. Check in right now and ask yourself: Do I feel spacious in my body? Do I feel spacious in my thoughts? Do I feel spacious in my soul? I invite you to honor the work to be done by each part of you by giving yourself time for each aspect of you to be well-nourished and well-resourced.

Allowing more rest into your life is not just setting aside time for resting. It is also about letting go of the belief that everything is a challenge, everything is a fight to be won, or lost. When you stop fighting your way through your day, you will end the day with more of your energy intact. The more resourcing you sprinkle throughout your day, the less your work will feel like doing battle with life. The less depleted you are, the less rest you will need. If you turn your effort to embody the Queen into a war with yourself, you are missing the point entirely.

Notice if you are tensing up as you sit down to "conquer" your inbox. Are you determined to "crush" your launch? Become sensitized to when you are "powering through" your to-do list. Instead, you might imagine that everything is a dance, or a song, inviting you to move and breathe and harmonize your frequency as you sashay and serenade your way through the day. You can dance through the laundry, sing through meal prep. You can magnetize in the help you desire and the students for your course. It's still up to you to take action, to make choices, and to follow through. But set your intention to work SOFT not hard.

When you notice you have hardened up, or when the energy starts to slow down or ball up inside, do a body scan and see where the energy is stuck or blocked. Locate the blocked area and imagine it melting or dissolving. Check your shoulders and jaw throughout the day. Ask them to relax downward and pull your attention inward for a few moments. Remove your tongue from the top of your mouth and open your mouth wide in Lion's pose with your tongue out. Growl! Howl! Or sing a quick tune:

"This little light of mine, I'm gonna let it shine!"

"Shake your groove thing, shake your groove thing, yeah, yeah!"

*"We all come from the goddess, and to her we shall return,
like a drop of rain, flowing to the ocean."*

"I do my hair-toss, check my nails. Baby how you doin'? Feelin' good as hell!"

Move the energy!

Moments of rest don't have to derail you. Rather they should refresh you so you can carry on with more grace and ease. Try Microdosing your rest: resting for 1-3 minutes several times a day and see how that improves your sense of wellbeing. Perhaps we fail at this because we try to take too big of a bite. Start small and build. If we aren't practicing living, growing, and working in sustainable ways, we risk hitting the wall and crashing hard. Adrenal fatigue, illness, despair and unhappiness, broken relationships, and neglected kids (including our own inner child) are too high a cost to continue paying. That's old school. And school's out!

Here is a list I call *Forms of Holy Rest* that help me make space for luscious living on a practical level. Some of these can be microdosed, while others require a longer time commitment:

- Getting 8+ hours of sleep
- Laying in the sun
- Reading a fiction book like a mystery or romance novel
- Eating lunch away from the computer, on a table, with a placemat, napkin, and silverware
- Going for a meandering walk and taking time to look at nature, smell the flowers, and even sit a bit
- Napping in the daytime
- Doodling
- Anointing the body with essential oils and smelling them throughout the day
- Yawning, stretching, especially on the floor, in sunlight, like a cat
- Self-massage
- Staring into space, out a window, or daydreaming of any kind
- Spontaneous dance break or song break
- Spontaneous play time with kids, pets, friends, or beloved
- Shaking out hands, arms and, for bonus points, shaking out booty and legs
- Listening to music while drinking hot tea or a favorite beverage
- A long hot soak in the bath, preferably with essential oils
- Chatting with a close girlfriend
- Lying in child's pose or savasana
- Drinking a glass of water, bonus points for walking outside while drinking it
- Meditating for 3-5 minutes (anything longer is more of an active practice as opposed to rest)
- Saying a centering prayer or invocation that fills the soul
- Self-Hugging for 60+ seconds (ya, that's a thing!)
- Massaging temples with lemongrass or peppermint oil
- Putting on hand lotion with loving intention

INTEGRATING RESTING AS A WAY OF LIFE

I still have to consciously nurture my commitment to stay in feminine flow as the main energy / speed of my life. I invite myself into the practice of resting as I work daily. My invocation is, "Work Softly." I whisper this to myself as I sit at my desk. I use ritual to set my space so that my office feels more like a temple and my work more like devotion. I keep my oils nearby. I have candles and orchids in my office. The more I infuse my day with moments of connection with the sacred and affirmations of self-love, the more I see that they are an essential aspect of my productivity. I can usually do more in less time when I am nourished, aligned with my soul purpose, and well-resourced.

But while I seek a kind of daily flowing balance between productive activity and moments of Holy Rest, sometimes that balance works itself out over a longer period of time. I may choose to put in more time than usual in order to meet a deadline. My masculine capacities of structure, goals, focus, and productivity are not at odds with my feminine creative flow as long as I don't forget who is in charge when I call up my masculine warrior energy. Even warriors need rest.

Completing this book project is a great example of how I needed to turn up the volume on my inner masculine energy so I could be more productive and reach my goals. I had more late nights in a row than I prefer, but I also slept in so as to not shortchange my sleep. I made sure I used my priestess practices to set up a crystalline energy field and align with my soul purpose before each writing session. I made a master grid and anointed it with oils to hold the energy for the project. I tried to be gentle and understanding through the periods of non-writing by embodying patience and honoring the silence as part of the creative process. And I leaned heavily on the magic of sisterhood in my online writing program. All of this allowed me to birth this beautiful book with much more grace and ease than I ever thought possible.

One of the most joyful outcomes of being in flow with this book was how the exquisite art came into form. I knew I wanted to have powerful illustrations of each Queen. I knew I wanted my friend and uber-talented artist Jenny Hahn to do the work. Yet, every time I thought about commissioning her to paint the Seven Queens, I told myself it just wasn't possible, that I didn't have the budget, that she wouldn't be available. I talked myself out of that desire more times that I care to admit. It was scary delaying the decision as long as I did. Still, I trusted myself. I knew if I rested into it, and waited until I felt clear, the action would flow forth naturally. Eventually, I could no longer ignore my deep desire to have Jenny on board. In my resting, surrendering, waiting, I found courage. I sent her an email explaining what I had in mind. We had a brief Zoom call and we both knew she was absolutely the right artist for the Queens. The arrangements were made easily, and everything flowed so beautifully we could feel the Divine Flow supporting the endeavor. For more information on Jenny's work, see the afterword.

This is how things work when we are on our throne and creating from our sovereign Queen. That doesn't mean there won't be obstacles. But we flow around and over them in due course, without resistance. Resting before we need to, for the joy of it, because it feels good in our bodies.

More often than not I am resting into things these days, rather than leaning into them. When all of my energy is in alignment, life is full of ease and joy. Tapping into the wisdom of my womb, of my body, of my heart, and yes my mind is important. There is intelligence in every part of us, including that which may feel as though it comes from beyond us. It is a huge blessing in my life to feel connected to guidance from my Soul, Higher Self, and the Divine. And I am so grateful every time I have the courage to act on that guidance. From that place I can be in a state of ecstatic surrender and the practice of non-resistance.

Surrendering and resting into your soul purpose and divine guidance is by no means a getting out of the way. It's more of a joining without hesitation or anxiety, in acknowledgment of the union between you and the Divine. As you embrace your Queen, know that she is Divinely ordained. In your world, you are the monarch. You have the right and the responsibility to rule your lands softly and sovereignly, well-rested and well-resourced, in wholeness and wonder. The world is better for it in every conceivable way.

Here's to you.

Long Live the Queen!

Afterword

Become a part of the **Awakening the Queen** Facebook community. This is a private group for women seeking to awaken and embody the Queen archetype. It's a great place to learn more about this work and to be in a community with others as we talk about all things royal. **https://www.facebook.com/groups/awakeningthequeen**

To learn more about Dr. Rima Bonario and her work and her powerful line of Bloom Fine Egyptian Oils, visit **RimaBonario.com**

To learn more about artist Jenny Hahn and her work, visit her online studio at **JennyHahnArt.com**

The Seven Queens
Energy Practices & Affirmations

The Grounded Queen Energy Practice:
BECOMING ROOTED
(Add Red Amber Oil)

The daily practice of grounding or rooting yourself is the best way you can help yourself avoid the two shadow queens. In this practice you will visualize yourself connected to the earth using the image of roots descending from your feet and tailbone into the heart of the earth and anchoring there. This gives you three anchor points—one coming from each foot, and one from your tailbone. Close your eyes now and imagine them in place. Feel the increase in stability you gain as you lock your roots into place deep within the earth. Once your roots are well connected, imagine sipping pure clean energy up through your roots from the heart of Mother Earth into your body. Allow that energy to pool in your pelvic bowl. As that energy enlivens you, say the following affirmations out loud:

It is safe for me to be in physical form.
Mother Earth supports me and meets my needs.

My body is wise and worthy of love.
I love my body and trust its wisdom.

It is safe to have my needs met.
Abundance is everywhere.
I am allowed to be cared for.

The Passionate Queen Energy Practice:
Containing
(Add Musk Oil)

The daily practice of creating a safe container for your life-force energy is a wonderful way to ensure that your Shakti will be available for your own vitality and enjoyment. Imagine that you are sitting in the center of an egg-shaped bubble that stretches about 12 inches above and below you and is about as wide as when your arms are fully open. This bubble is your auric field or your personal energy field. On the edge of this field is a membrane, and it is intelligent. Just like the membrane of a cell, it has a job to do in managing what goes in and what comes out. When we don't have a solid energetic boundary to our personal energy field, we are often depleted as our energy is free to leak out. If we never learned good personal boundaries as a child, we may find that our bubble's edge is barely functioning. Conversely, we may have created a super thick wall to hide behind as a youngster in an attempt to feel safe. Sometimes we have a little of both. Maybe we wanted to withdraw from those people who hurt us, but we couldn't as they were the only source of love and resources. No matter your story, we all have an energy field and every field has an edge.

In order for you to get the full benefit of your Life-Force energy, you want to be sure that the edge or your energy field is free from holes, tears, or dents. Take a moment to put your hands out all around you and make contact with your edge. Greet it and acknowledge its existence. If you can't feel anything at first, it's okay. Just imagine it. Notice if it has a color or an attitude of some kind. Is it thick and smooth or thin and bumpy? Imagine using your hands to smooth it out and thicken it up. Call on your life-force energy to make it glow and infuse it with strength. Imagine it like the glass walls of a greenhouse and you as a precious orchid sitting within it. Notice how the glass allows in sunlight but keeps out wind and rain. Notice how it keeps the heat from escaping so the orchid can flourish. Because this membrane is intelligent, you can give it instructions and consciously direct how it operates. Up until this moment it may have picked up its operating instructions by osmosis from your parents or others in your life. Take a moment now to consciously choose how you want it to operate. Make it clear that no one else's energy should be inside your energy field. The space inside your bubble is for you and you alone. Ask it to help you from leaking your energy or upsets out on others. Notice how it is responding to these new instructions. Do you see a change in color, thickness, attitude/can you feel it heating up or firming up? Now as you feel your Shakti nicely contained inside your new "greenhouse," say these statements out loud:

My energetic space is safe and secure. I can unleash my Shakti without guilt.

Life is pleasurable and I deserve to have pleasure in my life.

I embrace and celebrate my sexuality. My sexuality and sexual expression is sacred.

My hips open easily and I move my body gracefully, easily, and effortlessly.

The Empowered Queen Energy Practice:
Inhabiting your Core
(Add Jasmine Oil)

This Queen is all about embracing your personal power. The energy practice that goes along with her is mastering your energetic core. When you are in your core you are able to engage with the world. People can feel your intentions, your commitments, and your boundaries. They can feel you in residence. Your core is one of the most potent places that the Queen energy is felt. It's the seat of your sovereignty. Some people are naturally good at inhabiting their core, but many are not. Energy follows attention, so if you regularly exercise your core muscles, your physical strength can help you stay in your core. You can build strength with the plank exercise. Paying attention to your posture is also helpful. Opening the chest, rolling back the shoulders, and straightening your head is a good start. Think of the elegance and strength of a ballet dancer—male or female. That is what a powerful core looks like.

To build your core, begin by bringing your attention to the base of your skull where it meets your spine. Then in your mind's eye, trace your spine all the way down to your tailbone. Picture each of the cervical vertebrae which start out fairly small in the neck, then the thoracic and lumbar vertebrae which increase in size and strength as they snake their way toward the sacrum. Finally at the very bottom, visualize the smallest of the vertebrae, the coccyx and tailbone. Now imagine your spine growing, thickening and glowing with light that stretches from the skull through the entirety of the torso. I like to imagine the glow becoming a column of light that beams up through my head above me and down from my tailbone right into the earth. Like a powerful pole of light I can lean on, I feel it helping me to stand more erect. Next tighten your stomach muscles and imagine yourself "sitting" back into yourself along the interior of your spine. When I connect with this feeling it's like I can suddenly "feel" myself. I will often sigh or relax and spontaneously say, "There I am!" Once you feel yourself in core say the following affirmations out loud:

I have the right to be me. I can act without shame.

I honor the power that is within me.

I have the will to accomplish tasks easily and effortlessly.

I use the fire in my solar plexus chakra to burn away hesitation and doubt.

I complete what I commit to doing.

The Loving Queen Energy Practice:
The Inner Fountain
(Add Rose Oil)

Begin by grounding and sending your roots into the earth as you learned with the Grounded Queen. Once you feel them connected into the earth, imagine drawing pure loving energy from the Earth Mother up into your pelvic bowl as though you are sipping a milkshake through a straw. As you feel the energy enter your pelvic bowl, allow it to begin pooling there. In a female body, this is where we receive energy. See the energy as light filling in the entirety of your pelvic area. Once that feels full, you can imagine drawing it up another level to your heart. In a female body, this where energy moves outward. Imagine a smaller chalice there and see it filling with this pure energy. Then allow the light to flow out from your heart. See it falling like rain back down and refilling your pelvic bowl. It should look like a double layered fountain. Bring the energy up and let it naturally spill back down and be caught in the larger pelvic bowl. In this way you are running a full circuit through your body. Continue visualizing the energy moving like this for several minutes. Allow that energy to cycle within you, say the following affirmations out loud:

My body holds an inexhaustible supply of energy and love.

I am worthy of love from myself and others.

I am allowed to keep some for myself and to give some away.

I commit to being gentle and kind to myself.

I am loving toward myself and others.

I live in balance with others and with the earth.

I create and live from harmony.

The Expressive Queen Energy Practice: Authentic Clearing

(Add Amber Cashmere Oil)

The daily practice of clearing your energy field and removing outside influences will support you in activating the power of this Queen. This is the practice of visualizing moving anything that is not YOU out of your body and auric space and calling back to you any and all parts of you that have been consciously or unconsciously left elsewhere (outside of your auric field). Begin by imagining a light source tuned to the frequency of your name scanning your auric field and body from the top down. Every time it hesitates or hits a block of some kind you've uncovered something that is not you. Imagine it melting, vaporizing, disappearing in some way. If you know where it belongs, send it there. Otherwise let Mother Earth have it. She will transmute and reuse the energy. Continue scanning all the way down your body and beyond to about a foot below your feet. Keep sending out anything that is not you. Once the space inside you is clear, imagine calling home or magnetizing to you any and all parts of you, aspects of your attention, or energy that are not currently inside your body or auric field. As they feel the pull, visualize them gently returning back to you from wherever they are now. As they come home, your unique vibrational frequency will become stronger. Notice how it feels to be filled up with you and only you. As that frequency increases, say the following affirmations out loud:

*I release any and all cords, ties, bonds, and agreements
made by me or others under false pretenses.*

*I love being authentically me.
I express myself and my desires and dreams clearly.*

My body and field are mine alone and inhabited solely by me.

*I make time for my creative expression.
Creativity flows in and through me.*

*My voice is necessary. I deserve to speak and hear the truth.
My Dharma is a gift to the world.*

The Visionary Queen Energy Practice:
Chakra Balancing

(Add Sandalwood Oil)

The daily practice of connecting with the chakra system, and especially the third-eye chakra, can go a long way toward restoring and preserving a clear view of yourself. By balancing and connecting all of your body's energy centers you will have access to a more holistic understanding of life. Use this chakra meditation and visualization to access this holistic viewpoint. Start by visualizing a ruby red orb at the base of your spine, imagine the sphere spinning, then glowing and radiating red light out into your body and auric field. Breathe deeply and imagine this red light soothing and healing your body, mind and soul. When you are ready, visualize moving up to the sacral chakra and connect with its vibrant orange orb. See it spinning and then glowing and radiating orange light out into your body and auric field. Breathe deeply and imagine this orange light soothing and healing your body, mind and soul. When ready, move up to the bright yellow orb in the solar plexus, then the verdant green orb in the heart, the sky blue sphere in the throat, the deep indigo orb in the third eye, and the brilliant violet orb in crown. After opening and balancing all these chakras, allow them to connect with and communicate with each other. As you feel peace and calm coming over you, say the following affirmations out loud:

I am open to the wisdom and insight that resides within me.

I see myself and the world with clarity.

I create and manifest my vision for my life.

I trust myself to see what needs to be seen.

The Divine Queen Energy Practice:
Soul Connection
(Add Blue Lotus Oil)

The daily practice of connecting to your Soul Essence can be extremely rewarding. There are an infinite number of ways to make this connection including meditation, contemplation, using prayer beads or traditional prayer, or chanting and singing. I like to make it physical by imagining capturing my Soul in my hands and bringing her into my body. There is a Native American practice I like that invites us to imagine that there is a unique sunray that belongs only to us. Within that ray is our Soul's unique frequency. To do this practice stand with your feet shoulder width apart and drop into your womb and heart. Set the intention of connecting to your Soul. You may already feel that connection, or you may feel nothing at all. Either is okay. Next bring your attention to the sunlight streaming onto the planet. Tune into your unique ray that is on its way to you now. Stretch your arms out and bring up over your head. As our hands get closer, imagine capturing your unique sun's ray between your hands. Holding it between your hands, slowly lower your hands all the way to your abdomen while imagining that ray is entering your body and moving down through all of your chakra centers. Tune into how the unique frequency that belongs to you is organizing and harmonizing the energies within your chakras, your body, and your auric field. Allow yourself to enjoy this pleasant sensation. When you are ready, say the following affirmations out loud:

I am a walking expression of the Divine and
Divinity resides within me.

I take time to connect with my Soul Essence and
my unique frequency.

I receive guidance quickly and easily and
live a life of never-ending Grace.

Every moment is filled with untold magic and mystery and
I see the Divine inner wisdom at play in all things.

The Seven Queens
Master summary charts

Queen	Archetype	Shadow Queens	Chakra	Energy Practice	Anointing Oil Stone
Grounded Queen	Earth Mother	Flighty Queen Frozen Queen	Base/Root Chakra	Grounding Roots in Earth	Red Amber/ Red Jasper
Passionate Queen	The Lover	Siren Queen Stagnant Queen	Sacral Chakra	Strengthening Your Edge	Musk/ Carnelian
Empowered Queen	The Warrior	Beheaded Queen Cut-Throat Queen	Solar-Plexus Chakra	Inhabiting your Core	Jasmine/ Tiger's Eye
Loving Queen	The Healer	Sacrificial Queen Solitary Queen	Heart Chakra	Energy Fountain	Rose/ Rose Quartz
Expressive Queen	The Artist	Silent Queen Starring Queen	Throat Chakra	Clearing: Me/ Not Me	Amber Cashmere Sodalite
Visionary Queen	The Seer	Foolish Queen Arrogant Queen	Third-Eye Chakra	Chakra Balancing	Sandalwood Lapis
Divine Queen	The Goddess	Empty Queen	Crown Chakra	Unique Sun Ray	Blue Lotus Amethyst

Goal	Challenge / Need	Royal Focus	Royal Right	Blessing to Bestow
Self-Preservation	Fear / Safety	Grounding, Nourishment, Prosperity, Trust	To exist and have needs met	Gratitude for what we have Earth Care - restoring and honoring Mother Earth
Self-Gratification	Guilt / Desire	Emotions, Desire, Needs	To feel and have pleasure	Permission to indulge and live life to the fullest
Self-Definition	Shame / Power	Energy, Action, Will, Power	To act and be an individual	Be Discerning (Yes/No): reduce and release what doesn't serve
Self-Acceptance	Grief / Connection	Love, Balance, Self-Love, Giving & Receiving	To love and be loved	Forgiveness and Reconciliation: removal of debt
Self-Expression	Lies / Truth	Finding your Voice, Listening, Resonance	To speak and hear truth	Service: giving time/energy to a sacred cause
Self-Reflection	Illusion / Clarity	Intuition, Insight, Vision, Dreams, Wisdom	To see clearly	Generosity and Understanding: seeing others as self
Self-Knowledge	Attachment / Detachment	Union with Higher Power, Embodied Divinity	To know	Transmit Light and Love: embody Divine Presence

BIBLIOGRAPHY

Alli, Antero. Iconoclastic Ritual: The Underlying Instinctual Sources of Paratheatre ©1991 http://www.paratheatrical.com/iconoclasticritual.html.

American Medical Association 2021. *Applications to medical school up big. Is it the "Fauci effect"?* [online] Available at <https://www.ama-assn.org/residents-students/preparing-medical-school/ applications-medical-school-big-it-fauci-effect/> [Accessed 31, December 2020].

Badenoch, Bonnie and Cox, Paul. "Integrating Interpersonal Neurobiology with Group Psychotherapy," International Journal of Group Therapy, April, 2010.

Bly, Robert. *The Little Book of the Human Shadow.* New York, NY: HarperCollins Publishers, 1998.

Bowlby, John. "The making and breaking of affectional bonds. I. Aetiology and psychopathology in the light of attachment theory. An expanded version of the Fiftieth Maudsley Lecture, delivered before the Royal College of Psychiatrists, 19 November 1976." *The British Journal of Psychiatry* 130, no. 3 (1977).

Brene Brown, "The Power of Vulnerability: Teachings on Authenticity, Connection, and Courage," Audio CD, Sounds True; 1 edition (November 15, 2012).

Caesara, Lynda, *The Dance of the Masculine & Feminine Workshop Study Guide,* The Next Practice Institute of Mobius Executive Leadership, 2017.

Diamond, Diana. "Attachment Disorganization, The Reunion of Attachment Theory and Psychoanalysis," *Psychoanalytic Psychology,* Volume 21, No. 2, 2004.

Guerin, Philip J. *Family therapy: theory and practice.* Gardner Press, 1976.

Henes, Donna, *The Queen of Myself: Stepping into Sovereignty in Midlife.* Monarch Press, 2005.

Judith, Anodea, *Eastern Body Western Mind, Psychology and the Chakra System as a Path to the Self,* Celestial Arts, 1996.

Levine, Peter A. *Waking the Tiger: Healing Trauma: The innate capacity to transform overwhelming experiences.* North Atlantic Books, 1997.

Levine, Peter A., and Kline, Maggie. *Trauma through a child's eyes: Awakening the ordinary miracle of healing.* North Atlantic Books, 2010.

Maslow, A. H. "Some basic propositions of growth and self-actualization psychology." *Personality: Critical concepts in psychology* (1998).

Miller, Kenneth D. "Synaptic economics: competition and cooperation in synaptic plasticity." *Neuron* 17, no. 3 (1996).

Miller, William A. *Your Golden Shadow: Discovering and Fulfilling Your Undeveloped Self.* Harper & Row, 1989.

OnlyYouForever. 2020. *Disorganized Attachment in Marriage - OnlyYouForever.* [online] Available at: <https://www.onlyyouforever.com/disorganized-attachment-in-marriage/> [Accessed 19 October 2020].

Rothschild, Babette. *The Body Remembers.* New York: Norton, 2017. Print.

Schore, Allan N. "Back to basics attachment, affect regulation, and the developing right brain: linking developmental neuroscience to pediatrics." *Pediatrics in Review* 26, no. 6 (2005).

Scimel, Pyszczynski, Greenberg, O'Mahen and Arndt, "Running From the Shadow: Psychological Distancing From Others to Deny Characteristics People Fear in Themselves," *Journal of Personality and Social Psychology,* 2000, Vol. 78, No. 3.

Siegel, Daniel J. *Mindsight,* Bantam Books, 2010.

Siegel, Daniel J. "Reflections on Mind, Brain, and Relationships in Group Therapy," International Journal of Group Therapy, April 2010.

Siegel, Daniel J. *The Developing Mind,* The Guilford Press, 1999.

Siegle, Daniel J. "Toward an Interpersonal Neurobiology of the Developing Mind: Attachment Relationships, Mindsight, and Neural Integration," *Infant Mental Health Journal,* 2001.

Stevenson, Betsey, and Wolfers, Justin, "The Paradox of Declining Female Happiness," *National Bureau of Economic Research, Working Papers* 2009.

Tononi, Giulio. "Consciousness as integrated information: a provisional manifesto." *The Biological Bulletin* 215, no. 3 (2008).

Zweig, Connie, and Jeremiah Abrams. *Meeting the Shadow: The hidden power of the dark side of human nature.* JP Tarcher, 1991.

ABOUT THE AUTHOR

Rima Bonario, Th.D speaks and teaches on women's empowerment and embodiment practices through online and in person women's circles. She also leads sacred travel journeys to places like Egypt, France, and Hawaii to awaken and activate a deep connection to the Divine Feminine within. Rima's decades-long personal journey of discovering her feminine superpowers, embracing her self-sovereignty, and coming to deeply love and fully inhabit her body informs her work with her students. Her passion is helping women create and live a life they love by cutting through energetic clutter, dissolving emotional baggage, and forming wildly fulfilling habits of attention. Rima holds a doctorate in Transformation Psychology and has studied with master teachers in body-based energy work, sacred sexuality and Tantra, and the sacred art of Anointing. Rima is the creator of Bloom Fine Egyptian Oils and she loves initiating women into the use of these high-vibration oils and the ancient practice of self-anointing. She lives in Las Vegas, Nevada with her family and enjoys the sunshine and desert mountains that surround her home.

More Books By Flower of Life Press

 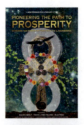   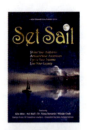

  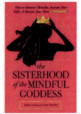 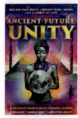 

    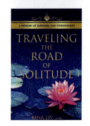

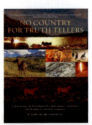  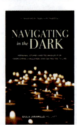 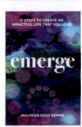 

www.floweroflifepress.com

FREE TRAINING: www.bestsellerpriestess.com/bestseller-priestess

Made in the USA
Coppell, TX
04 March 2021